PLAYBOY'S BOOK OF WINE

PLAYBOY'S BOOK OF WINE

by
Peter A. Gillette
and
Paul Gillette

Special Photography by Fred Lyon

A Ridge Press Book
Playboy Press

Editor-in-Chief: Jerry Mason
Editor: Adolph Suehsdorf
Art Director: Albert Squillace
Project Art Director: Harry Brocke
Managing Editor: Moira Duggan
Associate Editor: Mimi Gold
Associate Editor: Barbara Hoffbeck
Associate Editor: Carla van Splunteren
Art Associate: Nancy Louie
Art Associate: David Namias
Art Production: Doris Mullane

Published simultaneously in the United States and Canada
by Playboy Press, Chicago, Illinois.
Library of Congress Catalog Card Number: 74-81258.
ISBN: 87223-411-8. First edition.
Playboy and Rabbit Head design are trademarks of
Playboy, 919 North Michigan Avenue, Chicago, Illinois 60611 (U.S.A.)
Reg. U.S. Patent Office, marca registrada, marque déposée.
Printed and bound in Italy by Mondadori Editore, Verona.

To our wives, Helen and Shelly

CONTENTS

INTRODUCTION

We have, between us, enjoyed wine for almost one hundred years. For most of that time, we were quite ignorant of its academic aspects. The extent to which we have been educated is only the extent to which we have talked about wine with people who make it, read other wine books, and consulted wine academicians about questions to which we could not find satisfactory answers elsewhere.

Why, then, have we decided to write a book about wine? Frankly, because no other book we've seen approaches it from our perspective: that is, as a thing to be enjoyed. To be sure, there are many that tell you everything you ever wanted to know—and then some—about which wines are grown where. We don't think of these as wine books; we think of them as geography books. There are many others that celebrate individual wines or the wines of specific locations. Finally, there are the tastemaker books; the ones that tell you what their authors have decreed are "good" wines (i.e., the wines they themselves like), and how you too can learn to like them. What they don't tell you is that their authors often are in the business of selling these wines themselves, or are on the payroll of someone in the wine industry.

What the world needs, we felt—though not as much as a generation of peace, or an end to inflation, or a more singable substitute for "The Star-Spangled Banner" —is a book that tells the story of wine honestly, irreverently, without reliance on the clichés most would-be wine lovers have let themselves be fooled into believing, and, most importantly, without bias.

Change that to *without unacknowledged bias.* Everyone who has opinions has biases. Let us tell you some of ours up front, so that if we inadvertently let unlabeled opinion slip in among the facts, you'll quickly recognize what we're up to.

We have a bias against the idea that there's such a thing as a "good" wine. There are wines that are carefully made and there are wines that are carelessly made. There are wines made from cheap grapes and there are wines made from expensive grapes. There are wines we like and wines we don't. But if you like one that we don't, that's your business. And the one you like is just as "good" for you as the one we like is for us.

We've got a bias against the idea that there's a

"correct" wine—as in, "the correct wine to serve with x is y." We've got favorite wine/food combinations, and it appears that there are certain combinations that a majority of people find most palatable. But if you're in the minority, well, you're every bit as correct as the next man.

We've got a big bias against overpriced wines—by which we mean those priced disproportionately to the costs their purveyors incurred putting them before us. We appreciate that some grapes are costlier than others, that some methods of winemaking are costlier than others, that some wines are taxed more highly than others, and that some cost more than others to transport from the winery to your door (owing mainly to the distance between the winery and your door). Naturally, these costs will be reflected in the price of the wine. But some wines are priced 1,000, 2,000, or even 5,000 percent the aggregate expenses incurred by their purveyors. Often these inflated prices are the result of artificial shortages created by wine merchants—and by those who pay the inflated prices. We don't think it's illegal or even immoral, but we do tend to judge high-priced wines more harshly than medium- or low-priced wines. If we are asked to pay $5 an ounce for a glass of wine, it better be one fantastic glass of wine! (At this writing the celebrated Château Lafite-Rothschild, a red still wine produced in the French region of Bordeaux, is selling retail in New York City at $72 per 24-ounce bottle, 1966 vintage, and $175 per 24-ounce bottle, 1955 vintage. Comparing the purveyors' costs to those of other wine purveyors, a fair price for the 1966 would be about $25 and for the 1955 about $50.)

We also have palate biases—as does every wine drinker we know, although many are reluctant to admit it. The senior author (hereinafter, for simplicity's sake, we'll refer to him as G-1) developed his palate in the south of Italy and still leans toward the full-bodied, highly acidic red wines of the region. Give him a delicate Traminer-based wine of the sort frequently found in Germany's Rhine Valley and he tends to be less appreciative than of a lusty, spicy Gamay-based wine of the sort for which the Beaujolais district of France is famous—even though the German wine costs more to produce and is widely regarded in the wine trade as a "better" (that is, more carefully made) wine. The junior author (hereinafter G-2) leans toward fruity white wines and reds with high tannin

characteristics. He thus prefers a 1967 Mayacamas Cabernet Sauvignon, from California's Mayacamas Mountains, to a 1969 Domaine Maurice Chévillon Nuits-Saint-Georges, from the French region of Burgundy. The former costs about $15 a bottle at this writing, the latter $72. The latter is overpriced—in terms of purveyors' costs it should be about $20—but this has nothing to do with G-2's preference. Given a choice between the two bottles free, he still would pick the Mayacamas Cabernet. Why? That's the bias of his palate. He simply prefers that type of wine! And as a noble Roman once said, *de gustibus non est disputandum*, there's no disputing tastes.

Not long ago G-2 was the dinner guest of a senior executive of a large New York bank. The man has spent many years living and working in Europe and South America, and currently makes an average of two foreign trips a month. If travel is broadening, a man could hardly be broader. And his impeccable manners and considerable charm reflect his international exposure.

Dinner, served in his apartment, was built around Mediterranean foods and comprised seven courses with nine wines. The choice of wines revealed great sophistica-tion. Each (to G-2's palate and those of the other diners) was an incomparable match with the food it accompanied. The vintages invariably were among those the wine industry regards as the best years for these wines, and the little-known wines in the group were every bit as exciting as the internationally celebrated ones—more so, in fact, because of their unfamiliarity. G-2 looked forward to discussing them with his host when they had a private moment.

Then, as the *vin de résistance* (Château Margaux 1953, one of the world's most prized wines and vintages) was being served, G-2 noticed the butler pour wine from a different bottle into the host's glass. Intrigued, G-2 kept an eye peeled for a glimpse of the label. The wine was Taylor's Port.

The Taylor Wine Company, of Hammondsport, New York, is a widely respected producer of carefully made inexpensive wines. Taylor Port, a high-volume seller throughout North America, retailed at the time for $1.85 for a 25.6-ounce bottle, a price with which it is hard to quarrel. The Château Margaux 1953 had been sold out for several years and therefore could not be purchased

except at auction, where it would draw bids of perhaps $150 for a 24-ounce bottle. In any case, wine "authorities" agree unanimously that one does not serve Port, a sweet wine, with one's main course.

G-2 later got the opportunity to ask his host how it happened that he had bypassed the Château Margaux for the Port. "I always drink Taylor's Port," he replied, "unless my guests are drinking white wine. Then I drink Taylor's Sauterne. I can force down one of the better wines when I have to, and I usually will when I eat out. But here at home, it's easier to drink what I like."

G-2 asked how the banker, not liking the highly prized wines he served his guests, had gone about selecting them. "Simple," he said. "My butler does it."

When we told that story to a friend of ours who sells wine, he told us about the time he played host to a Florentine architect who was an annual visitor to the United States. Knowing the Florentine had been away from home for several weeks and thinking he might appreciate a potable reminder, our friend planned to serve with dinner a well-known Orvieto he himself had brought to the U.S. on his last trip to Italy.

Before dinner the two men repaired to the host's wine cellar for a sherry apéritif. Our friend then proudly produced the Orvieto. Whereupon the professor noted a bin of Almadén Dry Sémillon and said, "Would you think me terribly bold if I suggest we have the Almadén? It's one of my favorite wines, and I look forward to drinking it every time I come here—but my friends always serve me Italian wines!"

This is not a brief for inexpensive wines. One reason expensive wines continue to sell is that many people deem them worth the price. A few buyers may be interested primarily in the status of the label, but the majority, we are sure, are interested in the wine. (If not, it would be a relatively simple—if illegal—thing to buy one bottle of a celebrated wine and keep refilling it with inexpensive wine, changing the cork each time. As a matter of fact, we know of a restaurateur who regularly did just that until state beverage commission agents caught him at it!)

Item: A friend of ours at the William Morris office, our literary agency, drinks only Inglenook Navalle Chablis. It sells for $1.69 a fifth. The same winemaker produces another Chablis for $2.15 a fifth and a Pinot

Chardonnay for $5.15 a fifth. The main reason the Pinot Chardonnay is more expensive is that Chardonnay grapes are more expensive. The other two Inglenook Chablis are attempts—using cheaper grapes—to duplicate the taste, smell, and look of the Chardonnay.

Item: A burglar in Miami took thirty cases of wine from a liquor store. They were not simply taken at random: They comprised three cases each of wines that had been stored in different areas of two rooms. They included a $30-per-case Bardolino, and $18-per-case Spanish Chablis, a $48-per-case Hungarian Cabernet Sauvignon, and a $36-per-case Alsatian Gewürztraminer. In taking them, he bypassed wines selling at $60, $90, and even $150 per case.

Item: André Tchelistcheff, dean of California winemakers, discovered in a New York liquor store a 1941 Beaulieu Cabernet Sauvignon selling at $72 per case. Tchelistcheff, who had made the wine, knew it was selling at auction for up to $300 per case. Obviously, the liquor store didn't know the value of what it was selling.

Tchelistcheff promptly bought all the store had in stock, then loaded it into his car for the drive back to California. In Indiana he stopped at a pleasant-looking roadside restaurant and found no wines to his liking on its list. He asked the proprietor's permission to bring in one of his Beaulieu 1941's, and permission was granted. It was a memorable meal, solicitously served and more than reasonably priced. In gratitude, Tchelistcheff not only tipped the waitress generously, but also gave the proprietor a gift bottle of the 1941 Beaulieu Cabernet, suggesting that he serve it next time some extra special guest was at the restaurant.

A month later, Tchelistcheff, back in California, got a thank-you note from the proprietor. "We really appreciate your gesture of giving us the wine," it read. "Unfortunately, there was something stuck in the neck of the bottle. We finally got it out, but then the wine was sour, so we had to pour it down the drain. However, we realize it was given in the spirit of friendship, so we thank you anyway."

The "something" stuck in the neck of the bottle was a cork. Apparently the restaurateur didn't recognize it because he had served only wines with screw-top bottles. As for the wine being "sour," the tasters apparently were

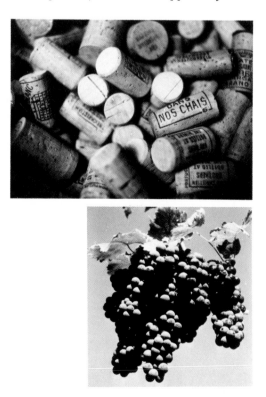

unfamiliar with the tannic taste characteristic of a fine Cabernet Sauvignon, and so poured down the drain a wine most cognoscenti would prize!

The point, of course—let us not belabor it—is that enjoying wine is a highly subjective enterprise. This is not to say that the only way to enjoy it is to charge into a wine-shop, buy the cheapest bottle you can find, and drink it until you get bored with it and must move on to a more expensive bottle (although that's one method, and certainly not to be despised). We do believe most people will enjoy wine more if they know something about what's involved in making it, different ways to serve it, and guidelines to follow in discovering new wines. At the same time, let no wine snob say that there are immutable laws or irrevocable rules about wine, because there quite obviously are not.

On the subject of wine companies, let us here declare that we are not now and never have been on the payroll of any wine company—or of any public relations agency or other organization involved in selling, promoting, or otherwise advancing the fortunes of the wine industry. In the interest of broadening our knowledge on the subject, we've accepted free trips to wineries and sample bottles of wine (as has just about every other person who has written about wine). But we are not on the take, salarywise or otherwise.

As to wine stocks, we have never owned at any one time more than one hundred shares of stock in any company in the wine industry.

In short, we're writing about wines because the subject appeals to us and because we think we have something interesting to say to readers. Almost three-quarters of a century ago, when G-1 was a four-year-old boy in Nicastro, Catanzaro, Italy, he was promoted from sleeping in his parents' bed to sleeping with his widowed grandfather. On the morning after his first night with *nonno*, he awoke to find the old man kneeling alongside the bed. It appeared at first that *nonno* was praying. But he wasn't. Reaching under the bed, he produced a jug of wine and two glasses. Then he wandered out into the yard and returned with two fresh eggs. He broke the eggs into the glasses, then covered them with wine, and handed one glass to G-1. "Drink," he said. "You'll like it."

He was right.

1.
THE JUICE DIVINE

Opening pages: Painting of grapes in baskets hangs
in Calvet Winery, Beaune, France. In
foreground is grape-picker's knife (serpet). In
background, typical Vendanges costumes.
Left: Detail of Trajan's Column shows Roman
soldiers transporting wine in amphorae.

he ancient Greeks thanked Dionysus for δωρον οινοι, "the gift of wine." The Egyptians believed the gift came from Osiris, while the Armenians and Hebrews credited Noah. Probably wine predates all these peoples. The celebrated *Vitis vinifera*, the grape-producing vine from which most wines are made, preceded man on earth.

Prehistoric man almost certainly made wine. Paleontologists have found the fossilized remains of what appear to be batches of crushed grapes. Cretan vessels of the Minoan civilization appear to have been used for wine. Paintings on the walls of Magdalenian caverns depict what could only have been winemaking. And the earliest of man's writings, including cuneiform tracts from Babylonia and papyri from ancient Egypt, contain numerous references to the fermented fruit of the vine.

Various legends purport to explain wine's invention. Our favorite has it that a Sumerian king, Gilgamesh, who liked grapes, frequently found his supply eaten by his wives and children. To insure that he'd always have some for himself, he stored a batch in a cask labeled "Poison." The cask somehow got mislaid, and a few years later it was happened on by one of the wives. She, as chance would have it, planned to kill herself because she resented Gilgamesh's preference for his other wives. Drinking the liquid she found in the cask, she felt a strange and wondrous glow. She promptly brought a cup to the king, who felt the same glow. Her discovery returned her to his favor, and they lived happily ever after.

Well, as our Italian forebears say, *se non è vero, è ben trovato*, if it isn't true, it should be. In any case, winemaking definitely was practiced in the Middle East and parts of China three millennia before Christ. The so-called "Standard" panel from Ur, currently in the British Museum, depicts wine drinking. It dates to about 2500 B.C. Chinese literature contains the account of a man who was sent into banishment in 2285 B.C. for making wine from rice. And in Egypt, wine was part of the funeral services of kings from about 3000 B.C.

During the second millennium B.C., each Egyptian king apparently had two vineyards: one for his funeral wines, the other for table wines. When he died the vineyards went public and wines were distributed under the king's name. One of the better-known varieties was Kankomet, from the vineyard of Ramses III (1198-1167 B.C.). Judging from descriptions of the wine, though the king's life was short it was a happy one.

The Egyptians introduced wine labeling, and some of the labels were quite detailed. A second millennium precursor of today's labels proclaimed vintage, vineyard, and winemaker: "In the year XXX, good wines of the large irrigated terrain of the Temple of Ramses II in Per-Amon. Chief winemaker: Tutmes."

Reliefs and murals in Egyptian tombs give a thorough account of contemporary winemaking. Grapes were harvested with sickles much like those currently in use. They were crushed by foot, then further dejuiced in wooden presses like some still used. The juice was fermented in vats of acacia wood, then portioned into barrels from which the wine was served.

Essentially the same procedures were followed in Babylonia in 2000 B.C., where winemaking was regulated under the Code of Hammurabi. These first wine laws stipulated conditions under which the beverage could be bought and sold. The punishment for a seller who misrepresented the volume of a container was to be thrown into a vat of water. But innkeepers who served intoxicated persons were dealt with much more severely: The punishment was loss of one limb for a first offense, and in certain circumstances death. The Greek historian, Herodotus, wrote of the Babylonians: "They are accustomed to deliberate on matters of the highest moment when warm with wine; but whatever they in this situation may determine is again proposed to them on the morrow, in their cooler moments, by the person in whose house they had before assembled. If at this time also it meet their approbation, it is executed; otherwise it is rejected. Whatever also they discuss when sober, is always examined a second time after they have been drinking."

Laurence Sterne wrote in his novel *Tristram Shandy* (1767): "The ancient Goths of Germany…had all of them a wise custom of debating every thing of impor-tance to their state, twice; that is, once drunk, and once sober; drunk that their councils might not want vigour; and sober that they might not want discretion." Oh, well, *se non è vero.…*

Biblical scholars have counted more than 150 refer-ences to wine in the Old Testament. There are additional dozens in the Talmud. Genesis records that King Mel-chizedek blessed wines and offered them to Abraham. The Book of Numbers reports that one of the regrets of the Hebrews, at the time of the Exodus, was having to leave behind the wines of Egypt. Happily, the wines they found in Palestine were equally palatable.

Dionysus—or someone—brought wine to Greece

*The whole process
of winemaking is depicted in
Theban tomb painting. In section below
the grapes are gathered, then
crushed by foot in a trough. Wine is
stored in large pottery jars.*

about 1000 B.C. The first Greek imports reportedly came from India—perhaps originally shipped from Damascus, as today many Algerian and Spanish wines become "French" before ultimately arriving in North America. But Italian wines soon became the Greek favorite. Significantly, the Greek name for Italy translates as "land of wine." More precisely, these wines were Sicilian; viticulture evidently flourished on the island as early as 2500 B.C.

The Greeks apparently were the first people to age their wine. Some sweet wines which matured in earthenware crocks seem from their descriptions not too different from the modern Portuguese wine, Malmsey. Many others were diluted with sea water and some were perfumed. The wines then were stored in vessels lined with pitch, which could not have failed to add a taste element most modern drinkers would find unpalatable.

Like the ancient Greeks, Julius Caesar also favored wines from Sicily. He personally selected the one to be served at the banquet honoring his investiture as consul in 50 B.C. It was a golden, hearty, and robust Mamertino from the province of Messina. The wine continues to be made today. Caesar deemed wine and women essential ingredients of a successful military campaign. Not only did doxies follow the Roman troops to battle, but vines were planted wherever the army triumphed. The vineyards of Bordeaux, Burgundy, the Loire, the Rhône, Champagne,

*Right: "Noah in the Vineyards,"
fifteenth-century Italian fresco. Left: Priests
offer wine in detail of Theban tomb painting. Below:
Woodcut by sixteenth-century Venetian artist
depicts genii bringing grapes to Bacchus. Bottom: Vine
motif dominates rich, romantic Persian miniature.*

*Right: Bacchus, god of
wine in classical mythology
(also called Dionysus), depicted in
"The Youthful Bacchus,"
sixteenth-century painting by
Michelangelo Caravaggio.*

Alsace, the Rhine, and the Moselle all were planted originally by the Romans.

Students who have forgotten most of their high-school Latin often remember the opening passage of Caesar's account of his Gallic campaigns: *"Gallia est omnis divisa in partes tres, quarum unam incolunt Belgae, aliam Aquitani...."* ("All Gaul is divided into three parts, of which one is inhabited by the Belgians, another the Aquitani....") This same Aquitaine is today's great French wine region of Bordeaux.

However, the Romans were not the first to bring wine to France. Five centuries earlier the Greeks planted some of their vines (originating, presumably, in Sicily) near Marseilles. Caesar's troops complained of the wines as being "smoky," which may have been the first round in a still-running battle between Italian and French wine lovers. A favorite joke of many Italians involves the French tourist in a small Roman café who refused the local wine and demanded a French import. The café did not stock one, but the owner promised to send out for one. The waiter he sent, contemptuous of French wine snobbery, mischievously brought back a bottle of vinegar, which he poured into a carafe and served. The Frenchman studied the color, nosed the wine, then tasted it, and smiled contentedly. "Ah," he reflected, "we French are so generous. We always export our best wines." Many Frenchmen tell the same story about an Italian tourist in a Parisian café.

The conquerors of the Christian church who took over the Roman Empire from the Caesars promptly dispensed with the troop-following harlots. Still, and perhaps as compensation, the churchmen preserved Roman viticultural traditions. The celebrated Clos de Vougeot, a vineyard on France's Côte d'Or, was planted by Cistercian monks in the twelfth century. The equally celebrated Steinberg Vineyard in Germany's Rheingau was planted

by Cistercians a century later. Pope Clement V, early in the fourteenth century, established vineyards at Avignon; the wines came to be known as Châteauneuf-du-Pape—the new Papal Castle—as they are today.

During this time in the Americas, grapes were growing abundantly. The Vikings who arrived in Canada at the turn of the eleventh century dubbed the land, "Vinland the Good." The name "Vinland" persisted in Icelandic literature for six centuries. The grapes the Vikings found probably were the hearty *Vitis labrusca*, which still grows in southeastern Canada and the northeastern United States and is the principal grape used in the making of several highly regarded wines.

If native North Americans made wine, history fails to record it. But European immigrants soon began using not only native grapes but also transplanted vines and hybrids. Captain John Hawkins, leader of a sixteenth-century English foray into Florida, found in a Spanish settlement some twenty hogsheads of wine made apparently from wild native grapes—most likely the *Vitis rotundifolia*, which grows along the Atlantic seaboard from Maryland to Florida. He didn't care much for what he sampled, but forty years later Captain John Smith wrote enthusiastically of the grapes and wines of Virginia:

"Of vines there is great abundance in many parts, that climbe the toppes of highest trees in some places, but these beare few grapes except by the rivers and savage habitations, where they are overshadowed from the sunne; they are covered with fruit though never prunned nor manured. Of these hedge grapes we made neere twentie gallons of wine, which was like our British wine, but certainly they would prove good were they well manured."

So much for Captain Smith's opinion of British wine. It was, by the way, widely shared, which may explain why England imported so much table wine from

Daubigny del   Ed. Willmann sc.

Bordeaux and so much sack and sherry from Spain. However, several modern English wines are well regarded both at home and abroad.

Captain Smith continued: "There is another sort of grape neere as great as cherry, this they [native North Americans] call messamins; they be fatte and the juyce thicke, neither doth the taste so well please when these be made in wine." It remains true today throughout the world that the fattest, juiciest, and most abundant grapes generally produce the least satisfactory wines.

Lord Delaware, Governor of Virginia, wrote the London Company in 1616 that he believed the American colonies might serve as the locale for a wine industry rivaling that of France. The company promptly recruited French viticulturists, who brought their own vines. The European cuttings could not survive the severe winters of the Northeast or the sandy soil of the Southeast, and the French winemen did not like the native American grapes. The project was abandoned, with interest in native North American wines not reviving for two centuries.

In the West, conquistador Hernando Cortez planted Spanish vines that grew so well he ordered every land-grant holder in his territory to plant ten vines per year per native American living within the grant area (the formula assumed, correctly, that the native Americans could be conscripted to tend the vines). The crop was so good that Spanish vintners feared American competition. Spain ultimately ordered the American vines destroyed. Some of them were, but others were carried north into California, where they—and various other imported cuttings—continue to thrive.

In the seventeenth century in France, a Benedictine monk, Dom Pérignon, made (dare we say "stumbled upon"?) a discovery that revolutionized winemaking in the province of Champagne. Winemakers had long known that certain wines, crushed and pressed and fermented in the fall as are all wines, refermented in the spring. When this happened, the wines popped the covers of their bottles (cotton wadding was used in those days rather than cork). The troublesome wines, which seemed particularly abundant in the Champagne region, came to be known as *vin diable* (devil wine), or *saute bouchon* (lid popper). Pérignon speculated that the problem was not in the wine but in the bottle cover. If a stronger cover were used, the wine would stay in the bottle and—who knows? —perhaps improve as much during the second fermentation as it did during the first.

Pérignon ordered that the bottles in the Benedictine Abbey of Hautvillers, of which he was cellarmaster, be given thicker stoppers which would be held in place with string. When these held, the bottles broke, so he procured stronger bottles. Finally, both the bottles and the stoppers held, and Dom Pérignon was able to sample one of the wines that survived second fermentation. *"Venez vite, mes frères! Je bois des étoiles!"* he cried, creating a phrase which among wine lovers has become as celebrated as Alexander Graham Bell's, "Mr. Watson, come here, I want you." Said the Dom: "Come quickly, brothers! I'm drinking stars!" He was, of course, drinking the wine we now know as Champagne.

By the mid-eighteenth century, wine had become a near-universal beverage. It was being made as well as drunk on six of the continents—in China, Russia, Japan, Australia, New Zealand, Egypt, Cyprus, Palestine, Syria, Turkey, Persia, Bulgaria, Hungary, Rumania, Austria, Germany, Luxembourg, Switzerland, France, Portugal, Spain, Morocco, Algeria, Italy, Tunisia, Malta, Greece, Argentina, Brazil, Chile, Mexico, and the soon-to-be United States. Its production and consumption have been increasing annually ever since.

2.

2.
FROM THE VINE COMES
THE GRAPE

Wine is fermented fruit or vegetable juice; which is rather like saying that woman is a female human. The definition is correct as far as it goes, but it doesn't go nearly far enough.

Chemically speaking, wine is the closest thing there is to a miracle. Given the opportunity, it will actually make itself. Put enough fruit or vegetables into a container and the weight of the units on top will crush the ones on bottom. If the juice contains sugar, it will ferment automatically. Of course, human attention to various details will influence the quantity and especially the quality of the resulting wine. But the basic phenomenon is Nature's doing, not man's.

Gastronomically speaking, wine is also near miraculous. It is a food: a most nutritious beverage. It is a drug: tranquilizer, appetite stimulant, and mild sedative. It can also be a delight to the eye, nose, and palate.

There are well over ten thousand different wines currently available in North America, at least another ten thousand each in Europe and Asia, about five thousand in Africa, and about two thousand in Australia. Some of these differ substantially. Others differ only slightly. But each is a truly distinct wine. How does one classify them?

The simplest approach is geographic. But the origin of a wine doesn't tell very much about its character or characteristics. Another approach is in terms of the circumstances under which the wine is usually drunk. Thus we hear of "table" wines and "festive" wines, "apéritif" wines and "dessert" wines. But one man's meat is another's *poisson*, and the "when" of wine drinking is, in our view, strictly a matter of personal taste.

We prefer to categorize in terms of the wine's physical character: whether it is sparkling or still, fortified or aromatized, carbonated or flavored.

Still wines are the wines most people probably think of when they think of wine—the traditional "table" wines that are as much a part of the classic European meal as the food. They can, of course, be drunk away from the table also. Working-class Europeans have long used them as a recreational beverage, to be consumed anytime and under any circumstances. The practice has recently been adopted by young people all over the world.

Still wines, by legal definition in North America, contain no more than 14 percent alcohol. More than that results in classification as a fortified wine. Actually, most still wines contain between 11 and 12 percent alcohol. This is the result of natural fermentation, not addition of distilled spirits or other matter (sugar may be added to induce natural development of alcohol).

Still wines cover the full spectrum of dryness to sweetness, and of very dark to very light. The dark wines are usually called red, though the color would probably strike most non-wine-drinkers as purple. In a few parts of the world, these "reds" are called black.

The light wines usually are called white, though they are closer to yellow. In parts of North Africa, they are called gray, and in Portugal they are often called green. An intermediate shade, sort of pink, is called *rosé* by the French and Portuguese, *roze* by the Turks, *rosato* by Italians, and *rosado* by the Spanish-speaking people of Europe and the Americas. For simplicity's sake, we'll use red, white, and rosé.

Most wine—over 99 percent of the world's production—comes from grapes. The remainder derives from apples, cherries, mangoes, peaches, oranges, duhats (a plumlike fruit of the East), dandelions, blackberries, elderberries, parsnips, and various other fruits and vegetables. Surprisingly, wines made from the same fruit can differ substantially, even if processed quite similarly.

Cabernet Sauvignon

Chenin Blanc

Gamay

Catawba

Concord

Johannisberg Riesling

Chardonnay

Delaware

Niagara

Cabernet Sauvignon

This dull blue beauty is regarded by many as the queen of red-wine grapes. It is the principal grape of many celebrated California and Bordeaux wines and some of the delicate dry reds of Hungary, Yugoslavia, South Africa, Australia, and Chile.

Catawba

Henry Wadsworth Longfellow rhapsodized this native North American white grape, which dominates several semidry white and rosé still wines and appears as a blending grape in a number of sparkling wines.

Chardonnay

Regarded by many as the best of France's white-wine producing grapes, this pale green, low-yield variety is the only one used in the famous dry still whites of Chablis.

Chenin Blanc

Principal grape of France's Loire Valley and the only grape permitted in Anjou wines, the dull green varietal also grows prolifically in California.

Concord

A native North American, this blue-black grape has one of the highest per-acre yields and can withstand the fierce winters of Canada and the northeastern U.S. Very sweet, it normally is used only for religious wines or to add volume to other wines.

Delaware

Pale yellow with delicate skin, it is regarded by many vintners as the very best native North American wine grape. It appears in a number of highly regarded dry and semidry white wines, and sparkling wines.

Gamay

This huge, blue-gray grape predominates in the wine that made the French district of Beaujolais famous. It also appears in some distinctive California, Canadian, and Australian wines.

Johannisberg Riesling

Grape of honor in Germany's famous Rhine Valley, this big, brown-spotted yellow beauty has also become a favorite in Australia, California, and South Africa, especially for tangy, fruity, white still wines.

Niagara

One of the first hybrids, this hearty grape can withstand the coldest North American winters. It appears in a number of popular white still wines of Canada and the eastern United States.

Palomino

Sangiovese

Sémillon

Pinot Blanc

Sauvignon Blanc

Sylvaner

Pinot Noir

Seibel 7053

Zinfandel

Palomino

A Spanish native, this small yellow grape with almost translucent skin is the chief variety in sherry.

Pinot Blanc

This international favorite can be found in Germany, Austria, Italy, France, Australia, California, North Africa, Chile, and Argentina. It appears in many of the dry white still wines celebrated in France's Burgundy region.

Pinot Noir

Actually blue, this "black" Pinot is the principal grape of the celebrated hearty red still wines of Burgundy. It is also the basis of some highly regarded dry still red wines from California, Hungary, and North Africa.

Sangiovese

Deep purple, it is the principal grape in Chianti and most other dry red wines of Italy's Tuscany region.

Sauvignon Blanc

This versatile French native with yellow-green skin is used as a blending grape both in the sweet white wine for which Sauternes (France) is famous and the dry white wine of the Bordeaux district of Graves. In California and Australia, it is the dominant grape in several noteworthy dry whites.

Seibel 7053

Deep blue-black, this is one of several distinguished grapes bearing this hybridizer's name. Number 7053 has high yields and is a principal blending grape in red wines of Australia, North Africa, and the Americas.

Sémillon

Yellow-green and thin-skinned, this is the principal grape of the popular dry white still wines associated with Graves and the sweet white still wines for which Sauternes is best known.

Sylvaner

A Central Europe native, this peripatetic high-yield grape now can be found throughout Europe, South America, South Africa, and California. It is the principal grape used in making sparkling wines and fruity white still wines.

Zinfandel

Believed to be a native of Bari, Italy, this zesty purple grape gained its greatest acclaim in California, where it now is the most widely grown red-wine grape.

Take the grape. It is a member of the botanical family Ampelidaceae, which comprises eleven genera of berry-bearing vines. Almost all wine is produced from grapes of the genus *Vitis*; more precisely, from grapes of the subgenus *Euvites*; still more precisely, from three or four species within this genus or from hybrids of these species. It does not tax the imagination that grapes of the species *Vitis labrusca* will yield substantially different wines from those of the species *Vitis vinifera*. But most of the world's best-known wines are produced from *vinifera* grapes, and there are substantial differences even among the most similar of these.

Take two of the most popular *vinifera* varieties: Sémillon and Cabernet Sauvignon. The former has a green skin, the latter blue. Sémillon is one of the principal grapes (most wines are a blend of grape varieties) of the popular dry white still wines associated with the Graves district of France's Bordeaux region. It is also one of the principal grapes of the celebrated sweet white still wines for which the Sauternes district of Bordeaux is best known. Though the same grape is used, the wines, except for their color, could not be more different.

Cabernet Sauvignon is the principal grape of some celebrated California red still wines, usually marketed under the producer's name, followed by the varietal name (for example, Concannon Cabernet Sauvignon). It is also the principal grape of some celebrated Bordeaux red still wines, usually marketed under the producer's name alone (for example, Château Margaux), or under the name of the producer followed by that of the township or district in which the wine originates (for example, T. Jouvet [producer] Saint-Julien [township]). These wines are all generally dry and generally delicate, and they have many other similarities, but they have many more differences. More different still are the Cabernet Sauvignon-derived white wines of Italy's Trentino-Alto Adige and Friuli-Venezia Giulia regions. Simi Winery in California's Alexander Valley produces a rosé Cabernet Sauvignon. A similar rosé of Cabernet is produced in France.

Some differences can be explained by the blending formulas of the winemakers, others by the aging and other treatment of the wine, and still others by differences in the soil and climate where the grapes are grown. But the same grape, grown in the same vineyard, and processed in exactly the same way by the same winemaker will yield different results from year to year. To find out why, let's examine more closely the various steps of grape growing and winemaking.

Viticulturists have catalogued more than eight thousand varieties of grapes, but fewer than one hundred of these are used extensively in winemaking. Unfortunately for wine drinkers, the grapes that produce the wines drinkers like most usually have the lowest yield per acre and require the most delicate care. This is one reason the most sought-after wines usually are also the most expensive.

Most wines are blends of several varieties, with one predominating. The winemaker selects among varieties much as a painter selects among the colors on his palette. A grape high in tannic characteristics, such as the Cabernet Sauvignon, produces wines which have a very harsh quality when they are young. As the wine matures in a cask or bottle, the harshness abates and the wine acquires an extraordinary complexity of bouquet and taste. Unfortunately, this may take ten to twenty years, or even longer. To shorten the wait the winemaker may add a "softening" wine from a grape like the Merlot. The complexity of the Cabernet may suffer, but some drinkers will deem the sacrifice worthwhile.

This isn't to say that all blends compromise quality.

*Left: Mustard plants grow
between trellised vines in California.
The flowers will later be turned
into the soil to nourish the grapes. Below:
Newly-blossomed grapes.*

Some winemakers blend strictly for taste, others blend mainly for economy. By combining wine from a high-yield-per-acre grape like the Carignan or Thompson Seedless with a low-yield variety like the Cabernet Sauvignon or the Pinot Chardonnay, the winemaker reduces unit cost while at the same time preserving some of the characteristics of the more desirable low-yield grape.

The character of a wine begins developing long before the first grape appears on the vine. It begins in the soil of the vineyard. Logic might suggest that the more fertile the soil, the better the wine. Actually, something approximating the opposite appears true. There are prime vineyards in Germany so rocky that vignerons must carry up soil from neighboring lowlands to nourish the vines. An axiom in the cliff-like hills along the Rhine and Moselle rivers has it that

*Where a plow can go,
There no vine should grow.*

Vineyards along Portugal's River Douro are so rocky and hilly that vignerons cannot transport grapes to the wineries for crushing and pressing. Instead, they perform these operations on the slopes, then carry the juice to the winery in huge goatskin back-sacks called *borrachos* (the word translates as "drunkards").

The wine regions of most other nations are less mountainous, but usually no more fertile. The soil of Champagne is chalky, that of Bordeaux and California's Livermore Valley sandy gravel, that of the Moselle Valley predominantly slate, and that of Italy's Piemonte mainly clay. In Burgundy, where little else but grapes will grow, farmers have a saying: "If our soil weren't the richest in the world, it certainly would be the poorest."

One of the things the soil of all these lands holds in abundance is trace elements, and particularly iodine and the minerals manganese, molybdenum, nickel, vanadium,

and zinc. Viticultural studies suggest that these not only control the growth rate of vines but also contribute characteristics of taste and aroma to the grapes (and, by extension, to the wines made from them).

The soil and the elements it contains apparently react differently with different varieties of grapes. The Nebbiolo grape, source of so many celebrated wines in Italy's Piemonte region, has not produced wines of comparable repute when planted in other countries or even in other wine-producing regions of Italy. The Zinfandel grape, meanwhile, is virtually extinct in its presumed home, Bari, Italy, but has reached full flower in California. The Cabernet Sauvignon, dominant grape in the much-revered red wines of Bordeaux's Haut-Médoc, has yielded California counterparts which some people feel will soon surpass the best Bordeaux has ever produced. But the Pinot Noir, dominant grape of the celebrated hearty red wines of Burgundy, has not been transplanted with equal success.

Along with soil, a key influence on the character of a wine is climate. Wine grapes seem to fare best where summers are fairly long, fairly hot, and fairly dry, and winters fairly cold and fairly wet.

The vine becomes dormant shortly after the first cold spell of autumn. Nonetheless, if the ground becomes too cold most vines will die. *Viniferas* are particularly vulnerable; however, the hearty *labruscas* are able to withstand severe winters.

In spring the fruit begins to grow. Now a fairly steady temperature is essential. If there is frost after buds have appeared, the fruit may be killed. This explains why most prime·wine-producing regions are along riverbanks or near other large bodies of water. The water keeps the air cool during early spring days, delaying the start of the growing season. Once growth begins, the water keeps the air warm into the harvest season.

Left: Smudgepots burn through the night to protect vines against frost. Bottom: Spraying with sulphur is done by helicopter. Below: Young vines at Beaulieu Vineyard are sprinkled for irrigation and frost protection.

Slow, steady warmth is very important to grapes. Too hot summers ripen the outer grape too quickly, before its inner regions (which contain the juice) have had a chance to develop properly. Too much rain causes the grapes to rot on the vine, or, at harvest time, dilutes the juice of the grapes.

Because climate varies from year to year, the quality of the grapes—and the wines—varies, even though all other factors in the wine's production may remain the same. It is for this reason that wine's vintage is important in regions where climate varies substantially.

A Year in the Vineyards

The vigneron's year begins with the first frost and ends with the harvest. California winemaker Sam J. Sebastiani, of Sebastiani Vineyards, in the Sonoma Valley, traditionally keeps a month-by-month log of his activities. These excerpts from a recent year's log give some idea of the vigneron's life as well as the development of his wines.

"*December/January:* In Europe pruning traditionally starts in mid-January, on St. Vincent's Day. We start a month earlier, after the first cold spell forces the vines into dormancy. This season we began our pruning on December 11, just after severe frosts and even some snow. Even when there is no snow the ground may be frozen, but grapevines can survive temperatures down to zero degrees.

"The two primary purposes of pruning are to train the vines to grow in a shape that will facilitate cultivation, disease control, and harvesting; and to distribute the bearing wood over the vine in order to increase its productive capacity as far as possible consistent with its ability to bear high-quality fruit. Too little pruning causes the vine to produce large quantities of low-quality fruit. Too much pruning decreases the yield.

"The two methods of pruning that we use are head pruning and cane pruning. On our older, more mature vines we use the first method. The vine stands alone and is cut so that the bearing spurs (short growths whose buds will bear the crop) are evenly distributed about the head of the vine, much like the spokes of a wheel about the hub. The center, or top, portion of the vine is left open to allow room for nourishing sunlight during the growing season.

"New plantings or replantings, however, are cane-pruned. That is, the fruit-bearing canes are supported by trellis wires. Depending on the strength of the vine, two to four canes, with twelve to fourteen fruit buds each (one bud yields two bunches of grapes), will be trained to run along the trellis. Over the years, vintners have learned that cane pruning is a nearly ideal system. It not only facilitates picking and allows better fruit distribution, but also increases production without intimidating the vine.

"*February:* This is perhaps the slowest month in our yearly cycle of winemaking. Heavy rains this month have delayed our pruning. This will not affect the quality of the harvest, but it does add frustration to a normally organized activity.

"The current high mean temperatures are causing some grape varieties to break out of their winter dormancy early. This is evidenced by slight movement of the buds and bleeding at the pruning cuts. If this continues, early blooming will result and the danger of frost damage will become critical.

"*March:* Continued rains have held up disking; that is, pulverizing the soil with a disk harrow. This process breaks up crusted earth, aerates the soil, and turns under nitrogen-rich mustard plants growing in the vineyards.

"For the next two months, frost protection will be critical. During this period, we must keep a close watch on early morning temperatures. We use overhead sprinklers

*The terraced vineyards
of the Côte Rôtie in France. Lakes
encourage steady temperatures,
mountains provide favorable drainage
and sun exposure—all desiderata
for grape growing.*

for frost protection. When vineyard temperatures drop to 34 degrees Fahrenheit [about 1.2°C], we turn them on. Showering the vineyard with a fine mist of droplets the size of a medium raindrop, the sprinklers protect both the grapes and vines. The water continually forms ice around the tender new shoots. Water gives off heat when it freezes. Instead of harming the shoots, the ice insulates them against any further drop in temperature.

"Plant parts covered by the ice-water mixture will remain near 32 degrees [0°C] even when the surrounding temperature drops considerably. Since plant damage does not begin until the temperature of the shoots drops below 29 degrees [about −2° C], this method is the safest means of preventing frost damage. However, it is necessary to maintain a constant flow of water to insure uniform protection. This flow must continue until all the frost has melted.

"Our overhead sprinklers serve other useful purposes. They are used for irrigation and bloom-time cooling (in case of sudden increases in temperature during bloom period—late May, early June—when the potential fruit is highly vulnerable to heat damage).

"*April:* We are again threatened with frost. Bill Bailey, our ranch foreman, and I have been spending several nights in the vineyards (two nights began around midnight and lasted until almost eight in the morning), watching temperatures and turning on our sprinklers.

"We are signaled that trouble is ahead by our frost alarm, which sounds when the temperature reaches 35 degrees [about 1.6°C]. The few frosts we have had were mild and short in duration. Frost damage to our unprotected vineyards has been negligible to this point, but frost will remain a danger throughout May.

"Many vintners are making their crop predictions, which as always, are subject to change. To me, this year's

*Autumn mood: Vineyard in California's
Mayacamas mountains, planted with the
much-prized Cabernet Sauvignon.
Leaves turn multicolored as grape berries
reach their prime at harvest time. Cabernet
Sauvignon is the queen of red grapes.*

harvest looks promising. The vines are heavily laden with tiny flower buds where grape clusters will eventually form. However, we still have four more weeks to be concerned about frost. We must also be concerned with the problem of excessive heat during bloom-time. Normally after this, it should be clear sailing, but there are exceptions, such as last year's excessive heat spell during the summer, which cut our crop in some vineyards to 50 percent.

"One thing we are sure of, though: The grape harvest will begin two weeks early this year (mid-August). My father's barometers—his Canada geese—have already hatched out their young two weeks early.

"April is also planting month. We are preparing the soil for new vineyards at our Schellville ranch and for planting year-old cuttings in places where we lost vines to December's abnormal freeze.

"For our new plantings we begin soil preparation in the fall by ripping the earth to a depth of three feet. When the soil begins to dry out enough for our tractors, we begin disking (in February or March).

"All new plantings are with vines that are bench-grafted onto certified rootstocks. The vines are of European origin. The rootstocks are native to eastern America and are generally of the St. Georges variety. Such vines are resistant to phylloxera, the root louse which decimated California vineyards in the 1870's.

"This year our planting program will cover more than fifty acres, including such prime grape varieties as Cabernet Sauvignon, Merlot, Barbera, Pinot Chardonnay, Gewürztraminer, and Chenin Blanc. These vines will be trellised in their second year and will bear a crop in four or five years.

"*May:* So far the month has been promising. We have had no frosts. Our grapes are benefiting from moderately warm days without excessive heat. We are now seeing the beginning of bloom in many varieties. If this weather continues throughout the bloom, and we have a normal set (conversion of the grape flower to a grape), we will be well on our way to a fine harvest.

"We have begun installing pipelines to carry water from our reservoir to the new plantings. This is being done concurrently with our planting, which is going very smoothly.

"We are also in the process of improving our grape-handling operations in preparation for the harvest. In previous harvests we have utilized one crusher, washing it down when switching from red grapes to white grapes. This caused delay in handling the grapes. The sooner they are crushed after picking and put into a controlled atmosphere, the better will be the resulting wine. Before this year's harvest we will have installed a new crusher for our white grapes, so that they will be handled more rapidly when they arrive.

"We have also been tearing down the distillery building which my grandfather used in the old days in making high-proof spirits used for our dessert wines. Next year these grounds will contain new, stainless steel, individually temperature-controlled fermentation vats.

"*June:* Due to the cool, moist nights in the North Coast counties this time of year, we are faced with a mildew problem. Powdery mildew, called *öidium* in European vineyards, is our particular concern. It is a fungus which attacks the leaves of vines. If allowed to spread unchecked, it will dehydrate the leaves, halt berry growth in a green, pea-sized state, and eventually kill the vine. Fortunately, this fungus is easily controlled by annual spraying with finely ground sulphur, usually applied twice a year, once before the bloom and again immediately after the grapes have set.

"*July:* Most of our grapes have now completed

Clockwise from top left: Cheerful grape-picker in Lebanon; Barossa Valley in Australia; Château Carbonnieux, Graves, France; sorting the grapes, Italy; picking in Côte Rôtie, France; morning break, Fleurie, France; a good harvest, Puglia, Italy.

In the vineyards of Italy's Campania,
trellised vines grow as high as twenty feet.
Following a centuries-old method,
workers on ladders pick grapes and place
them in large wicker baskets. Right:
Baskets are lowered to the ground by rope.

their initial growth. They are about half their mature size and are shielded from the midday sun by a lush green canopy of foliage. Soon the grapes will put on their final spurt of growth and the harvest will be with us. In the meantime, there are certain minor operations that must be carried out to insure a fruitful harvest.

"Weeding is one. We must cut back weeds growing between the rows of vines lest they rob them of moisture in the soil, prevent complete fruit maturation, and interfere with field work. Earlier in the year we turned under (by disking) both weeds and any cover crops that were growing in the vineyards. During the summer, to prevent further growth of these weeds, we use a weed-cutter with a number of wedge-shaped blades that chop off the weeds below soil level. The cutter is followed by a culti-packer, which breaks up clods of soil and mulches the ground for better moisture retention.

"Suckering also is done at this time. This involves removing all shoots that originate either below the ground, or on the trunk of the vine if they are not fruit-bearing. These shoots, or suckers, grow quite vigorously and draw off sap that would otherwise nourish the whole vine. Since the vine should expend all its energy for fruit production, these suckers are removed before they can diminish any of its vigor.

"Grape leafhoppers have long been a vineyard problem. They attack the cell structure of the grape leaf. A minor infestation may be insignificant, but a medium infestation could cause enough defoliation to expose the grapes to sunlight and turn them into raisins. A major infestation could prevent the fruit from ripening at all. In our new vineyards, blackberry bushes are being planted randomly around the perimeters. These bushes serve as host for a wasp species, *Anagrus epos*, which feasts on grape leafhopper eggs, substantially reducing their numbers. By

Left: Emptying barrels full of freshly picked grapes into wagon, in San Martin, California. Right: Hilly vineyard in the south of France, with view on farmland. Dry, rocky ground is good for vines.

"*September*: We call it variously the harvest, the vintage, or the crush. Whatever you call it, it is the most exciting time of year at any winery. When the grapes are ripe, we transport them to the winery quickly, crush them, and pump the resulting must (pulp, skins, seeds, and juice) to either fermentation tanks or presses.

"Over the last five years we have begun the harvest as early as September 3 and as late as September 23; we have finished as soon as October 21 and as late as November 14. This year indicators point to an early harvest, currently projected to begin during the week of September 4. Here is a projected view of this year's harvest, giving the expected picking dates for ten of our most important varieties:

"*Week One (September 4–9)*: The bulk of our Gewürztraminer grapes will be harvested this week. Nearly a quarter of our Pinot Noir and Gamay Beaujolais will be picked. They are the earliest ripening black varieties.

"*Week Two (September 10–16)*: Our only slack week, involving a smattering of all varieties. We begin picking Pinot Chardonnay and Chenin Blanc.

"*Week Three (September 17–23)*: We normally pick ten to fifteen tons of Pinot Chardonnay and about the same of Chenin Blanc. This week and the following two we will receive the balance of our Pinot Noir and Gamay Beaujolais.

"*Week Four (September 24–30)*: We will bring in two-thirds of Barbera this week. Over half our Sylvaner Riesling is picked, along with another fifteen to twenty tons of Chenin Blanc.

"*Week Five (October 1–7)*: The biggest of the harvest. With the exception of Traminer and Chardonnay, virtually every variety sees the crusher this week. We begin bringing in Cabernet Sauvignon. We finish harvesting Barbera, Chenin Blanc, and Sylvaner. The major por-

encouraging the Anagrus wasp, we achieve an integrated system, eliminating the need for chemical pesticides.

"*August*: The black grape varieties are changing color. Where there were green berries, there now are bluish-purple grapes, growing larger by the day as they enter their final push toward maturity and harvest. This color change has always been the signal to grape growers and winemakers that the harvest is at hand. An old-timer's rule of thumb is, "When the grapes change color, the harvest is forty days away."

"We are fully occupied preparing our equipment for the harvest. Cleaning and inspecting for proper mechanical order is our highest priority. We are checking our hoppers, conveyors, electric hoists, crushers, must pumps, presses, fermentation vats, and all wooden cooperage to make them ready for the wine of the vintage. Even our grape-picking knives are being sharpened in preparation for their return to use.

tions of our Green Hungarian and Johannisberg Riesling are also picked.

"*Week Six (October 8–14):* The Cabernet Sauvignon will come rapidly this week (almost one-third of it). We finish Green Hungarian.

"*Week Seven (October 15–21):* This is Cabernet Sauvignon's week, with nearly 40 percent of this variety being harvested. Late to ripen, it finishes the harvest in fine style.

"*October:* The harvest is in now, and it was the kind of vintage winemakers dream of: a generous helping of superior-quality grapes. Our crush this year totaled nearly 4,500 tons, up from both our normal crush (some 4,000 tons) and last year's short crop (3,100 tons). The real blessing, however, has been the consistently high quality of the fruit.

"Largely responsible was some of the best grape weather we have experienced. The winter was wet, and the soil retained the moisture well. The spring saw no killing frosts and was followed by a moderately warm summer, devoid of excessive heat. The harvest went exceptionally well, with sporadic rains slowing down picking schedules only slightly. This spread out the harvest a week or two, which actually gave us more time to attend the newly fermenting wines.

"*November:* Hoppers and crusher-stemmers are now silent, the fields are barren save for an occasional truck dumping pomace between the rows of vines. Pomace (dried grape skins, seeds, and pulp), high in nitrogen, is a natural fertilizer. The vineyards themselves give visible indications of approaching winter. Leaves have gone through spectacular color changes during the last two months, showing off rust browns, flaming crimsons, and fiery yellows. Now they are falling to the earth, leaving the vines bare until the next growing season.

*Modern harvesting methods are employed
in vineyards of New York State's Finger Lakes
region. Left: Individual grapes are shaken
loose by harvester. Right: The grapes
ride conveyer belt before dropping down chute
into trailer pulled by tractor.*

"The winter rains have begun, the pruning will begin after the first hard frost lulls the vines into dormancy."

The Sebastiani operation is typical of vineyards the world over. It is larger than the average French château or German estate which grows its own grapes and bottles its own wine. It is smaller than the huge consortia like Ruffino in Italy, B&G in France, or Gallo or Taylor in the United States, which buy all or most of their grapes from private growers. But in every vineyard and winery, the same basic procedures are followed.

The Harvest

As the newly formed hard green berry of the grapevine ripens, it develops acid. Then it changes color and begins undergoing a series of complicated chemical changes as a result of which certain of its acids are converted to sugar. (The process is part of the ripening of all fruits.) The more heat the grape gets (from the sun), the more rapidly this conversion takes place. Early winemakers measured the sugar level of the ripening grape by tasting it. Modern winemakers measure more precisely with a hydrometer, a refractometer, and other instruments.

The hydrometer is a weighted glass tube, calibrated in degrees of balling (or, in French, *brix*). Immersed in a 100-gram solution, it will record 1 degree of balling for every gram of sugar. (In a pure water solution, it would record 0 degrees.) The refractometer measures the bending of light as it passes through a solution. A gram of sugar causes light to bend 1 degree of balling.

Shortly after the grapes change color, vignerons begin testing them for sugar. The more sugar a grape contains, the more alcohol there will be in the wine fermented from it—and, usually, the less acid. Different winemakers have different standards as to the perfect sugar-acid bal-

ance for each variety of grape. This is determined to some extent by the intended use of the grape. For example, the Pinot Noir not only is the principal grape of the red still wines for which Burgundy is best known but also for many of the sparkling white wines characteristic of Champagne. Most winemakers prefer 17 to 20 degrees balling for a sparkling white (with acid of 1 degree or higher) and 21 to 23 degrees balling for a still red (with .9 degree or less acid).

Some grapes, if left on the vine beyond normal ripeness, will simply dry up. Others will develop characteristics of sweetness which many wine drinkers prize. Among the varieties which develop these characteristics are the Chardonnay, Sémillon, Sauvignon Blanc, Riesling, Gewürztraminer, and Palomino. There is a danger, however, in leaving the grape on the vine too long. With most grapes the occurrence of frost is fatal; what yesterday was potentially a rich crop may today be nothing more than frozen garbage.

A protection against frost is the fungus, *Botrytis cinerea*, which forms on the ripest grapes during an exceptionally long and even growing season. This "noble rot," as English-speaking wine producers call it (the Germans call it *Edelfäule*, the French *pourriture noble*), concentrates sugar and glycerine content and at the same time reduces acidity and water volume. The grape thus produces less wine, but sweeter wine.

Noble rot appears almost every year in Germany, France, and South Africa, about one year in seven in Italy and the United States, and rarely elsewhere. Wines produced from it are described as *Spätlese* in German—a term adopted by North American wine producers. South Africans simply translate it "late vintage." The French and Italians do not have a special designation for the wines made from late-picked grapes. These grapes most often are reserved for production of specific wines (for example, the better Sauternes wines of France and Sémillon-based sweet white wines of Italy).

When the winemaker gives the word, the grapes are picked. In some vineyards the picking is done by hand, in others by mechanical harvester. Hand-pickers take entire bunches of grapes and generally are expected to harvest a ton a day. They go to work at dawn and try to accomplish as much as possible before the midday heat. Mechanical harvesters knock the grapes individually from the vine. They work around the clock to bring in the grapes at their peak of readiness.

In some vineyards each bunch of grapes is examined and those containing imperfect grapes are put aside to be used for wines of lower quality. The French call the process *épluchage* (picking), the Germans call it *Auslese* (selection). In some German vineyards, the process is further refined. The bunches of grapes are spread on a large table, and the individual grapes are sorted: *Beerenauslese*, the less ripe (but the entire group, it will be remembered, comprises riper grapes than those normally harvested), and *Trockenbeerenauslese*, the riper. The yield of the *Trockenbeerenauslese* grapes generally is only one-tenth that of normally harvested grapes, and the prices of most *Trockenbeerenauslese* wines doubly reflect the difference: These wines usually cost twenty times the price of normal wines.

In extremely rare years, the *Edelfäule* on German grapes will protect them not only against frost but also against ice and snow. These very late-picked grapes produce that super delicacy among German wine delicacies, *Eiswein* (ice wine). The grapes freeze and are harvested in the middle of the night. The unfrozen center, which has a high sugar-water ratio, yields a very sweet and highly alcoholic wine.

3.
FROM THE GRAPE COMES
THE WINE

The procedures of making wine vary from place to place, but the basic steps are the same everywhere. Probably no one's techniques are more basic than those G-1 and G-2 follow for home-made wines.

To begin, we buy a ton of California or New York grapes. We prefer Zinfandel, which produces a wine closer than any other variety to the dry red wines of G-1's native Italian province of Catanzaro. When Zinfandel isn't available we usually buy Gamay or one of the Seibel varieties.

The grapes are shipped by rail to our northeastern Pennsylvania hometown of Carbondale. When we tell this to commercial winemakers, they cringe. They like to crush their grapes as soon as possible—only rarely more than five hours after picked—and in an undamaged state. By using bruised grapes that have been in transit for up to a week, we risk mold, mildew, and disruption of the acid-sugar balance. Of course, we would rather not take these risks, but it's a case of the only port in a storm. Wine grapes do not grow well in Carbondale. In any event, we've been lucky. We've managed to produce wines that satisfy us almost every time.

While we're waiting for the grapes to arrive, we clean and prepare our equipment, which is about as rudimentary as wine equipment can get. It consists of a crusher, a press, and three barrels of Kentucky oak, formerly used for bourbon.

To make sure our barrels don't leak, we fill them with water. This swells the wood. The water escapes through any holes until they are swollen shut. This usually takes about three days for the leakiest of barrels.

When the grapes arrive, we crush them. The crusher is placed on top of an open barrel and the grapes are inserted a basket at a time. The juice, skins, stems, and seeds all go into the barrel. The resulting mixture, or must, ferments automatically—the result of a chemical reaction between the sugar in the grape and the yeast enzymes in the film that develops on the skins as they mature.

Each day we stir the must, then cover the barrel with a cloth to keep its contents clean and to help retain natural heat. In warm regions, heat can be a problem, causing the must to ferment too rapidly to develop desired acids and other properties. To slow fermentation, especially for white wines, winemakers use refrigerated tanks. We Pennsylvanians have the opposite problem, shared by many German winemakers: too slow fermentation, resulting in overly acidic red wines (but just right for naturally fermenting whites). If the weather is unseasonably cold when we're crushing, we bring the operation indoors.

After the first few days of fermentation, we taste the must daily. When G-1's taste buds tell him that it's ready, we press it. The solid remains of the skins, stems, and seeds are discarded. The juice is transferred into fresh, covered barrels that have been treated with sulphur to kill harmful bacteria. These barrels, made firm on a massive rack, lie side by side with their bungholes upright.

The prepress stage of fermentation lasts eight to fifteen days, the postpress another fifteen to twenty. Sometimes, to produce a white wine, we draw off a barrel of juice early in the prepress phase and let it continue fermenting without its skins, stalks, and seeds. It is the skins that impart color to a wine. If they aren't permitted to ferment in the wine, it will be white, even though the grape was red. In any case, we let fermentation continue until it halts naturally. We don't use chemical additives or other techniques to halt it.

During the postpress phase, the wine ferments at a more leisurely rate. Instead of bubbling violently, it just sort of gurgles (described poetically as "the music of the

*Wagonload of grapes from
vineyard in Burgundy is unloaded at Beaune
cellar of shipper Louis Latour. Grower
will be paid according to weight and sugar
content of grapes. Right: Weigh-in
at Balaruc-la-Vieux in Provence.*

wine"). The foam produced by escaping carbon dioxide seeps through the barrel's bunghole and over the sides of the bilge.

When it is obvious that fermentation has ended, the bung (that is, the stopper) is put into the bunghole and the wine begins to age. After three months we begin to drink it—"from the wood," as the expression goes. A spigot is placed a few inches from the bottom of the barrel; solid particles settle below it, and the wine that comes out is clear.

Our average consumption is a barrel every six months (we have a big family). When the first barrel is finished, we clean and resulphur it, then transfer wine from the second barrel. In the process, we eliminate the

solids that have accumulated in the bottom of the second barrel. This barrel then is cleaned and resulphured, and the wine from the third barrel is transferred. Six months later, with two barrels empty, we remove the solids from the third and bottle the wine. It will be drunk only on special occasions in future years. Meanwhile, the first barrel of the new year's batch is ready for everyday drinking.

Producing wines in this manner is, of course, risky. Sometimes we're happy with the results, sometimes very disappointed. Commercial winemakers often use concrete, glass, or stainless steel fermenting tanks. They can't afford the same wide fluctuations in quality, so they control their operation much more tightly.

In early times crushing was done by foot. Residents of the wine-producing village would march around in a grape-filled trough. When they were thigh-deep in juice, the trough would be drained and new grapes added. In parts of Spain and Portugal, the practice persists today. In most places, however, mechanical crushers or combination crusher-stemmers are used. These range in size and sophistication from hand-cranked barreltop types like our own to the enormous (five stories high) unit at the Château-Gai winery in Niagara Falls, Canada. With the latter, grapes are dumped into a trough, pulled via steel-worm into chutes, mechanically separated from their stems, and squeezed. The free-run juice is then routed through pipes to fermenting vats, while the solids are carried to presses. Not once in the process are the grapes touched by human hands, much less feet. Not that this ever presented a problem in hygiene: Fermentation sterilizes the wine.

Some mechanical harvesters not only pick grapes but also crush them *in situ*. In addition to being more efficient, the method insures against quality failures resulting from too much time between picking and crushing. But most vineyards are on terrain too hilly for mechanical harvesters, and winemakers have not been able to find comparable soil/climate conditions in flatter places, so hand-picking probably will remain part of the scene for quite some time.

To make white wine, the vintner presses his grapes immediately after crushing them. The juice then goes into a fermenting vat. Fermentation normally continues until the alcohol concentration in the solution reaches 14 to 16 percent, then automatically stops. If there was more sugar in the grape than necessary to produce this quantity of alcohol, the excess will remain in solution and the wine will taste sweet. If there was less, fermentation will stop

*Left: Steel worm draws grapes
into a crusher-stemmer. Below: In Fleurie, a
worker shovels grapes into basket press.
Bottom: An ancient basket press.
Right: Modern bladder-type press at Widmer's
Wine Cellars in Naples, New York.*

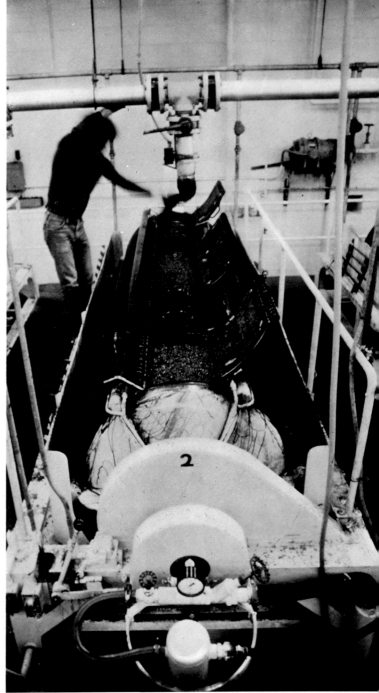

when the sugar runs out, at an alcohol concentration somewhere under 14 percent. The wine will taste dry.

Generally, sugar content is no problem in Italy or California, where the growing season is both long and sun-filled. But in many parts of the world, grapes occasionally must be harvested with less than the desired amount of sugar. To bring the wines up to the desired alcohol concentrations, winemakers may add nongrape sugar—sucrose, maltose, or whatever—to the fermenting must. The process is called *chaptalization* in France, where it was pioneered by a chemist named Chaptal. In Germany it is called *Verbesserung* (improvement) or *Gallization,* after the local pioneer, a chemist named Gall. The process is illegal in California.

Some vintners make a lower grade of wine, or "near-wine," by adding sugar and water to already pressed grape skins. Fermentation is induced, the acids and other substances remaining in the skins are freed, and the resulting liquid is marketed, usually as a jug wine (sold by the half gallon or in larger containers rather than in the standard 24- to 28-ounce bottle).

Various chemical additives also are legal in most countries and are regarded as legitimate by most winemakers. These additives include tartaric acid (used when a long, hot summer has baked too much of the natural acid out of the grapes); calcium carbonate (to de-acidify wines made from underripe grapes or which are otherwise overly acidy); and diatomaceous earth (a fine clay-like substance), which is subsequently filtered out, to remove un-

An Italian winemaker inspects free-run juice passing from crusher to fermenting vat. This luscious-looking liquid is squeezed from the entire grape. Fine red color of quality Italian wines like Bolla and Bertani is a notable characteristic.

wanted solids. In some circumstances some winemakers also pasteurize wine or heat it short of pasteurization. Others use charcoal to filter out unwanted color.

To make red wine, the vintner follows basically the same procedures as to make white, except that the entire grape—skin and pulp, and seeds, and sometimes also stalks—goes into the fermenting vat with the juice produced by crushing. Depending on the deepness of color desired by the winemaker, the skins (and other solids) may be left in the vat until fermentation stops, or they may be removed earlier. For a rosé wine, they will be removed after only a day or two of fermentation.

Note well that the grapes have not yet been pressed. The liquid in the fermenting vat is what flowed freely when the grapes were crushed. Wine people call it the free-run wine. The pressing doesn't take place until the skins have been removed from the vat. They will yield about one-fifth the volume of wine as the free run. It will be of substantially lower quality and very dark. Some commercial winemakers, like us amateurs, will blend it with the free-run wine, but most will put it aside for blending with lower-grade wines in their line or for sale to other producers of wine. (Under U.S. law, you may describe a wine by its varietal name as long as 51 percent of its volume was produced from that grape and the wine contains the "characteristics" of that grape.)

Let's return now to the fermenting vats. When the grapes were crushed, the juice which resulted was not pure liquid. Like most substances which we call liquids, including water, it contained solid particles. These particles are what give the liquid its density. They are called lees. When fermentation has ended, the wines are transferred to other containers for aging. These may be vats as large as 100,000 gallons or barrels that hold as little as fifty gallons. The lees that now remain in the fermenting vats will be discarded. The wine, meanwhile, will continue to retain many solid particles. These will make it look cloudy, almost muddy. Over the next weeks and months many of the particles will settle and the wine will clarify. Periodically the winemaker will transfer the clear wine into a new container and discard the current batch of lees. The process is called racking.

While being clarified, the aging wine also undergoes a change in character. This is partly a chemical reaction to the material of which the storage container is made. Red wine usually is stored in wood. Most winemakers prefer oak, specifically limousin or soane from France. Some use redwood, especially for less expensive wines. Usually, the more expensive the wine happens to be, the smaller the storage container likely to be used.

It is extremely interesting to observe the wine at this stage. One place to look, as the big and potentially great vintage of 1959 was being processed, was at Gevrey-Chambertin. This is among the cluster of little Burgundian villages that make up the Côte de Nuits and produce magnificent and world-famous wines.

At the *cave* of Armand Rousseau, huge wooden vats sat monolithically in the cool dimness. Because of their height, their contents could be inspected only by climbing a ladder and peering over the brim. The deep pool of wine looked almost black in the pale light, and it bubbled and blurped gently, like an old gentleman after a handsome dinner. Monsieur Rousseau said with a twinkle, "We call that 'the music of the wine.'"

To the inexperienced, the music was dissonant, for this early in the life of a wine it tastes thin and acrid. But the vintner was not dismayed. To him, wine always presents discernible qualities that find counterparts in a catalogue of tastes assimilated over a lifetime. Matching present with past permits an educated prediction as to the degree of glory the wine will achieve at maturity.

Even after a year the character of a developing wine may be evident only to experts. At La Romanée-Conti, the birthplace of Burgundies of unsurpassed quality—and rarity—the *caviste* withdrew a sample of one-year-old La Tâche with a wine "thief"—a glass pipette—and released it into a little silver winetaster's cup. Its color was pale, its bouquet faint, its taste not even a glimmer of the wine-to-be. Yet the *caviste* was beaming. All was as it should be. His one-year-old La Tâche tasted precisely like well brought up, one-year-old La Tâche should taste. All his children were headed for greatness.

And, of course, the experience of Burgundy is matched and repeated by the other wine regions of France, each in its distinctive way. New wine everywhere contains clues, for those who know how to look, to its future promise.

The importance of the wood to the wine is dramatically apparent to experienced tasters who sample quantities of the very same batch of wine from different barrels or casks. Certain containers, after being used fifty or sixty years, develop highly individual characteristics, which they then impart to all wines stored in them. In some wineries, when a superior barrel or cask is identified, the wines from it are separated and sold either as the winemaker's "private reserve" or under some similar designation. A few wineries, like Buena Vista in California's Sonoma Valley, put the cask number right on the label. The drinker who finds a wine he especially likes can then look for the same cask number.

White wines may also be aged in wood, but more frequently stainless steel, glass- or fiberglass-lined metal, or concrete containers are used. This is less in the interest of economy than of taste. The qualities most drinkers prize in white wine—lightness, fruity taste, the fresh aroma of the grape—are not always enhanced by wood aging.

Red wine ferments in the cellars
of shipper Louis Latour, in Burgundy region.
In foreground, châpeaux (hats) of grape
skins form atop vats. Wine from the
bottom of the vats is pumped over them. Pigment
in the skins gives wine its color.

Left: Gamay grapes ferment in refrigerated tanks at the Robert Mondavi winery. Below: Wine is pumped from tanks, filtered, sampled, and transferred to aging-tanks. Gamay-based wines are usually bottled within weeks of the harvest.

The aging period may last anywhere from a few weeks to a few years. White wines generally get less aging than reds, but there are exceptions. The characteristic red wine of the French Beaujolais district is traditionally brought to market on November 15 of the harvest year. Until fairly recently, horse-drawn carriages of the wine literally raced north to Paris on that date to meet patrons waiting for them at bistros. The new wine, Beaujolais *nouveau*, then was drunk at parties celebrating the harvest.

Most inexpensive wines, white or red, are bottled after less than a year's aging. Among more expensive wines, dry whites usually are aged for a year to eighteen months, sweet whites eighteen months to three years, and red for two to six years.

This doesn't mean that the more aging a wine gets, the better it will be. The character—or "quality," if that word can be applied to something so highly subjective—of the wine depends on many factors: the grape(s) from which it was made, soil in which the grapes were grown, weather during their growing season, treatment of the must during fermentation, etc. Some grape varieties seem to reach their peak after a relatively short aging period, others take quite a while. The trick is to give each grape the amount and kind (oak, redwood, etc.) of aging that brings out its "best" (that is, most desired) properties. When that's been done it's time to bottle the wine.

Blending may take place at any time before bottling. Some vintners actually blend in the field, planting different grape varieties side by side and harvesting them all together. Others blend in the crusher, or immediately after fermentation. Some blend only mature wines, while others blend several times during the wine's development.

Many winemakers consider blending their highest art, for by judiciously choosing the varieties to be blended and the times at which it is done, they exercise their great-est control over the ultimate character of the wine. Not only are different varieties of grapes blended but also wines from different years. Mature wines usually lack the freshness and fruitiness of young wines; young wines usually lack the complexity of mature wines. Adding a small quantity of young wine to a mature wine often provides freshness and fruitiness without detracting from the complexity or other desired properties of the mature wine.

Eventually the aging wine will reach a point of clarity where relatively few solids will separate automatically from the solution. Yet many will remain in solution, keeping the wine cloudy. To remove them, winemakers dump egg whites, gelatine, or other neutral matter into the wine. These substances attract the solid particles and carry them to the bottom of the solution. The clear wine then is pumped off. The whole process is called fining.

In some wineries one more clarifying procedure, filtering, is employed immediately before bottling. Nylon powder, diatomaceous earth, or some similar neutral substance is dumped into the wine. The wine then is run through a filter, which takes out both the neutral agent and additional solid particles.

Many people believe that, once bottled, the wine stops aging. This is untrue. The myth probably owes to confusion with distilled spirits, which do not change character after they have been bottled (but do continue to age, —as, for better or worse, do we all—for as long as they exist). But while a bottle of twelve-year-old bourbon (the twelve-year designation refers to the amount of time the bourbon was stored in wood) remains a twelve-year-old bourbon fifty years later, a twelve-year-old bottle of wine becomes a sixty-two-year-old bottle of wine fifty years later. And the differences between that same bottle at age twelve and age sixty-two are enormous.

Not all wines get better as they get older. In fact,

Great vats of Barton-Guestier's new winery in Blanquefort, near Bordeaux, have a capacity of one and a quarter million gallons. B&G has the distinction of being the oldest of the négociants of Bordeaux.

no wine improves indefinitely. Each reaches a peak—again, bear in mind the high degree of subjectivity in these matters—at a certain age, depending on the grape(s) it contains, the way the wine was made, and so on. White wines generally peak earlier than reds, and inexpensive wines generally peak earlier than more expensive wines. Very few Rieslings, for example, are palatable more than five years after the grapes were picked. Very few Cabernet Sauvignons are at their best less than five years after the grapes were picked. Some Cabernets do not peak for twenty to thirty years. As a rule, the longer it takes the wine to peak, the "better" (that is, more to the liking of most experienced wine drinkers) it will be. Also, the longer it takes to peak, the longer it will stay at its peak and the longer it will take to decline.

Our rule of thumb for this—by no means applicable without exception, but pretty reliable in our experience—is that the wine will stay at peak for approximately one-half as long as it took to get there and then take twice as long to decline into undrinkability. In other words, a Sylvaner Riesling that reaches its peak two years after the grapes were crushed will stay that good for another year, then will begin to decline until, four years later, at age seven, it will be undrinkable. Meanwhile, a Cabernet Sauvignon that takes twenty years to reach its peak will stay there for ten and then decline for another forty, not becoming undrinkable until age seventy. We stress that there are exceptions to this rule, particularly among the more carefully made wines (which tend to stay at peak longer and decline more slowly). But all wines eventually turn into vinegar, and some of those 150-year-old bottles sold at auction for upward of $1,000 prove more suitable for sprinkling on a salad than drinking.

The usual problem, however, is not that wines are kept too long but that they are drunk too soon. To prevent

Left: In Sicilian cellar, wine is racked in the classical manner: by being pumped "off its lees" from one barrel to another. Below: At the Corrado winery in Luciano, Campania, wine is drawn from aging vat, then tested by winemakers.

this, some winemakers store bottled wine for years in their own warehouses before releasing it to retailers.

If a still wine is aged under certain circumstances, its overall volume decreases more rapidly than its alcohol volume. Thus, the percentage of alcohol rises. When it passes 16 percent, the wine is classified as fortified. Most fortified wines are in the 17 to 21 percent range, although some have been known to go as high as 30 percent. (Distilled spirits are usually 43 to 50 percent alcohol.)

The alcohol content of wine is not an indication of the wine's quality, only its potency. Most drinkers of fortified wines prefer those with 21 percent or less. The wine is drunk not for its ability to induce intoxication, but for its ability to gratify the senses.

Like still wines, fortified wines cover the full spectrum of dryness to sweetness. Dry ones frequently are served as apéritifs, sweet ones with dessert or as after-dinner drinks; accordingly, the classifications apéritif and dessert wines. But these terms are misleading. Dry or sweet fortified wines can be enjoyed away from the table as well as at it. Most hosts would not serve a sweet fortified wine with a meal, because most diners would not find its taste compatible with their food, but an occasional drinker does enjoy ruby Port or some other sweet fortified wine as a dinner wine, and who's to say he's wrong? Another reason most people do not drink fortified wines with meals is that the higher alcohol content does not permit the diner to consume enjoyably the volume of liquid he desires with his meal.

Except for ruby Port, fortified wines generally are not spoken of in terms of color. Actually, they occupy a fairly broad yellow-gold-brown spectrum. As a rule, the drier the wine, the lighter the color.

The first fortified wine probably was produced by accident. We envision a vintner leaving a barrel of wine in some sunny place, perhaps even forgetting it is there. Some time later he remembers it and tastes it to see if it is still good. The moment is somewhat like Pérignon's when he discovered sparkling wine. Our vintner finds that his wine not only is still good, but that it also has acquired a unique character, a combination of qualities that resemble those of brandy almost as much as wine. It also has acquired a brandy-like wallop.

What happened is that the sun heated the barrels in a way that caused some of the wine inside to evaporate through the pores in the barrel. But the evaporation was uneven. Water evaporates more quickly than alcohol. Thus, for every unit of wine that evaporated, the alcohol concentration was increased in that which remained. (If the process were permitted to continue indefinitely, all that would remain would be alcohol and sediment.) Our absent-minded winemaker liked this powerful new wine so much that he began making it regularly. And thus sherry was born.

The classic sherry-making method, developed in the Spanish city of Jerez de la Frontera (a mispronunciation of the first word resulted in the English word, "sherry"), begins with the drying of the grapes—usually Palominos—on straw mats in the sun. This increases their sugar content and decreases their volume. They then are pressed. Because of the high sugar content, the early fermentation is quite violent and the resulting wine usually reaches 16 percent alcohol concentration, with additional sugar remaining in the solution.

When fermentation ends, the wine is stored outdoors in partially filled butts with loosely covered bungholes. The loose covering permits air to enter. In most parts of the world, this would eventually cause the wine to turn to vinegar. But in Jerez and the Jura Mountains of France, something mysterious happens: A yeast film, which the Spaniards call *flor* (flower), develops on the surface of the wine. It apparently protects the wine from vinegarization and at the same time imparts unique taste characteristics to it. Winemakers have been able to duplicate the phenomenon elsewhere by introducing *flor* yeast cultures taken from Spain or France, but they have not been able to create a *flor* naturally.

The *flor*-covered wine remains outdoors for a year to eighteen months, then is clarified and put into aging barrels. Usually these barrels are part of a network called a *solera*, which blends wines from various years.

The term, *solera*, derives from the Spanish *suelo* (ground)—not from *sol* (sun), as some writers have informed their readers. The network is created by laying down a number of barrels of a given type of wine. The following year, a second tier of barrels—containing the current vintage—is placed atop the first. In succeeding years, additional tiers are added.

As wine is drawn from a barrel in the oldest tier, it is replaced with wine from a barrel in the next tier. This wine is in turn replaced from the next tier, and so on, until the tier containing the current vintage has been tapped. The wines from the different tiers blend, and no matter how much wine is drawn from the final tier, some of the original wine remains.

The Spanish like to say that the older wines in the network serve as guardians for the younger ones, helping them overcome their lack of maturity. The young ones, conversely, inspire zest in the older ones. The marriage is a happy one. In any case, the concept is.

Some winemakers have applied short cuts to sherry making. These include baking the wine at 100 to 140 degrees Fahrenheit (37.8 to 60°C) for up to a year, either in barrels stored in a heated room or with stainless-steel hot-water coils in an aging tank. To compensate for the absence of the "woody" or "nutty" taste sun-aged sherries absorb from the wood in their aging butts, many short-cutting winemakers add oak chips to the baking wine. To raise alcohol concentration without permitting wine to evaporate, some winemakers add brandy.

There is no question that sherries produced by these methods possess some of the characteristics of sherries produced by the more painstaking and costlier traditional method. However, few if any experienced sherry drinkers will confuse the short-cut wines with the traditionally made product.

Port and most other fortified wines achieve their higher alcohol concentration via addition of brandy. The principal differences among these wines are a result not of the winemaker's methods, but of the type of grape used in the still wines which subsequently were fortified, of the amount of aging the wine has had, and of the type of wood in which it was aged.

Fermentation takes place when yeast enzymes (either those in a plant or others introduced by the winemaker) react chemically with sugar. Each sugar molecule is split into two molecules of ethyl alcohol and two of carbon dioxide. The carbon dioxide, a gas, forms bubbles which rise to the top of the solution, then escape into the air. This takes place in an open fermenting tank. If the tank were closed, or if the wine were bottled before it had stopped fermenting, the bubbles would remain in the solution. That's exactly what happens in sparkling wines.

As Dom Pérignon discovered in the seventeenth century, certain wines bottled in the fall referment in the spring. When the bubbles are imprisoned in the bottle until just before the wine is consumed, the wine develops a unique and tantalizing character. This type of wine came to be known as Champagne, after the region of France where Pérignon's abbey was located. Later winemakers

A priestly winemaker in Etna, Sicily, inspects for clarity by looking through his glass at an open fire. Right: French winemaker submerges a light through the bunghole to test barrel's content. Bottom: California wine man draws a sample.

found that when refermentation didn't occur spontaneously, it could be induced by adding sugar and certain yeast cultures. This is the way sparkling wines usually are made today, in Champagne and elsewhere.

There is some dispute as to which wines should be called "Champagne." The wine merchants of Champagne stoutly maintain that only they have the right to the name, and every few years they sue someone for using the word without permission. They have won some of the suits and lost others. In any case, sparkling wines of the same type as Champagne are made throughout the world.

Most of them are white. If they aren't called Champagne, either with or without a qualifying adjective (Canadian Champagne, California Champagne), they are called the local equivalent of "sparkling wine." In Italy, for example, they're labeled *spumante* (frothing); in Spain *espumoso* (foamy); in Germany, *Schaumwein* (froth wine), and in parts of France outside the Champagne district, *vin mousseux* (sparkling wine). A few are pink and are called that, with or without a qualifier (New York State Pink Champagne). A few others are red. These usually are called sparkling red wine, sparkling Burgundy, or Cold Duck, the latter a translation of the German, *kalte Ente*.

White sparkling wines traditionally have been "festive" wines, served at weddings, New Year's Eve parties, and so forth. But many hosts like to serve them as apéritifs, dinner wines, dessert wines, or after-dinner wines. The pinks and red are less frequently served with meals, but this is not unheard of.

Like still and fortified wines, sparkling wines cover the entire sweetness-dryness spectrum. The sweet ones usually are not served with meals (except with dessert). The dry ones are served just about any time. Like still wines, sparkling wines often are limited by law to 14 percent alcohol. In practice, most contain 11 to 12 percent.

Acre of aging sherry barrels on the roofs of Widmer's Wine Cellars, Naples, New York, is big tourist attraction. The barrels stay on the roof year-round. Bottom: California wine man Louis M. Martini inspects laboratory samples.

The essential characteristic of sparkling wines is natural effervescence—that is, the presence of carbon dioxide produced *by fermentation*. It is possible to infuse a still wine with carbon-dioxide gas, much as soft drinks are infused with it. But wines treated this way bear about as much resemblance to those with natural effervescence as a plastic glass with a stem on it bears to delicate crystal stemware. We are not saying, mind you, that one is "better" than the other, only different from it.

The first step in making a sparkling wine is to make a still wine—or, more precisely, several still wines. These are aged for several months, then blended. The blend is called a *cuvée* in France, where the process apparently originated, and most other countries that produce sparkling wines continue to use the term (along with several other French terms for various steps in the process). Some producers blend only wines of the current year. Others draw also on wines from previous years.

What happens next depends on the winemaker's choice of method, a choice dictated chiefly by economic considerations. The costliest method is the traditional *méthode Champenoise*, developed at the Benedictine abbey at Hautvillers in the seventeenth century. First the young wines are bottled. Then a small quantity of yeast and sugar, or syrup, is added to each bottle, and the bottle is capped.

The additive triggers a second fermentation (called, in French, *prise de mousse*). But the carbon-dioxide bubbles produced in the conversion of sugar to alcohol do not escape into the air, as they did during the first fermentation. The cap on the bottle keeps them in the wine. This is where it gets its sparkle. Fermentation slowly continues until all the sugar has been converted to alcohol. The wine then is aged for two to four years. During this period it never leaves the bottle and the cap never comes off.

During fermentation and subsequent aging solid particles are separated from the wine. The bottles initially are stored neck-downward on inclined racks, and the particles settle in the neck. To accelerate particle separation and sedimentation, winery workers lift and twist the bottles daily for several months. The procedure is called riddling (in French, *remuage*). After several months, the wine is clear, and the bottles are stored upside down to keep the particles in place in the neck.

When the winemaker decides that the wine has had peak aging, the sediment is removed. In the early process winery workers would simply uncap the bottle. The sediment would then shoot out due to the force of the carbon dioxide. The worker would then cover the top of the bottle with his thumb and hold it there until he could slip on another cap. Unfortunately, lots of wine was lost (and more than a few thumbs sprained) in the process.

Most modern winemakers simplify things by freezing the neck of the bottle in a brine solution. The cap is then removed and the frozen sediment slides out very easily—looking for all the world like a wine Popsicle.

Whichever variation the winemaker employs, the process is called disgorging (*dégorgement*). When the sediment is removed the empty space in the bottle is filled with more wine of the same type and usually a small dose of brandy and/or sugar (*le dosage* in French) to give sweetness. The bottle then is corked and put to market or returned to the cellar for more aging.

A less cumbersome—and considerably cheaper—method for making a wine sparkle is the transfer method developed in Germany. The second fermentation is induced as in the *méthode Champenoise*. However, the bottles are not riddled. Instead, when fermentation is complete, the wine is emptied into tanks under pressure. It is then filtered and rebottled.

Cheaper still than the transfer method is the Charmat process, named after its French inventor. Instead of bottling the *cuvée*, the winemaker stores it under pressure (again, 75 to 90 pounds per square inch) in a tank, usually one of five hundred to one thousand gallons capacity. Yeast and sweetening are added and secondary fermentation takes place, with the tank serving as one huge bottle. After two or three weeks of this secondary fermentation, the wine is chilled to stop its fermenting action, then is pumped through a filter into a second tank. From this tank it is bottled and given final aging.

A fourth process, designed in Russia, involves a series of Charmat-like tanks. A *cuvée*, yeast, and sweetening agents are stored under pressure in the first. While still fermenting, they are transferred to the second. But before the transfer is complete, enough new wine is added to keep the first tank full. When the second tank is full the still-fermenting *cuvée* is filtered and transferred to a third tank. During the transfer additional wine is taken from the first vat to fill the second, and enough new wine is added to the first to keep it full.

The process continues through another three to seven tanks, with the wine always under pressure and always fermenting. The flow is timed so that the wine reaches the final tank within twenty-one days. Here fermentation is stopped and the wine is filtered and bottled under pressure.

Users of the less costly methods often insist that there is little difference between the end result of their method and the *méthode Champenoise*. Most experienced sparkling-wine drinkers, however, readily perceive a number of differences—most obvious among which is the quantity and liveliness of the bubbles.

Moreover, on the theory that there is no point wasting a costly and cumbersome method on a cheap wine,

méthode Champenoise winemakers usually select from among the more expensive varieties of grape for their *cuvée* and employ greater care at each step of the wine-making process. The result is that *méthode Champenoise* wines usually cost double to quintuple the bulk-processed wines, or even more.

Even the cheapest bulk process, however, involves an added expense over the production of still wines, and all sparkling wines reflect this cost. In North America, they also reflect a luxury tax that is not applied to still wines— a mere $3.40 per gallon in the United States and $3 per gallon in Canada at this writing.

A few fortified wines are given certain aromatic characteristics by the addition of quinine or the essences of various herbs. Probably the best known of these in the western world are Dubonnet and the vermouths. Eastern counterparts are the tea-flavored plum wines of China. In the past, western aromatized wines were used almost exclusively as an ingredient in cocktails; they now are popular as apéritifs, dessert wines, or "anytime" drinks.

Among the additives used in aromatized wines are coriander, quinine, cloves, rose petals, camomile, juniper, orange peel, hyssop, and wormwood. It is from the German word for wormwood, *Wermut*, that the most popular aromatized wine, vermouth, gets its name. The skill of the maker of aromatized wines lies in his selection of aromatizing ingredients. As many as fifty may go into a single wine, and the wineries guard their mixing formulas zealously. The ingredients are added to the base wine (almost invariably a white) when it is less than two years old. First sugar syrup or mistelle (unfermented grape juice fortified with brandy) is added for sweetening. Next the brandy or other distilled spirit, to bring the alcohol concentration up to 18 to 20 percent. Then the aromatizing herbs. The mixture now is pasteurized, then cooled to

about 15 degrees Fahrenheit (about −9.4°C). It remains at this temperature for about two weeks, during which the tartrates in the solution crystallize and sink to the bottom of the storage tank. The wine then is aged at normal temperatures for another three or four months before it is bottled and shipped to its sellers.

Certain still wines with relatively high sugar content and some undissolved yeast particles undergo a very slight secondary fermentation in the bottle. These wines are not as effervescent as sparkling wines, yet they are not exactly still, either. They are marketed as still wines, sometimes with the adjective "crackling"—as in crackling rosé.

The popularity of these wines among newcomers to wine drinking has inspired some winemakers to give certain still wines—almost inevitably white or rosé—a slight dose of carbonation. These wines also are marketed as still wines—again, sometimes with the "crackling qualification," although this is illegal in the United States.

Other wines receive greater doses of carbonation and are marketed as "pop" wines, intended to be drunk recreationally rather than at table. Frequently these wines are flavored with the juices of other fruits. Most have about 7 to 9 percent alcohol. As with aromatized wines, the base wine itself is the least important ingredient, since the winemakers generally use the cheapest tolerable wine they can find. The "pop" winemaker's skill, like that of the maker of aromatized wines, lies chiefly in his selection and blending of nonwine ingredients.

Drinkers of these wines usually do not care much for other wines, and drinkers of other wines usually do not care much for these wines. In Mediterranean countries they usually are served only to children, although in summertime some adults like them as thirst quenchers. More often, Mediterranean adults quench their thirst by mixing effervescent mineral water with an inexpensive still wine.

4.

4.
THE ENJOYMENT OF WINE

*Opening pages: L'assaggiatore (taster)
Nino Franceschetti samples Valpolicella in the
North Italian city of the same name.
Left: English artist M. W. Sharp painted
another taster, holding the glass up against
the light to test for clarity.*

reek lore has it that the custom of clinking glasses in a toast started as an attempt to involve the one sense otherwise excluded from the enjoyment of wine: The clinking drinker could now hear the wine—or at least hear something pleasant associated with it—in addition to seeing it, smelling it, touching it, and tasting it. Many newcomers to wine don't involve even these four senses. They blindly hoist the glass to their lips and drink the contents down. They're missing an awful lot.

Sight: Wines are as individual visually as people, and sometimes almost as interesting. They range in color from the palest yellow-green to the deepest amber-gold, the pinkest rosé to an almost brownish red or deep purple. Some bubble, some merely crackle, and some, though still, give off a distinct sparkle.

Smell: For the experienced drinker, most of a wine's pleasure comes in its smell, or—in the term most frequently used by wine professionals—its "nose." There are only four taste sensations, but there is an almost infinite variety of olfactory subtleties which can be perceived in wine. (Researchers report that the nose can distinguish 16,000 different smells.) Without smell, most wines "taste" (seem to be) alike.

Tastes: There are four: bitter, sour, salt, and sweet. Bitterness is acrid, like the taste of aspirin, quinine, or a particularly strong cup of tea. Sourness is acid, like the taste of lemon or vinegar. Many people find a moderate degree of bitterness desirable in certain wines. This bitterness is the result of tannic acid. Wine professionals term these wines "tannic" or "tart." Sourness is regarded as an undesirable characteristic—an indication, in fact, that the wine has turned (or is in the process of turning) to vinegar. The degree of sweetness in a wine is a matter of personal preference. If sweetness is absent, the wine is termed "dry." We know no wines with a salt taste.

Professional wine men exploit all these sensations when judging a wine, and when they speak of "tasting" they really mean "sensing." They taste—using the term in their sense—at several levels.

First, they are interested in the wine's quality—not whether it pleases their palate, but whether it is free from defects. There is an element of subjectivity in this, of course, but there is virtually universal agreement on some principles. For example, a wine should not taste of vinegar, and it should not have a foreign odor, such as the mustiness that may develop from storage under certain conditions.

Next, they taste for character. They have a concept of what this type of wine should taste like, and they compare the taste of a particular wine to the concept. With wine made entirely from one grape variety, there would be little if any room for disagreement. But the majority of wines are blends, and traditional types have distinct characteristics. Margaux, for example, differs quite noticeably (to professionals) from Saint-Emilion, although both are made up predominantly of the same grapes.

Finally, the wine man tastes for excellence—the presence of certain characteristics which identify the wine as a superior example of its type. There is a great deal of subjectivity here, too. But most wine men share a general set of standards, and indeed, in a blind tasting, most will be very close on their ratings of the sampled wines.

The idea of a "blind" tasting often is misunderstood. Many newcomers to wine drinking imagine a wine expert blindfolded, attempting, by taste alone, to identify the origin of the wine. If he is a real expert, he will be able to name the region or district in which the wine was made, the community and even the vineyard. In an extreme exaggeration of the stereotype, the expert is assumed capable

of determining even the row of the vineyard.

This is nonsense. While most professional wine men can readily distinguish among typical wines of given regions (the average Burgundy, say, versus the average Bordeaux), it's entirely possible to make a Bordeaux that has more in common with the typical Burgundy than with other Bordeaux.

Among the essential contributors to a wine's character—or personality—are the choice of grapes, their treatment during fermentation, and the circumstances under which the wine is aged. A wine man—professional or amateur—may have a vivid memory of the wine of a particular producer and may promptly identify a glass of this producer's wine when he is served it without being told what it is. But most professional wine men asked to identify wines in this manner will politely tell you that they probably can't, apart from recognizing wines with which they're intimately familiar, and possibly identifying typical examples of given types. Certainly no one is going to identify wines from one particular row in a vineyard. Grapes are not processed individually by row.

In any case, the real blind tasting is not a test of the taster but of the wine. One or more wine men taste one or more—usually more—wines. The bottles are concealed to eliminate the possibility that the taster will be inadvertently influenced by his previous experience with the wine. The taster then rates the wine in terms of quality, character, or excellence. He may do so verbally or on a point scale. Most wine men use a point scale. G-2 does, also; however, G-1 prefers straight verbal ratings.

G-2's 20-point rating system follows. These criteria—we both agree—can prove helpful to anyone who wants to get more out of his wine drinking. One needn't taste wines blind (although that certainly is useful). The criteria can be applied to any glass of wine.

Wine Taster's Scorecard
(*Maximum points per characteristic given in parentheses*)

Visual

Color (2)	Clarity (2)
Good=2	Brilliant=2
Mediocre=1	Clear=1
Bad=0	Cloudy=0

Olfactory

Nose (4)	Indistinct=1
Varietal and sophisticated=4	None=0
Merely varietal=3	Unpleasant odors:
Distinct, but not varietal=2	subtract 1, 2, or 3

Gustatory

Sweetness (1)	Distinctly high or low=0
Correct=1	General acidity (2)
Too much or too little=0	Correct, well-balanced=2
Acetic acid (1)	Slightly high or low=1
None=1	Distinctly high or low=0
Some=0	Flavor (2)
Tannic acid (2)	Correct=2
Correct=2	Slightly off=1
Slightly high or low=1	Distinctly off=0

Other

Body (1)	Little or none=0
Correct=1	Overall excellence (2)
Too much or too little=0	Extremely high=2
Memory (1)	High=1
Significant=1	Not appreciable=0

Score:

0-5 *Undrinkable*	17 *Wine of excellence*
6-8 *Barely drinkable*	18 *Wine of high excellence*
9-12 *Drinkable, but with*	19 *Wine of outstanding*
a noticeable defect	*excellence*
13-16 *Sound commercial wine*	20 *Rare and memorable wine*

To begin, you should be in a quiet and comfortable room. It's possible, of course, to enjoy wine under other circumstances. But the ability to taste suffers when there are distractions or discomforts. Many professional tasters refuse to work in a room that is not quiet, and most prefer a room temperature in the 60's.

Ideally, the tasting should be done at a table covered with a white cloth. In European tasting rooms, candles frequently are used. The taster looks at the candle through the wine as one test of its clarity. In the Americas the typical tasting is by daylight or soft electric light.

The size and shape of your glass is important. It should be large, clear, and stemmed. Large means a minimum of six ounces, preferably eight or more; even thirty-two ounces is not too large. Also, the lip should be slightly turned in. Both factors enhance perception of the wine's nose. Clear means the glass should be colorless and not have inscriptions, designs, or other markings on its surface. Its clarity and its stem will enhance perception of the wine's visual character.

Pour three or four ounces into the glass; ideally it should be filled to no more than one-third its capacity. Under no circumstances should it be filled more than half. The nose of the wine—its aroma and bouquet—will be contained in the upper portion of the glass. A full glass (like one that is flat or cone-shaped) will fail to convey the wine's olfactory character.

Visual: The first visual test is for color. Holding the glass by the stem, tilt it so that you can look into the top and see *through the wine* to the white tablecloth. If you have no white tablecloth, a sheet or two of paper will do. In any case, the background against which you view the wine should be white. Don't hold the glass up to the light source. This technique is helpful in the second visual test—for clarity—but it tends to confuse color.

Left: G-2's scorecard for rating wines on a 20-point scale. Below: Decanting natural sedimentation at Château du Debez in Bordeaux. It is done by looking through the neck of the bottle at the flame and ceasing to pour the instant sediment appears.

Each type of wine, whether red, white, or rosé, has its own typical color characteristics. For instance, a Cabernet Sauvignon should be of a certain color density that would be different from a Pinot Noir; a Chablis should differ from a Sauternes. Likewise, an older wine of any of these types would have different color from a younger wine.

The taster develops his concepts of a wine type's color through experience. He tastes hundreds, then thousands, then perhaps even tens of thousands of glasses of this particular wine type, and his memory records those color characteristics which the various glasses have shared. He then compares each future glass to this standard.

In every test his comparison is tri-level. First, he determines that the wine is "good"—that is, not defective. (A deep amber color would indicate, for example, that certain white wines had been exposed to too much light and/or heat, and thus had gone "bad"—had lost their typical properties of nose and taste, as well as color.) Secondly, the taster determines that the wine is in character. A Neuchâtel should look like a Neuchâtel and not like, say, an Orvieto bianco. A wine, however, may be off-color without being defective. Finally, he evaluates the degree of excellence of color which this particular wine possesses. A Neuchâtel, for instance, can be both "good" (not defective) and "correct" (possessing typical color) without being especially vivid, rich, full, etc.

G-2 doesn't suggest that every taster arrives at this determination by way of three distinct steps, or that he thinks of these traits specifically by the terms quality, character, and excellence. But whatever he calls them, this is what he is looking for. While the characteristics are highly subjective, there is almost universal agreement among wine professionals as to what the "correct" characteristics of a given wine should be.

All this presumes that the taster knows the wine he is tasting. In the event of a blind tasting, he will fall back on a more general set of criteria. He evaluates whether this unknown wine has a good color, a true color, the kind of color he normally associates with a correct wine. As his evaluation proceeds, he decides, either deliberately or unwittingly, that this is a particular type of wine, and he bases his evaluation on his concepts for that wine type. Or he may merely continue to evaluate the wine as *a* wine.

The newcomer to wine who wishes to apply the professional's methods to his own tasting naturally will not have a comparable fund of tasting experience from which to derive standards. But the professional taster's approach may still be useful to him. The newcomer can decide whether a wine looks generally "good" (does he *like* the color, is it pleasing to his eye?). Then, as he continues to taste, he will learn to associate various color characteristics with good as opposed to defective wines, with varietal or regional correctness, and with excellence within a wine type.

Now, having examined the color of the wine in your glass, rate it on your scorecard. For superior color, give it 2 points, for merely correct color, 1. If you consider the color incorrect, give it no points. (If you have no concept of correctness for the wine, rate it 2 if you like the color very much, 1 if you merely like it, and 0 if you dislike it.)

The second visual test is for clarity and does not require a great deal of expertise. Either the wine is cloudy (muddy, incapable of being seen through) or it is clear. There is a borderline area where clearness ends and cloudiness begins, but few wines fall into it.

Some wines are not merely clear, they are brilliant. That is, they reflect light to such an extent that they appear to glimmer or sparkle, like jewelry.

An old wine may be clouded with sediment (the solid matter which has separated from the solution during aging). If so, the bottle was disturbed shortly before the wine was poured. It should be left untouched until the sediment has resettled at the bottom.

A wine that is cloudy under other circumstances is considered defective, and many professional tasters will reject it out of hand, not going any farther in the evaluation.

To rate the wine for clarity, continue to look through it at the tablecloth or other white background. If the wine is dark and cannot be seen through for that reason, hold it up to the light. If it still cannot be seen through, you may be sure it's cloudy.

On your scorecard, rate a brilliant wine 2, a clear wine 1, and a cloudy wine 0. (With sherry and a few other fortified wines, solid particles will appear even though the wine is clear. This is not regarded as a defect. With white wines, crystal-like particles will sometimes appear. This is an indication that the wine has been stored at a near-freezing temperature. Though the particles won't affect the nose or taste of the wine, they are evidence that this particular batch has been mishandled.)

Olfactory: To test for nose, swirl the wine several times in the glass, then simply put your nose into the glass and inhale. The swirling helps coax out the wine's olfactory properties.

One of these is aroma, the smell of the grapes from which the wine was produced. Each grape species has a distinct aroma, and various blends acquire aromatic characteristics of their own.

Bouquet is the smell of the wine itself. It reflects the "marriage" of a blended wine (the reaction the various blending wines have had on each other during the wine's development), the type of aging (whether in oak or redwood, or some other container), and other differences resulting from the techniques of fermenting and aging.

Older wines made from certain grapes will also develop a "bottle bouquet," that is, a sophisticated combination of olfactory sensations that most experienced drinkers consider one of the prime satisfactions of wine.

Again, all this is highly subjective. But there is broad agreement among experienced drinkers as to which wines are prized and to what degree.

On the other side of the scale, there are olfactory indicators that a wine has gone bad. The most apparent of these probably is the odor of acetic acid—an indication that the wine has oxidized and turned to vinegar. There is another odor characteristic of white wines which have been exposed to too much heat and/or light. And there are others that reveal defects resulting from incorrect corking, storage, or other treatment of the wine.

Professionals almost inevitably can tell by smell alone whether the wine is defective and how the defect was caused. Drinkers with less experience usually cannot identify specific defects, but almost everyone who likes wine can tell from smell alone whether a wine is defective, because, strangely enough, to someone who likes wine, good wines almost always smell good and bad wines almost always smell bad.

In scoring a wine's nose, tasters usually reject out-of-hand any wine with serious off-odors, such as that of acetic acid. If the off-odors are deemed less than serious, tasters simply subtract points from the rating.

Some wines—especially Italian reds—have little or no nose. This may explain why many Italian restaurants and hotels serve wine in small glasses. There is nothing to capture in the empty upper portion of a large glass. A taster who knows the wine's regional and varietal character may adjust his rating to reflect this. But other raters will simply down-point the wine, and this is one reason some experienced drinkers say these Italian wines can never be truly "great." Professional wine men almost always agree that the wines of France and California possess more nose than those of other nations, and they frequently give them higher overall ratings than other wines.

In G-2's rating scale, nose is responsible for 4 of the maximum 20 points. If there is no nose (or virtually no nose), he scores 0. If the nose is indistinct—if G-2 can perceive an olfactory character to the wine, but it is not identifiable with any other wines in his experience—he scores 1. If the nose is distinct but not identifiable with a specific grape variety or combination of varieties, the score is 2. If the nose is identifiable with a variety or varieties of grape, the score is 3. And if, in addition, there is the complexity of bottle bouquet, the score is 4.

Newcomers to wine drinking, not having an olfactory association with grape varieties, might alter the scale thusly: no nose, 0; faint traces of pleasant nose, 1; moderate degree of pleasant nose, 2; very pleasant nose, 3; extremely pleasant and interesting nose, 4; unpleasant nose, subtract 1, 2, or 3.

By the way, when swirling to coax nose from the wine, the simplest—and neatest—procedure is to put the base of the glass on the table and simply describe several small circles with it. Flamboyant tasters occasionally swirl the glass in the air. But the wine will spill if the glass is not held perfectly level.

Gustatory: It is now time to taste the wine. For the wine's full taste to register it must be brought into contact with taste buds at the tip of the tongue (they record sweet tastes), the sides (sour tastes), and the rear, just below the palate (bitter tastes).

Professional tasters usually take a sip of wine and position it behind the lower gum. They then touch it with the tip of the tongue to register sweetness. After this, they move the wine through the mouth so that acetic and other acids can be perceived by the taste buds along the tongue's sides. Then they move the wine to the back of the mouth so that the rear taste buds can react to its tannic content (bitterness).

To help this along, they sometimes "whistle in" or "suck in" a quantity of air with the wine. This tends to bring out the various taste characteristics more clearly. Some tasters also, after exposing the wine to the taste buds in the individual areas, squish it around in their mouth to perceive its taste sensations in combination. Obviously, these are steps that will not be employed when wine is drunk at table or in other social settings. But it's a good idea even in social drinking to leave the wine in the mouth for a few seconds before swallowing it, or much taste sensation will be lost.

In rating wines for sweetness, tasters match the current wine with their sweetness standard for wines of its type. On G-2's scale, a wine that is as sweet as it should be is rated 1. A wine that is too sweet or not sweet enough gets 0.

In rating wines for acetic acid, tasters look for its absence, not presence. If the wine has no trace of acetic acid, it gets 1 point. If there is some acetic taste, the wine gets no points. (If there is a clear taste of vinegar, the wine will be rejected out-of-hand—although in that case it probably would already have been eliminated on nose.)

The tannin test applies only to red wines—whites, fermented off the skins, develop no tannin. As with other taste properties, tasters seek a "correct" level. Correctness will relate both to the type of wine and its age. A young Cabernet Sauvignon, for example, will normally have a very high tannic character. This does not mean that the wine is bad. It simply means that it is not ready to be drunk.

In fact, high tannin in a Cabernet Sauvignon is very desirable. It indicates that the wine will be long-lasting and probably will develop considerable sophistication during its bottle-aging. The celebrated old vintages of Cabernet which wine men prize most—those wines

which at age thirty, forty, or fifty are still not past their prime—of necessity were undrinkably high in tannin when young. Their sophistication results from the chemical reaction of their tannin to other chemicals as the wine aged in the bottle.

On the other hand, high tannin in wines which lack other characteristics suitable for aging is considered undesirable. These wines are regarded as "wrong," not merely young.

The taster's evaluation of tannic-acid content, therefore, is aimed at determining not only the quality of the wine, but also whether it is currently at its peak.

With wines intended to be drunk young this will not be a consideration. But a red wine that has no tannic character whatsoever will usually be unsatisfying.

On G-2's scale, a wine with the "correct" tannin level for immediate drinking gets 2 points. One that is slightly high or low in tannin gets 1 point, and one that is distinctly high or low gets no points. With white wines, some professionals rate fruit acids in place of tannin. G-2 prefers to consider these under general acidity, and to assign the extra 2 tannin points to that category.

The general acidity rating is based on the taster's opinion of the balance of acids in the wine. Thus, a more

Home-winemaking paesano Sam Galati,
with G-2 (left) and G-1 (right), conducts
blind tasting of commercially
produced wines. In sequence, wine
is tested for color, held up to light
to test clarity, finally nosed and tasted.

highly tannic wine might be rated more favorably than a mildly tannic wine because the high tannin blends harmoniously with the wine's other taste properties. This presupposes a standard of what the well-balanced wine should be.

A wine whose acidity is considered correct—the acids are deemed well-balanced—gets 2 points on G-2's scale. If the acid balance seems slightly high or low, the wine gets 1 point. If the balance is distinctly high or low, the wine gets no points.

Flavor, like general acidity, is a matter of the taster's standards. He compares this wine to his concept of the wine type's "correct" flavor. If he finds the flavor correct, the wine gets 2 points. If he rates it slightly off, the wine gets 1 point. If he regards it as distinctly off, the wine gets no points.

In all these taste categories, the newcomer to wines will lack an experiential standard by which to judge the wine's characteristics, but he can rate each category in terms of his own general likes and dislikes in these taste areas. For example:

If a wine is too sweet or not sweet enough for his taste, he gives it no points. If it is just right, it scores 1 point.

If the wine has no unpleasant vinegar-like taste, he gives it one point on acetic acid. If it does have a vinegary taste, no matter how slight, he gives it no points.

If a red wine has a pleasant bitterness, it gets 2 points. If its bitterness is slightly unpleasant, or if the wine is slightly too bland, it gets 1 point. If the discrepancy is extreme rather than mild, the wine gets no points.

If the taster likes the overall acidic character of the wine—if it is neither too tart nor too bland, neither vinegary nor watery—it gets 2 points for general acidity. If it deviates slightly in one direction or the other, it gets only 1 point. If it deviates considerably, it gets no points.

Finally, with respect to flavor, if the taster likes the taste of the wine very much, he gives it 2 points. If he merely likes it, he gives it 1 point. If he dislikes it, he gives it no points.

Body and Memory: "Body" refers to the density of the wine—that is, the amount of soluble solids it contains. Colloquially that translates as "thickness," in the sense that molasses is thicker than lemonade.

The newcomer to wine might find it difficult to imagine one wine being "thicker" than another, but there are differences, and while they are not as pronounced as the difference between molasses and lemonade, they are nonetheless apparent to experienced wine drinkers. A Pinot Noir, for example, is substantially thicker than a Gewürztraminer; a Barolo likewise has more body than a Chianti.

The professional taster has a concept of what each wine type's body should be, and he compares the body of the present wine to his standard. If he considers it correct, the wine gets 1 point on G-2's scale. If there is too much or too little body, the wine gets no points.

The newcomer to wine may rate for body in terms of his own feel for the wine's thickness. Is it too light (thin)? Or too full-bodied (thick)? In either case, no points. Is it just right? One point.

"Memory" refers to the ability of the wine's taste to remain on the tongue after the wine has been swallowed or expectorated. Professional tasters usually expectorate. They claim that swallowing the wine dulls the palate. Also, there's a limit to the amount of drinking a taster can do without getting inebriated.

G-2 has found that he cannot fully appreciate the taste properties of a wine he doesn't swallow. Also, he's never felt comfortable about spitting out good wine. Accordingly, he limits his tasting to amounts he can consume without becoming inebriated—and swallows it all after mentally registering its taste properties.

In any case, certain wines have a strong, clear taste when you first apply them to your tongue. Then the taste vanishes as soon as the wine loses contact with the taste buds. The taste of other wines will remain for a number of seconds after contact has ceased. Many professional tasters count mentally the number of seconds they can continue to taste the wine after swallowing or expectorating. They'll speak of an eight-second wine or a six-second wine. The longer the wine's memory, the more highly it is prized.

On G-2's scorecard, a wine with a significant memory gets 1 point. A wine with little or no memory gets no points. How much is significant? That will depend on the wine. Again, the professional taster's experience with various wine types comes into play. A Chardonnay, for instance, is expected to have more memory than a Traminer.

The newcomer to wines, while building his experiences with wine types, might arbitrarily choose four seconds as the dividing line between "little/none" and "significant." Or he might sample three or four wines, take their average as his dividing line, and continue using this figure until additional experience provides him with a new standard.

Overall Excellence: Finally, the "overall excellence" rating is thoroughly subjective. The taster may rate the present wine against others of its type, or he may rate it against all wines in his experience. He may attempt to assess the balance of the other elements on the scorecard—visual, olfactory, gustatory, and other. Or he may simply use the 2 points as a bonus to boost the rating of a wine he prizes highly, whatever his reaction to its individual elements.

Some raters—G-1 among them—who do not use numerical scorecards insist that this personal, subjective rating is the only valid measure of a wine because the ultimate consumer does not taste individual parts, he tastes the whole wine. G-2 prefers a scorecard because he finds that reduction to individual elements permits greater precision in judgment.

G-1 demurs as follows about point-rating wines:

There is no question that G-2, with his numerical system, usually winds up feeling about the same about given wines as I, with my instinctive approach, do. As a matter of fact, it's almost uncanny how closely we've independently rated more than five hundred wines. But our ways of arriving at that result vary considerably. I really don't think you need numbers to distinguish between a clear wine and a cloudy one, a pleasant nose and an unpleasant one. Numbers spoil it a bit for me. And I don't care as much about the details as G-2. The color for instance. Does it really have to be absolutely right? As for memory, the day I've got to stand there ticking off the seconds that the wine remains on my palate—well, that's the day to lock up the wine cellar and break out the beer. Then the whistling in of the wine, the squishing it around in your mouth, the gargling with it. Well, that's not for me, either. I like to drink my wine—not guzzle it, mind you—but drink it, taste it, enjoy it, and, without undue delay, swallow it. So whistle away, if you must, but I don't really think it necessary.

The most important taste characteristic of a wine for me is the harmonious balance of various individual taste sensations. G-2 probably takes this into account when he rates the items individually and again in the overall rating at the end of the scale. But I prefer to concentrate only on the balance. The question I ask myself is, do I like the way this wine tastes? If I can answer yes, I'm satisfied.

Developing a Wine-Tasting Palate

Do experienced drinkers enjoy wine more now than when they were inexperienced? Almost without exception they say they do. But this is hardly surprising. Knowledgeability enhances appreciation of the "finer points" of almost anything, whether music, sports, food, or wine.

Knowledgeability can be developed by trial and error, and this is as true in wine as in anything else. If you buy the cheapest bottle you can find (or the most expensive), then drink it, then buy the next cheapest (or next most expensive) and drink that, and so on—or even if you simply buy bottles at random—eventually you will reach the point where you have a memory bank of distinct associations with various wines. Subsequently, whether deliberately or unthinkingly, you will relate future wines to those in your memory bank. If you are sufficiently adventurous, and have enough time and money, you may ultimately reach the point where you have sampled thousands of wines. Among them you will have certain favorites and certain semifavorites. You also will have established—and perhaps verbalized—a broad set of parameters to guide your future wine buying, so that you can avoid sampling those nine in ten bottles which do not warrant further investigation.

Most people, of course, have not the time, money, or endurance to arrive at this point by trial and error. That's why they buy books like this one. Fortunately, it is possible to develop a reasonable knowledgeability about wine without spending one's lifetime and total resources doing it.

The first step, we believe, is to establish a pattern of drinking wine regularly. The difference between the professional palate and that of the amateur is the professional's memory bank, which is built on many tasting experiences. A knowledgeable counselor can provide valuable advice about things to put into your memory bank, thereby sparing you the trial-and-error approach's biggest drawback: wasting time and money on wines you won't like at the time you try them. But counsel alone isn't enough. You must reinforce its lessons with experience.

Most *aficionados* drink wine daily. For G-1 and G-2, wine is an essential part of dining and always has been. Drinking wine daily doesn't require a lot of money. People of great wealth may find it financially feasible to consume a $25 bottle every evening at dinner, and professional wine men may tap the prime bottles in their own cellars at considerably less than it would cost an outsider. But the typical wine amateur will limit his everyday drinking to what North Americans call jug wines and the French call *vins du pays*: young, mass-produced, blended wines selling at $10 a gallon and under, usually in bulk (liter, half-gallon, or gallon) containers rather than the traditional 23- to 28-ounce bottle. It's possible to drink a 6-ounce glass of wine each day for $2 a week. That's only a few cents more costly than a daily bottle of beer or Coke.

Next, it is necessary—or at least expedient—to think about, and preferably make notes about, the wines you drink. If you proceed from bottle to bottle thoughtlessly, the characteristics of the wines tend to blur in your mind. A month later you probably won't remember which wines you've drunk, much less the distinguishing characteristics of each. If you makes notes about each wine, you'll not only discipline yourself to think about wine systematically—and thus approach each wine as a professional taster would—but you'll also have a means of refreshing your memory when you open another bottle of the same wine or sample a different producer's wine of the same type.

G-2 keeps a 20-point taster's scorecard on just about every wine he tastes. G-1 keeps a card with verbal

*They swirl
to coax out nose. Turned-in lip of glass
helps capture the wine's olfactory properties.
By filling large glass no more than a third,
tasters get the most out
of a wine's nose.*

ratings and descriptions. Naturally we don't carry these cards around to dinner parties, but if we taste a new wine (or a new vintage of a familiar wine) on some social occasion, we usually make notes on it later.

We don't rate jug wines or other blends with which we're familiar and the characteristics of which tend to remain pretty much the same from bottle to bottle. However, the newcomer to wine probably will find it helpful as well as interesting to rate all wines he tastes, and to rate the same wine a number of times on separate occasions. This should encourage familiarity with wine-tasting concepts as well as disciplined and systematic thinking about the disparate properties of wines.

If you'd like to go into palate development even more deeply, here is a series of exercises G-2 has devised based on more elaborate programs developed at the famed French national wine school in Montpellier and the Department of Enology and Viticulture at the University of California at Davis. Many readers will have neither the time nor the inclination to perform the entire eighteen exercises, but even a few, taken in succession or selected at random, can be useful. For a rough rule-of-thumb to measure your progress, regard the first eight exercises as Level A, successful completion of which will give you rudimentary wine-tasting skills; the next four (through Exercise 12) as Level B, successful completion of which should develop a formidable varietal memory bank; and the remaining six as Level C, the professional's course, which should develop the ability to distinguish very precisely among very subtle wine differences.

Advanced Palate Development

Exercise 1: Buy an inexpensive bottle of grape-based still wine. Any of the following would do: Gallo's Rhine, Gallo's Chablis, Italian Swiss Colony Rosé, M. LaMont California Vin Rosé, Widmer Naples Valley Pink, Taylor's Rhine, Bon Frère Blanc Superieur, Briault Vin Blanc, Château-Gai Crackling Rosé (marketed as Château Bon in the U.S.), Gomez Cruzado Spanish Chablis.

Each night for one week, taste this wine and fill out a 20-point scorecard on it (unless you find the wine unpalatable, in which case switch to another after the first try). You needn't taste alone. In fact, it usually is more instructive to taste with friends. When tasting in company, it's a good idea for each person to fill out his own scorecard without discussing the wines with anyone. Then, when all the scorecards are complete, the assembled tasters can compare and discuss their ratings on each point. If everyone is game, a second rating might then be made and this also discussed.

After the second night's rating is complete, compare it with that of the first night. As you continue through the week, compare each night's ratings with those of the previous nights, but always after each night's tasting. This will insure against bias—against the likelihood that you will try to support your judgment by duplicating your previous ratings, or try to establish your "objectivity" by deviating substantially from the original rating. (Many conditions affect the palate, and a taster's evaluations frequently change somewhat; so if your scorecard differs from day to day, it doesn't mean you're fickle. It may merely mean that your palate has been subjected to different influences from the previous day. Or it may mean that the wine has changed—especially likely if you use a gallon jug over an entire week.)

Exercise 2: A different wine for the second week, but the same color—don't change from white to rosé or rosé to white. Buy one from the above list (or any other wine in the same price range) and taste it in the above manner.

We recommend whites and rosés rather than reds because newcomers to wine usually find these lighter, fruitier wines more enjoyable. Greater experience usually leads to an appreciation of the tarter, more tannic reds. But this generally is a while coming.

Exercise 3: Select a third wine from the list (or any comparably priced white or rosé wine) and taste it for a week. If your first two weeks' wines were white, make this one rosé, and vice versa.

Exercise 4: For one or two nights only, taste the wine of week 3 against another wine of the same color. For example, if your Week 3 wine was Italian Swiss Colony Rosé, taste it against one of the other rosés. Fill out a score-card on each wine and, if tasting with friends, talk about your reactions.

Use a different glass for each wine. If you're short on glasses, wash each thoroughly before pouring a different wine into it. Traces of the first wine in the glass may influence your reaction to the second wine.

It is essential, of course, that the glasses be free of all traces of soap and detergent. It's also a good idea to reserve your wineglasses exclusively for wine. Under no circumstances use them for milk, the fats of which often influence future beverages served in the glass, even if it has been washed many times.

Exercise 5: For one or two nights, conduct a blind tasting of the wines you used in the first four exercises. That is, taste all four without knowing which is in which glass. Rate the wines, then identify them to yourself. You might also compare these blind ratings to those made in previous weeks, when you knew which wine was which.

Remember, the purpose of the blind tasting is not to test yourself but to test the wine under circumstances which reduce subjectivity to a minimum. The tasting may lead to your identifying one producer's wine as preferable to the other of the same type. But the real goal of the exercise is to develop your ability to perceive differences between the wines and types.

Exercise 6: Conduct a multinational blind tasting. From the above list (or using other wines of the same type and in the same price range), select at least four, and preferably more, from different nations. Within the U.S., consider California and the eastern wine-producing states separate nations (they use different grapes and have substantially different growing conditions).

Exercise 7: Buy two inexpensive red wines and conduct several nights of comparative tastings. Among those we suggest (although any costing less than $2 a fifth will do): Taylor's Lake Country Red, Great Western Baco Noir Burgundy, Gallo's Hearty Burgundy, Louis Martini Burgundy, Almadén Mountain Red Claret, Italian Swiss Colony Chianti, Hernandez Burgella, Briault Vin Rouge, Rouge Pedoque.

Exercise 8: Conduct a multinational tasting of red wines using those of at least four nations. Select from the above group or from other wines costing less than $2.

Exercise 9: We move now from generics to varietals. These wines cost a bit more, so you may find it prudent to share the tastings—and their costs—with friends.

Varietal wines, it will be recalled, are named after the grape from which they are principally made. For the first tasting in the series, select one of each of the following varieties: Sauvignon Blanc, Johannisberger Riesling, Chardonnay, Sémillon, and Gewürztraminer. They need not be from the same producer, but the exercise will be more effective if they are.

When tasting the wines, in addition to rating each on your 20-point scorecard, think about the character differences which distinguish them from each other. They are five varietals of widely differing properties, so the

Procedures for opening and sampling a bottle are demonstrated by G-2 in family wine cellar. Left to right, top to bottom: Remove foil; Insert corkscrew and extract cork; Feel cork for dryness and sniff for off-odors; Pour, Swirl, Nose wine.

character differences should be quite apparent to you.

Exercise 10: Repeat Exercise 9, using reds instead of whites. Select any five of these varietals: Cabernet Sauvignon, Merlot, Nebbiolo, Sangiovese, Pinot Noir, Barbera, Grignolino, Charbono, Carignan, Gamay, Zinfandel, Seibel, Baco.

As with the whites, these varietals all differ substantially. Thus, when tasting them, in addition to rating them on your 20-point scorecard, focus on the character differences which distinguish them from each other.

Exercise 11: Take each of the white varietals in Exercise 9 and taste it against the same varietal of two or more additional producers, tasting one variety per night.

Exercise 12: Take each of the red varietals you used in Exercise 10 and taste it against the same varietal of two or more additional producers, tasting one variety per night.

Exercise 13: Using the white varietals of Exercise 9, pour three glasses of each, fifteen glasses in all. Have someone arrange the glasses in three rows of five, with one example of each varietal in each row. The arrangement should be such that you have no way of identifying which wine is in which glass, but the person who arranged the glasses does.

Now, taste the five glasses in Row A. Next, taste one glass from B, and attempt to identify the glass in Row A to which it is identical. Then taste another glass in Row B and attempt to match it. After you've finished all the glasses in Row B, move to Row C and attempt to match these too with the glasses in Row A. Then review your choices with the person who arranged the glasses, and determine how many you correctly matched.

This, obviously, is a test of your palate rather than of the wines. In fact, it's a test the Department of Viticulture and Enology at the University of California/Davis

School of Agriculture administers to potential California wine tasters. But it not only tests your palate; it also teaches you to distinguish varietal characteristics.

The exercise should be repeated until you consistently identify all the wines correctly. If you get bored with it, go on to the next exercise, but return to Exercise 13 periodically in the future.

Exercise 14: Using the red varietals you previously selected in Exercise 10, repeat Exercise 13 until you can consistently distinguish among them.

Exercise 15: Buy a bottle of Gallo Hearty Burgundy and another of Great Western Baco Noir Burgundy. Arrange a row of five glasses. Into the first pour only the Gallo, into the fifth only the Great Western. Into the third, pour exactly 50 percent Gallo and 50 percent Great Western. Into the second, pour exactly 75 percent Gallo and 25 percent Great Western. With the fourth, reverse these percentages.

Now taste the wines and, using G-2's rating scorecard, evaluate their differences.

On the second day of the exercise, arrange three rows of glasses, as in Exercises 13 and 14. Then attempt to match the glasses in rows B and C with their counterparts in Row A. Repeat this exercise until you can consistently make correct matches.

Exercise 16: Repeat Exercise 15, using a 100 percent Cabernet Sauvignon (as opposed to a blend that is merely predominantly Cabernet) and a second bottle that contains 100 percent Merlot, Carignan, or Charbono. These will be difficult to find, but it should not be impossible in most North American cities. Few European winemakers produce 100 percent varietals with these grapes, but in California's Napa Valley Souverain produces a 100 percent Cabernet, Louis Martini a 100 percent Merlot, and Inglenook a 100 percent Charbono. North in the Alex-

Nineteenth-century engraving by W. Dendy Sadler depicts dessert drinking of a fortified wine—probably cream sherry. High alcohol content preserves a decanted fortified wine for many days without much loss of character.

ander Valley, Simi produces a 100 percent Carignan. If none of these wines is available in your area, a knowledgeable wine merchant should be able to locate counterparts.

Exercise 17: Arrange three rows of three glasses each. In the first row, have someone pour a glass each of the same producer's dry, extra dry, and *brut* or *nature* white sparkling wine. The second and third rows should contain the same three wines, but in a different order. Attempt to match the glasses in the second and third rows with those in the first.

Exercise 18: Repeat Exercise 17, using three different producers' dry vermouth instead of the white sparkling wine.

Having completed the above exercises, you will be able to devise others for further testing and development of your wine palate. Future tastings probably will be most profitable if confined to specific varietal or regional types. You might, for example, taste a group of California Cabernet Sauvignons or Chardonnays. Or a group of Chiantis or Barolis. Or a group of Saint-Emilions, Margaux, Pauillacs, or Pomerols.

In regional tastings, it is interesting to compare wines of varying price—and if enough people participate in the tasting, the per-person cost of higher-priced wines can be reduced to a level which many people can afford who might otherwise never sample the wine. For example, a Margaux tasting might include Château Margaux, about $35 per bottle in an off-vintage year, along with a *petit château* (little-known château-bottled wine) from the same region, costing less than $10, and two shippers' blends bearing the *appellation Margaux controlée.* More affluent hosts might add a bottle of old, prime-vintaged Château Margaux (at a cost of $75-$100 per bottle). Since the amount of each wine tasted by each person need not be more than an ounce or two, a fairly large number of people can share one bottle of wine.

There is no reason why these tastings cannot be social events as well as palate-developing experiences. In fact, many people currently are giving wine-tasting parties in place of the traditional cocktail party. G-1 and G-2 prefer limiting their tastings to four or five couples at most, but there are hosts who enjoy giving tastings on a much larger scale, and can do so successfully.

For a social tasting, we recommend a limit of seven or eight wines. They may be of diverse types, but we prefer sticking to one or at most two types. When diverse types are served, the generally preferred order of service is dry to sweet, young to old, and white to red.

Sparkling or fortified wines may also be made the subject of a tasting. Usually, these tastings are best confined to one class of wine (sherry or Port, not both). They may be limited to one producer's line (a tasting of Duff Gordon or Harveys or Williams & Humbert or Llords & Elwood sherries), or one type of sherry (a tasting of Duff Gordon's cream versus Harveys versus Williams & Humbert versus Llords & Elwood).

It's a good idea to serve bread and cheese to clear the palate between wines tasted. More elaborate fare may, of course, also be served.

Wine-Tasting Groups and Wine Touring

One way to get to taste a number of new wines is to join a wine-tasting group. These groups hold tastings regularly, featuring as many as thirty or forty wines (you don't sample them all, of course), usually presented by one or more producers and/or importers. Often vintages of celebrated wines will be available that otherwise could not be found except at prohibitive prices.

Unfortunately, in our experience the groups that hold the best tastings often restrict their membership and

*Before elegant tapestry of a
vineyard scene, taster at Château Figeac
in Saint-Emilion noses the winery's product.
Bottom: Silver tastevin displays wine's
color most accurately. Right: Members of the
German Wine Academy at Kloster Eberbach.*

guest lists to people in the wine industry and politicians or celebrities who can be expected to benefit the industry.

An alternative is to organize your own group. This need not be a case of the blind leading the blind. Most wine merchants will be delighted to help you set up tastings. In Illinois, wine merchants often conduct tastings in their own shops—a frequent practice also in Europe. Unfortunately, legislators in most of the other United States and in Canada, ostensibly for our own good, have passed laws prohibiting us from tasting wines in places where they are sold by the bottle.

Probably the best way to sample new wines—and, in the process, learn a great deal about winemaking—is to visit one or more wineries. Most wineries welcome visitors hospitably, providing guided tours of the winery itself, followed by a free tasting of its products.

One of the most enjoyable days G-1 and G-2 and their wives ever spent started with a drive to Hammondsport, New York. We first visited the good folk at Great Western, with a 9 A.M. sherry tasting to get us off on the right foot. Then we trekked over the mountain to Naples, where Widmer's wine cellars include the most impressive array of sherry-aging barrels we've ever seen—even in Jerez de la Frontera. Widmer's puts its barrels up on the roof, and a snow-covered half-acre of them, stretching out toward Lake Keuka, is the kind of sight you don't forget, even if you're jaded old winery-buffs like us.

After Widmer's, we headed around Lake Keuka and popped in at Gold Seal, where we tasted some exquisite white sparkling wines and the company's Chablis Natur—then just being readied for market. It's now one of the firm's top sellers. Then we doubled back to Taylor's to taste more sparkling wines. All four wineries welcome visitors daily, and there's no need for appointments or other preparations. You need only drive, bicycle, or other-

wise propel yourself within range and the wine folks will take it from there. (Taylor's guided tours, with immaculately clad college kids ushering tourists through the no-less-immaculate winery, have become one of the Finger Lakes' top tourist attractions.)

Hospitality is equally high in California, where we've spent many delightful hours sipping and chatting with wine people. The wineries don't reserve the red carpet treatment only for the press. At the very least, anyone who drives up is greeted cordially and shown around, then brought to the tasting room for drinks on the house. The bigger wineries have staff guides, who conduct tours at appointed hours. In the smaller ones, whoever is handy takes you around—it may be the winemaker himself. (At some of the very small ones, visitors are welcomed only when they've phoned ahead for an appointment—as the signs outside invariably proclaim.)

For the names and addresses of California wineries welcoming tourists, write to the Wine Institute, 717 Market Street, San Francisco, CA 94103. No comparable organization coordinates touring of New York State wineries, but most of them are located within a twenty-mile radius of Hammondsport. If you're planning a trip to the Finger Lakes region, write to one or more wineries in which you're interested (the name of the winery and the city will be sufficient address—you'll find both on the wine label) to determine times and dates of public tours.

Though many Canadian and foreign wineries do not welcome tourists, many others do. For details, write the winery directly or write foreign wineries in care of their U.S. importer. (A letter to Schieffelin & Co., Cooper Square, New York, NY 10003, will bring an invitation to the celebrated champagne cellars of Moët et Chandon at Epernay, France, open daily to tourists from Easter to November 1.)

European wineries are not nearly as hospitable as they were a couple of decades ago when G-2, as a student in Florence, spent weekends bicycling with his fellow *studenti* through Chianti country sampling the *vino* with *prosciutto*, country *formaggio* and huge chunks of home-baked *pane*, to say nothing of the days when G-1 meandered thereabouts, glass in hand. But hospitality is still high, especially in the smaller, family-run wineries. Last year, G-2 and his wife, summer-coursing at the University of Paris, drove down into wine country each weekend and were treated regally. Only rarely did the wineries know that G-2 was writing a wine book.

Air France offers a "Wine Countries of France" fly-drive program in Paris, Bordeaux, Burgundy, and Chablis, between April 15 and September 2. The fifteen-day tours include six days in Paris and an eight-day detailed itinerary in the wine regions, with *dégustations* (tastings) at well-known wineries. Some other national airlines offer comparable programs.

Germany and Switzerland are among nations which have annual wine festivals at harvest time, featuring tastings and more folklore than you'd imagine. For more information, write the German Wine Information Bureau, 342 Madison Avenue, New York, NY 10017, and the Swiss National Tourist Office, 608 Fifth Avenue, New York, NY 10020.

Some travel agents will have details on other wine tours. Lee Stewart, founder of Souverain Cellars in California's Napa Valley, currently conducts tours, limited to thirty persons, through wine regions of the world. These are aimed primarily at people in the wine industry but laymen are welcome. Among places toured are New Zealand, Australia, Argentina, and Europe. For more information, write Wine Tours International, 1367 Main St., St. Helena, CA 94574.

5.

5.
HOW WINES ARE NAMED

The Ancient Greeks called it οινος, the Hebrews *yayin*, the Egyptians *arpu*. The words all translate as wine, and in the ancient world that apparently was all you had to say. Whether in a restaurant or wine store or private home, you asked for wine and were given the local product, made from native grapes by whatever method had evolved among local winemakers. There were no types of wine. There simply was wine.

What happened to transform the semantic simplicity of those days into the hodgepodge of geographical, botanical, and proprietary names that prevails today is anyone's guess. Ours is as follows:

Sometime—perhaps around the time of Homer—a traveler noted that the wine he drank in Greece was in many ways different from the wine he drank in Syria. As trade developed, the demand grew for wine from certain places. What the drinker wanted, of course, was not necessarily wine produced in a specific location; he simply wanted wine of the type he associated with the place. Since the colors of wine are few and the properties of taste and smell quite difficult to describe, people fell into the habit of referring to wines in terms of their origin. Thus, one said he preferred Phoenician wine over Egyptian wine—much as modern drinkers might say they prefer Spanish wines over French wines. The preference, if real, is based on comparison of only a few of the many different wines produced in—and not necessarily typical of—these places.

As ancient travelers became more knowledgeable about the variety of wines within a country, they narrowed their terms of description. Thus, one spoke of Sicilian wines as opposed to Etruscan wines—or in later years, Burgundy wines as opposed to Bordeaux wines. There were, to be sure, many similarities among wines from each region, but there also were important differences.

Pierre of Bordeaux, for example, used only the free run from crushed grapes and aged his wine in a certain type of oak. His neighbor Marcel used press wine and aged it hardly at all. Both were Bordeaux wines, but their differences were greater than their similarities. Sophisticated drinkers quickly learned that the producer of the wine was more important than the place where the grapes were grown, crushed, pressed, or aged.

Enter the importer. Let us headquarter him in Beirut and call him Khalil. He brings in a few cases of Château Pierre and distributes them among his friends. They implore him to bring them some more. He takes their orders, returns to Bordeaux, and finds there is not enough Château Pierre to satisfy the demand.

Enter the shipper. We call him Claude. He points out to Khalil that there are several vineyards in the very same township as Pierre's, and these have more wine than they know what to do with. Khalil tastes these wines. None quite comes up to Pierre's, but some come close. He takes them as substitutes. He also buys some wines from neighboring townships, plus some the shipper has blended himself. Back in Beirut, the wines are sampled and new orders taken. The demand for Château Pierre is greater than ever. Khalil raises the price, then offers some of the other châteaux' wines as substitutes. Khalil's customers have no clear preference for one particular château, but they do show a general preference for wines from the townships of Pauillac and Saint-Julien in the district of Médoc, several miles up the Gironde River from the city of Bordeaux. "Next trip," they say, "if you can't get me Château Pierre, bring back as much Pauillac or Saint-Julien as you can get." As for the shipper's wines, Khalil can hardly give them away.

Back in Bordeaux he confers with Claude. They know that if they place all their orders at once for the wines of Pauillac and Saint-Julien, the producers will start raising their prices in the manner of Pierre—who currently is lighting his cigars with 1,000-franc notes. So they fill only half of Khalil's orders with wines bottled at the châteaux. Claude buys bulk quantities of other wine in Pauillac and Saint-Julien, blends these in his own warehouse, and labels them "Pauillac" and "Saint-Julien." Khalil brings these back to Beirut as substitutes for the unfilled orders for château-bottled wines.

The generically labeled wines are a hit. Because Claude bought in bulk and cut a few corners in blending and aging, he is able to sell them for half the price of the château wines. Meanwhile, Khalil's customers are delighted to have an additional option. Those who are able and willing to pay the price can drink Château Pierre, or the château-bottled Pauillacs and Saint-Juliens every day. Others can enjoy the shipper's Pauillacs and Saint-Juliens daily, reserving the château-bottled wines for special occasions and Château Pierre (which now is more expensive than blood) for super-special occasions.

Enter the public-relations man. At the behest of certain vintners of Pauillac and Saint-Julien, he begins spreading the word that the reason these wines are so good is the soil and climate conditions of the two townships. The public-relations man downplays the fact that the techniques of the winemaker are most important to the character of a wine. His clients happen to be vintners who produce wines rather hastily and inexpensively. If they can make buyers believe that the wine's origin is more important than the producer, they will get more for their wines.

Enter Jean-Luc, a Bordeaux shipper who does not share Claude's high ethical standards. He knows that

Pauillac and Saint-Julien cannot produce enough wine to fill the demand. And so he blends the Pauillacs and Saint-Juliens with wines from other townships which can be bought for much less. At first he uses only 10 percent foreign wines, then increases it to 20, then 30. Soon the wine he calls Pauillac contains only an eyedropper full of Pauillac per barrel.

Enter the lobbyist. On behalf of Pauillac and Saint-Julien producers, who ostensibly seek to protect the public but actually are concerned primarily with their profits, he persuades legislators to enact regulations limiting the labels "Pauillac" and "Saint-Julien" to wines from grapes grown in those regions. Later the regulations are changed to permit 15 percent foreign grapes.

By this time the French wine label is so confusing that most people—Frenchmen included—can't decipher it. Some wines prominently feature the name of a château. In much smaller letters they identify the township and district where it is located, the shipper, and the year of production (vintage). Other wines do not contain a château name. They prominently feature the name of a location, followed in small letters by the name of the shipper and the vintage. Still others feature the name of the shipper, or a trade name —for example, Mouton-Cadet.

Another unscrupulous shipper, Maurice, is headquartered in LeHavre. He buys the discards of everybody in Bordeaux, blends them, and ships them under his trade name: Château Maurice. Nowhere on the label does it say the wine is château-bottled. But many buyers assume the word Château is a guarantee of quality.

And that's only in the Bordeaux region. Over in Burgundy, there are no château names. Wines produced by the vintner himself carry a vineyard name, like Clos de Vougeot or Richebourg. Others feature a village name, like Chassagne-Montrachet, followed by a vineyard name like Morgeot. Still others feature the village name without the vineyard. Some may also contain the name of the proprietor of the vineyard, the district in the Burgundy region where the vineyard is located, and the name of the shipper.

Which information is important? Generally, the seller gives greatest prominence to the thing he's proudest of. This leads to the general rule that the more specific the featured information, the more highly valued the wine. Thus, a wine called Château Pierre or Clos d'Antoine, being produced by the vintner himself, is most valued. Next is a wine from a narrowly limited region (for example, the township of Pauillac). Then, a wine from a larger district (for example, Médoc, which contains Pauillac). After that, a wine from a still larger region (for example, Bordeaux, sometimes described as Gironde, which contains Médoc). Then a wine featuring the actual or trade name of the shipper.

But the rule has many exceptions. Some shippers have developed such a reputation for reliability that their own name has become more important than the territorial name. In other cases, a wine features a château or vineyard name, but the château or vineyard is one of very low repute. The producer is trading on the fact that unsophisticated buyers will assume the wine must be good because it's sold as château-bottled.

Confusing? We've only scratched the surface. Let's go back to our mythical tale. Enter Charlie from California and Harry from Hammondsport. Until recently, Charlie, a Sonoma County farmer, has grown prunes. Now that North Americans have begun drinking wine in respectable quantities, he has decided to become a winemaker. Harry, meanwhile, has always been a winemaker, one specializing in sacramental wines (those used in religious ceremonies). He now sees an opportunity to expand his market.

Charlie comes back to California with some vines from Burgundy. He plants them, grows grapes, and produces two types of wine: one white, the other red. On his label he identifies these as—simply enough—"California Charlie's White Wine" and "California Charlie's Red Wine."

The wines don't sell. Which puzzles Charlie considerably, because he happens to know—not only from his own evaluation but also from the opinion of experts brought in from Burgundy—that his white wine is very much like one from the Burgundian district of Chablis which sells at ten times the price. What's the problem?

Enter the ad man. "The problem," he informs Charlie, "is that people have no idea what type of wine yours is. The label doesn't tell them enough. Is it a Chablis, a Sauternes, a Graves, or what?" Charlie points out that, strictly speaking, Chablis, Sauternes, and Graves are not wines, but districts in France. "Strictly speaking," replies the ad man, "you will soon go back to growing prunes if you don't start selling your wines. You'd better start giving them names people can recognize, like Chablis, Sauternes, and Graves."

So Charlie renames his white wine "Chablis" and his red wine "Burgundy." And people start buying them. Then Charlie expands his line. He introduces some wines made predominantly from one grape and starts marketing them under the grape name: "California Charlie's Cabernet Sauvignon." Once they catch on, demand is very high. Before long he is producing twenty different wines under generic names like Chablis and Sauternes and varietal names like Cabernet Sauvignon and Pinot Noir.

Meanwhile, Harry, using blends of wine made entirely from native New York State grapes, has come up with a wine that closely resembles the celebrated sparkling wines of the French district of Champagne. Guess what he calls it. And back in France, Claude, learning of the tremendous demand for California Charlie's Cabernet Sauvignon, quickly runs up a batch of labels for Cabernet Sauvignon de Claude—perfectly honest, since the wine is made 100% from Cabernet Sauvignon grapes (though the week before it was selling as Médoc de Claude).

And so it goes. Today it's possible to find wines named after the producer, the shipper, the region of production, the regional type (Canadian claret, New York State Burgundy), the grape, a trade name, and in rare cases the importer. None of these names in itself is an indicator of much more than the general character of the wine and the seller's idea of his strongest selling point. But there is other information on most wine labels which can be used to give you some advance idea of how the wine compares to others with which you may be familiar. Let's examine some labels from various countries and see what they reveal about the contents of their bottles.

Australia

Australian wine labels are probably the world's most explicit, most informative, and most forthright. We've only once or twice seen one that attempts to mislead. Indeed, though our presentation here is alphabetical by nation, Australia would merit lead-off position in any list, because its labels could—and perhaps should—serve as a model for all labels.

The important information on a label is: (1) the winemaker; (2) the wine's general type or character; (3) the bottler—was it bottled by the grape grower himself, a shipper, or some other agent who purchased grapes or wines in bulk and blended them? (4) the place where the grapes were grown (very revealing if you know other wines from the same area, because similar grape-growing conditions result in many similar characteristics); (5) the year in which the grapes were grown, if the wine was made exclusively or predominantly from one year's growth; (6) the alcohol concentration (it may range from 7 to 22 percent, depending on the type of wine); (7) the size of the bottle (very important, sometimes a 23- or 24-ounce bottle looks as big as a 32- or 33-ounce bottle); (8) on foreign wines, the name of the shipper and importer.

Labels of most nations give only some of this information. In Europe, for example, grape varieties are rarely identified. The absence of the information doesn't mean that a wine is bad; indeed, some of the world's most celebrated wines are described only meagerly on their labels. But the label should tell you enough about a wine to give you some idea—before you buy your first bottle—whether you'll like what's inside. Australian labels generally tell you everything you need to know.

Seaview Moselle and Seppelt Shiraz/Cabernet

Producer's Name: The most important consideration in any wine is the producer. Some producers limit themselves to a single type of wine, particularly in France; others make as many as two dozen types. In either case, the producer generally runs true to form. (Seppelt and Seaview are among Australia's more prestigious.)

Grape: Seppelt's Shiraz/Cabernet is a blend of wines from these two grape varieties. The Cabernet is actually Cabernet Sauvignon. The Shiraz, rarely found outside Australia, is a blending grape with some characteristics of the more common Merlot, Carignan, or Malbec.

Seaview's wine is generically named—that is, the type, Moselle, describes a wine which the producer hopes

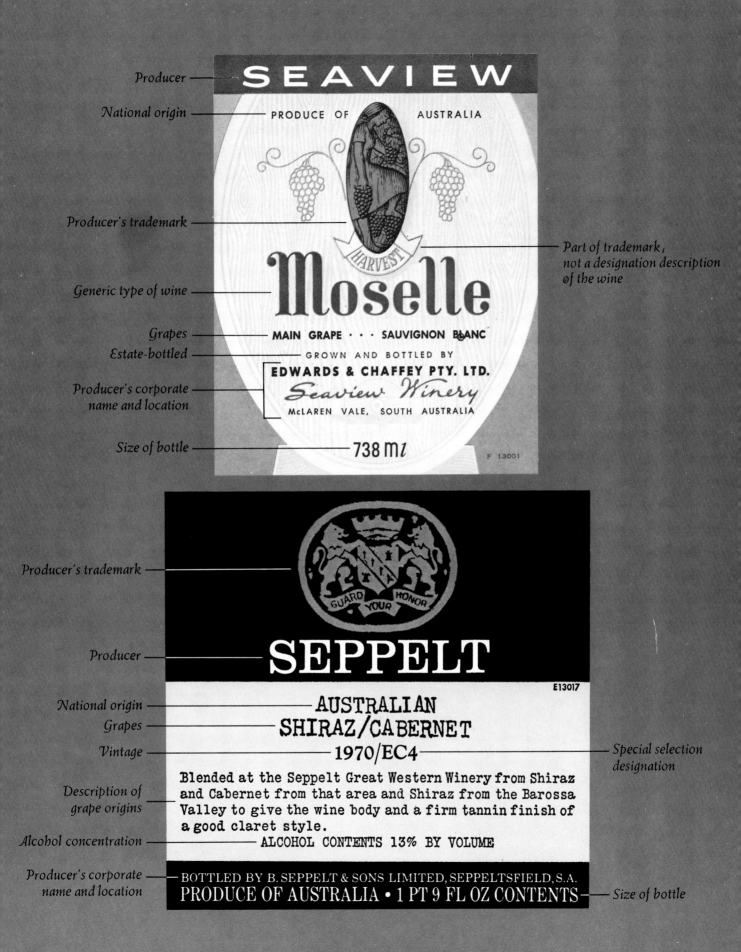

Producer — **SEAVIEW**

National origin — PRODUCE OF AUSTRALIA

Producer's trademark

Part of trademark, not a designation description of the wine

Generic type of wine — Moselle

Grapes — MAIN GRAPE · · · SAUVIGNON BLANC

Estate-bottled — GROWN AND BOTTLED BY

Producer's corporate name and location — EDWARDS & CHAFFEY PTY. LTD. *Seaview Winery* McLAREN VALE, SOUTH AUSTRALIA

Size of bottle — 738 Ml

F 13001

Producer's trademark — GUARD YOUR HONOR

Producer — **SEPPELT**

E13017

National origin — AUSTRALIAN
Grapes — SHIRAZ/CABERNET
Vintage — 1970/EC4 — Special selection designation

Description of grape origins — Blended at the Seppelt Great Western Winery from Shiraz and Cabernet from that area and Shiraz from the Barossa Valley to give the wine body and a firm tannin finish of a good claret style.

Alcohol concentration — ALCOHOL CONTENTS 13% BY VOLUME

Producer's corporate name and location — BOTTLED BY B. SEPPELT & SONS LIMITED, SEPPELTSFIELD, S.A.
PRODUCE OF AUSTRALIA • 1 PT 9 FL OZ CONTENTS — Size of bottle

will be regarded as typical of those characteristic of the Mosel Valley of Germany and Luxembourg. Opponents of generic labeling—usually winemakers from the region whose name is being borrowed—decry the tactic as an attempt to capitalize on their reputation. Proponents say that generic labeling is helpful to consumers who would not recognize varietal names but who have a concept of what certain regional wines (Moselle as opposed to Rhine, Bordeaux as opposed to Burgundy) are like.

Vintage: In Australia, which enjoys a relatively consistent climate, vintage is not as important a consideration as in France and Germany, where one year's crop may be very good and another's horrible. However, a vintage designation helps consumers keep track of the wine's age. Many reds and almost all whites start downhill within five years.

One reason the Seaview Moselle is not vintage dated may be that the blended wines are of varying ages. In this case, a bottling date would be helpful (some California winemakers employ this technique for nonvintaged wines). If a bottling date is not provided, the year of the bottle's manufacture usually is stamped in the glass on the bottle's underside; most bottles are filled within a few weeks of their manufacture.

Description: The Seppelt description is extremely helpful, telling not only the regions where the grapes were grown, but also the intended effect of the blend. It is very useful to know that the winemaker has attempted to make a full-bodied, high-tannin wine with strong memory. The cognoscento of California wines will recognize that this one purports to be much like California's better Cabernet Sauvignons; the cognoscento of French wines will anticipate a wine like those of the Haut Médoc in Bordeaux. This sort of information almost never appears on wine bottles outside Australia.

Top: Winemaker uses glass "thief" to draw a sherry sample at the Renmark winery in South Australia. Bottom: Sherry barrels absorb the sun—and reduce their contents via evaporation—at Seppelt winery in Seppeltsfield, Barossa Valley.

Special Selection Designation: Many Australian winemakers designate different batches as "bin x," "cask y," and so forth. These are batches which have received special treatment—extra aging, for example, or aging in particular casks or barrels which over the years have been found to impart unique characteristics to the wines they have contained. The "EC4" on this label is such a designation. If the consumer likes the wine in this bottle, he can be assured of getting exactly the same thing by buying another bottle labeled EC4; whereas other batches of Seppelt's 1970 Shiraz/Cabernet might be slightly different.

Kaiser-Stuhl Rosé

Grape: Though the wine is named generically (in this instance, after its color rather than a geographic region), the producer helpfully informs us that it is made 100 percent from the Grenache grape. The Grenache is a relatively low-yield grape compared to such grapes as the Catawba, Concord, and Seibel, from which many rosés are made. Thus, we know Kaiser-Stuhl's to be a more expensively—and presumably more carefully made—wine. Knowing that this rosé is not merely a Grenache blend but 100 percent Grenache may be useful to someone who is familiar with the character of the Grenache grape.

Winemaker's Comments: Not merely a commercial message of the sort that often appears on a back label, they helpfully tell us where the grapes were grown.

Barossa Valley Australian Pearl

What do the winemakers mean by "celebration" wine? A bona fide sparkling wine (one that underwent a second fermentation)? Or merely a carbonated wine? Nowhere on the Australian Pearl label does either word appear. But we get a hint when we look at the alcohol concentration—only 9 percent. This is almost certainly a carbonated wine, which doesn't mean that it's bad, only that it is not a doubly fermented (thus costlier to make) wine.

Canada

Canadian wine labels are simple and to the point. Normally they tell only the producer's name and location, the type of wine, the size of the bottle, and the alcohol concentration. If the type of wine is a generic, the adjective "Canadian" must by law appear before the word in letters of at least the same size and density. Occasionally the wine will be produced under a trade name, in which event the producer's name usually is appended. A commercial message may also be included. Most material will be in both English and French.

The labels here are all from one winery: Château-Gai at Niagara Falls, Ontario, the nation's largest. It uses Château-Bon on wines it exports to the United States. A perusal of the labels reveals as much about the winery's intended selling points as about the wines.

Château-Gai Claret

"Claret" is an English word applied by the British to wines of France's Bordeaux region. But rather than take the producer's general assurance that we are buying a Bordeaux-type wine, we'd prefer to be told the grape variety (or varieties) and judge the wine's character for ourselves. Fact is, this claret is made from a Seibel hybrid variety, as a phone call to the winery promptly revealed. The producer apparently does not mention this on the label because he does not think most prospective buyers will care. Recently, however, other North American wine producers have begun including varietal information on generically named wines. We encourage the trend.

There is no regional designation within Canada for the wine, although we learn from the label that Château-Gai is at Niagara Falls. Regional designations normally are not given for generically named wines—reasonably enough, since they are made in an attempt to duplicate the characteristics of wines associated with a different region.

Canadian Pink Catawba

The other wine is a varietal. Catawba is a native North American grape. The wines made from it usually are pink, but we've also seen some whites and reds, sparkling and still. This pink Catawba is a still wine, sometimes served as a table wine, often as a recreational drink.

Producer's Name: Though Château-Gai made both wines, it identifies itself on the Catawba label only in the small type at the bottom, and uses the national designation "Canadian" in the style of a trade name. Presumably this is to enhance drinkers' association of Catawba as a native grape. The French-sounding proprietary name might discourage this.

Size of Bottle: Note that these bottles hold 26 ounces. Many consumers erroneously assume that bottles smaller than a quart and larger than a split are fifths (25.6 ounces), but this is not so. Sizes can vary up or down. It is not a terribly important consideration in wines priced under $2 (less than £1), but it takes on importance when dealing with more expensive European wines, many of which are sold in 24 ounce bottles.

Sparkling Life and Dry Vermouth

Both the Vermouth and Sparkling Life labels contain a minimum of information, and nothing else really need be known about either of these wines. Vermouth is traditionally produced with the least expensive base wines available; it acquires its character as a result of the producer's formula of herbs and other aromatic additives. Thus, the producer's name is all you really need to know— assuming he will not disclose his aromatizing formula (in our experience, no producer ever has). Likewise, on the Sparkling Life—a trade name for this "pop," or carbonated, wine—the flavoring formula is what counts, not the base wines. Note, by the way, that the alcohol concentration is only 7 percent.

Château-Gai
CANADIAN CLARET
Dry Red Table Wine
Vin de Table Rouge

6 FL OZ/738 ML/ALCOHOL 13%/PRODUCED BY CHATEAU-GAI WINES LTD. NIAGARA FALLS, CANADA
RODUIT DE CHATEAU-GAI WINES LTD. NIAGARA FALLS, CANADA/26 FL OZ/738 ML/13% ALCOOL

Sparkling Life wine

FROM THE SKILLED VINTNERS OF CHATEAU-GAI WINES LTD.
NIAGARA FALLS CANADA. (ALCOHOL 7% BY VOLUME.
CONTENTS 26 FLUID OUNCES — 738 MILLILITRES.)

CANADIAN

SERVE COLD

SERVIR FROID

26 OUNCES

Pink Catawba

Provenant des cépages les plus nobles du célèbre vignoble de la vallée du Niagara, ce vin fin et délicat est élaboré dans les caves de Château-Gai Wines Ltd., à Niagara Falls, Canada.

From select grapes grown in the vineyards of the famous Niagara Valley comes this fine, delicate wine produced by the skilled vintners of Chateau-Gai Wines Limited, Niagara Falls, Canada.

CONTENTS 25/32 QT.—ALCOHOL BY VOLUME 13%

DRY VERMOUTH

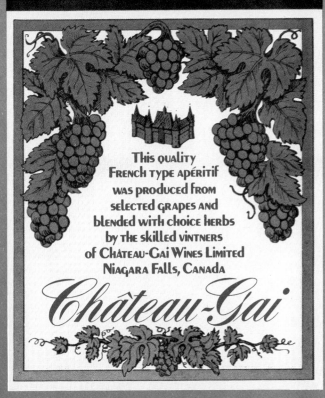

This quality
French type apéritif
was produced from
selected grapes and
blended with choice herbs
by the skilled vintners
of Château-Gai Wines Limited
Niagara Falls, Canada

Château-Gai

124

Chile

Chilean wines are simply labeled—perhaps too simply.

Concha y Toro Cabernet Sauvignon

Producer: Concha y Toro is a trade and corporate name. Many Chilean producers offer a Cabernet Sauvignon, and the characteristics of the different ones vary considerably. Hence, the producer's name is important.

Estate-Bottled: Under Chilean law, a wine may be described as estate-bottled only if the producer grew his own grapes, made his own wine, and bottled it on his own estate. This proscribes blending the wine with one of lesser repute and selling it under the estate name.

Gran Vino: Under Chilean law there are four classes of export wines. A one-year-old wine is labeled "courant"; a two-year-old, "special"; a three-, four-, or five-year-old has "reserve" on the label and one that is six or older, "gran vino."

Vintage: A wine that carries a "vintage" designation is made predominantly or exclusively of grapes grown during that year. Growing conditions during the year will affect the wine's quality, particularly in regions with un-

certain climate. *But,* this wine, carrying a 1970 vintage date, was bought in 1974. As a *gran vino,* it is supposed to be at least six years old!

So much for the worth of wine legislation. The ultimate test, as we shall repeat frequently in this tome, is the reputation of the producer. Actually, though it was mislabeled, we enjoyed this bottle of wine very much and believe it was worth more than we paid for it.

Vineyard Location: Note that none is revealed on the front label. The back label makes passing reference to "the famous Pirque vineyards," but their fame has not extended to any reference work on Chilean wine we've consulted. It would be helpful to know if they are in the Aconcagua or Maipo valleys, widely regarded as the best terrain for Cabernet Sauvignon (owing mainly to a high percentage of limestone in the soil). Still, the ultimate test of any wine is in the sensory satisfaction it provides, and this one scored very high. Our lament is that, because of the sparseness of information on the label, we might not have been attracted to the wine unless a friend had recommended it.

China

Very few wines are exported by the Republic of China and fewer still by the People's Republic of China. In either case, labeling is simple and efficient. A back label gives the English translation of the text on the front label and provides additional material required by U.S. regulations on imported wines.

Shao-Hsing Rice Wine

Producer: The government's tobacco and wine monopoly bureau.

Type of Wine: Shao-Hsing is a generic name for wine of a type most commonly found in the east central provinces, and is made from fermented glutinous rice, aged in earthenware jars. It is normally served at body temperature (98.6 degrees Fahrenheit or 37° C) in small cups during dinner. China also produces wines from grapes, but none, to our knowledge, is exported. As an alternate, New Dynasty, the importer of Shao-Hsing, offers a Chinese-type wine made in Portugal; Schiefflin & Co. offers another made in France.

Size of Bottle: Note that it is only 20 ounces.

Cyprus

Cyprus labeling is a model of simplicity, a welcome relief to anyone who has had to test his patience on the old German and current French labels. But many consumers would prefer a little more information.

Aphrodite

Producer: Keo Ltd. Trade names for individual wines are a common practice in the Greek-speaking world and can be confusing to consumers who expect either a varietal or a generic. Note well that Aphrodite is the name of this wine and this wine alone—not of a product line.

Description: It's hard to get more succinct ("white dry Cyprus wine"), but it's possible to be more explicit. As chance would have it, we liked this wine very much. But the producer takes the risk that prospective buyers will find the information given insufficient and pass by Aphrodite for something more familiar.

Producer's Motto: "Be happy and drink well!" is taken from a two-handled drinking bowl dating from 500 B.C., discovered on the site of the ancient Cypriot town of Marion, and now in the national museum at Nicosia.

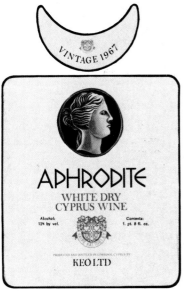

Pole-toting vineyard workers harvest grapes at Salisbury Topes, England. Once the largest importer of French wines, England today produces many of its own wines, and even exports a few. Facing page: Bottles of some celebrated Bordeaux wines.

Denmark

Denmark makes wine from apples, cherries, black currants, blackberries, elderberries, and strawberries. Most of these wines are sweet and are served as recreational drinks.

Cherry Kirsberry

So few of these nongrape wines are produced that it is difficult to distinguish their individual character and make comparisons. For that reason, about the only information of significance on a nongrape wine label is the name of the fruit from which the wine was made, the added ingredients (if any), the alcohol content, the size of the bottle, and the producer and his location. That, give or take a trade name, is what you'll find on Danish wine labels.

England

The nation's exported wines usually are made from apples, gooseberries, elderberries, raisins, red or black currants, oranges, or mead (a fermented mixture of honey and water, sometimes blended with apple or grape juice).

Merrydown Orange Wine

As in Denmark, the limited production of nongrape wine varieties makes comparison difficult. Thus, detailed information concerning the varieties of a given fruit or the areas where the fruit was grown is not necessary.

France

Now the chaos begins. French wine labels are, without question, the most disorganized and generally misleading of any country in the world. Even the French, if not knowledgeable about the wines of a given locality, will have trouble divining the important facts on the label— mixed up as they are among irrelevant material and, in some cases, words and phrases that can only be intended to deceive.

The newcomer to wine drinking, faced with this confusion and with the incredible prices of many French wines, might be inclined to avoid them entirely. But he will do so, we think, at his own great loss—for France produces some of the most exciting wines we've ever drunk. The only solution is to wade into the morass and attempt to make sense of the labels. Hopefully, the following discussion will provide some useful guideposts.

Château Margaux

Producer: It is not without reason that the name of Château Margaux, the producer, appears most prominently on the label pictured here. This is one of the world's most celebrated wines.

Grand Vin: The term frequently is used to describe a wine of extraordinary reputation, and most experienced drinkers would apply the term to Château Margaux whether or not it appeared on the label. However, this phrase on the label does not necessarily guarantee that the wine in the bottle is of comparable repute. Any producer can legally use the term.

Château-Bottled: Under French law, the term may be used only if the producer grew all his own grapes, made his own wine, and bottled it on his own estate. This proscribes blending the wine with one of lesser repute and selling it under the estate name.

Classification: In 1855, a group of Bordeaux wine brokers divided sixty-two of the region's most prestigious vineyards into five classes, termed growths. The top class—*premier cru classé*—comprised four châteaux: Château Lafite (now marketed as Château Lafite-Rothschild), Château Margaux, Château Latour, and Château Haut-Brion. Not surprisingly, Château Margaux boasts of its class on its label (the *grand* in *premier grand cru classé* is a fillip).

Controlled Name: The *Institut National des Appellations d'Origine* at Paris prescribes certain conditions under which the controlled name of a given region may be applied to a wine. All grapes must be grown in the region in question, they must be of one or more specific varieties, certain viticultural and vinicultural practices must be observed, the harvest must be limited to a certain quantity of grapes per acre, and the wine must contain a certain minimum alcohol level. As a rule, the smaller the geographical area whose controlled name is applied, the narrower the requirements. Thus, all wines that carry a township appellation (*appellation Pauillac controlée*) are more tightly regulated than those carrying the appellation of the district in which the township is located (*appellation Médoc controlée*). Likewise, those carrying the appellation of the district are more highly regulated than those carrying the appellation of the region (*appellation Bordeaux controlée*, or simply *appellation controlée*). Propagandists for the French wine industry try to persuade the public that all this is a guarantee of quality. It isn't. It is possible to follow the law scrupulously and still produce an unpalatable wine. Ultimately, the producer's reputation is far more important than the appellation.

Ginestet Margaux

This is a regional, or shipper's, wine rather than one that was bottled at the château. In other words, the

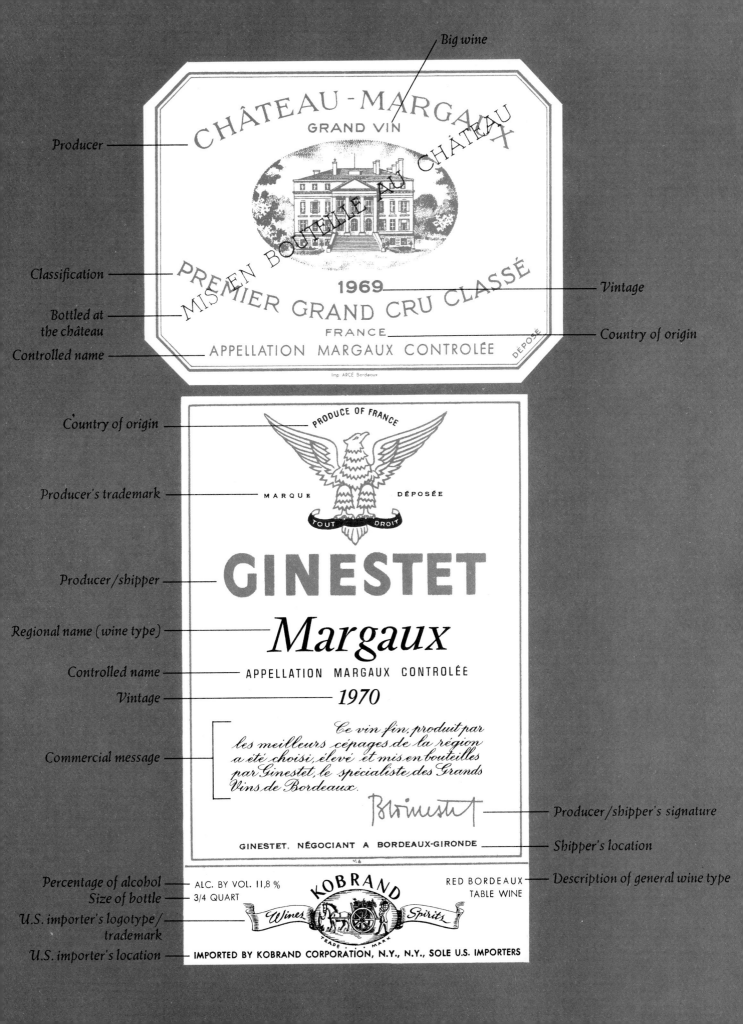

Big wine

Producer — CHÂTEAU-MARGAUX
GRAND VIN

MIS EN BOUTEILLE AU CHÂTEAU

Classification — PREMIER GRAND CRU CLASSÉ

Bottled at the château

Controlled name — 1969 — Vintage

FRANCE — Country of origin

APPELLATION MARGAUX CONTROLÉE — DÉPOSÉ

Imp. ARCÉ Bordeaux

Country of origin — PRODUCE OF FRANCE

Producer's trademark — MARQUE   DÉPOSÉE
TOUT DROIT

Producer/shipper — GINESTET

Regional name (wine type) — Margaux

Controlled name — APPELLATION MARGAUX CONTROLÉE

Vintage — 1970

Commercial message — Ce vin fin, produit par les meilleurs cépages de la région a été choisi, élevé et mis en bouteilles par Ginestet, le spécialiste des Grands Vins de Bordeaux.

Producer/shipper's signature — B. Ginestet

Shipper's location — GINESTET, NÉGOCIANT A BORDEAUX-GIRONDE

Percentage of alcohol — ALC. BY VOL. 11,8 %   RED BORDEAUX — Description of general wine type
Size of bottle — 3/4 QUART   TABLE WINE

U.S. importer's logotype/trademark — KOBRAND Wines Spirits

U.S. importer's location — IMPORTED BY KOBRAND CORPORATION, N.Y., N.Y., SOLE U.S. IMPORTERS

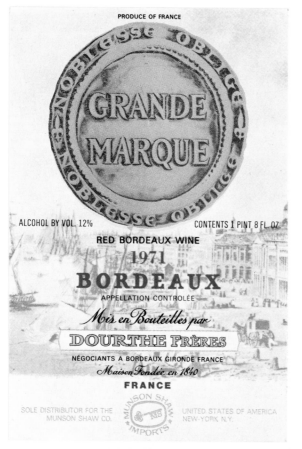

shipper bought wines in bulk from various vineyards, then blended and bottled them. This does not mean that the wine is necessarily of poor quality. In fact, this particular wine is quite highly regarded. But it does not have the prestige of a château-bottled wine, nor the price.

Producer: On a regional wine the producer is the shipper rather than the grower of the grapes. Ginestet proclaims his identity loudly, and this is no surprise. He is one of the more prestigious Bordeaux shippers, and his name is what distinguishes this Margaux from those of other shippers. Note well that the full name of the wine is Ginestet Margaux, both the producer/shipper's and the regional name. To refer to it simply as Ginestet would be meaningless. He produces an assortment of regional and varietal wines: a Ginestet Saint-Julien, a Ginestet Pomerol, a Ginestet Cabernet Sauvignon. Likewise, to describe the wine only as Margaux is insufficient. There are important differences between the Margaux of Ginestet and the Margaux of another shipper.

Regional Name/Wine Type: Here is where things really get confusing. Calling a wine a Margaux on a label that also contains the inscription *appellation Margaux controlée* identifies the wine as a product of the township of Margaux, district of Médoc, region of Bordeaux, country of France. But there are other wines not even produced in France that are called Margaux. These are the generic wines, named after the region whose wines they *purport* to characterize. Sometimes they are made from grape varieties specified under the *appellation Margaux controlée* regulations, sometimes from varieties never seen in Margaux. Usually they attempt to duplicate the character of Margaux wines, but do not succeed. Actually, they need not bear any resemblance to the wines of Margaux. There currently is being marketed in Japan a sweet white wine named Margaux. The original is dry and red.

This sort of thing makes French wine men very unhappy. They argue that no wine should be called Margaux that is not made under *appellation Margaux controlée* regulations. Makers of the other Margaux respond that the generic name has become common usage and describes a type of wine rather than a specific locality's wine.

Whichever side of the controversy you're on, the fact remains that there are lots of generic wines around. So the name Margaux without the designation *appellation Margaux controlée* identifies only a type of wine, not that type of wine from a specific place; and even with the appellation designation it fails to identify the most important factor in the whole affair, the producer.

Commercial Message: Usually printed on the back label. This message says that the fine wine in this bottle was produced from the best grape varieties of the region, harvested at their peak, blended and bottled by Ginestet, a specialist in "big" wines of Bordeaux.

Shipper's Location: Strictly speaking, Bordeaux is the principal city of the region of Gironde, but most people refer to the region as Bordeaux.

Percentage of Alcohol: As with most table wines, the alcohol in this one is about 12 percent. The alcohol concentration must under law appear on the label of every wine sold in North America.

Size of Bottle: Note well that this is three-fourths of a quart, or 24 ounces, the standard size in Bordeaux. In the United States, the standard size is four-fifths of a quart, or 25.6 ounces.

U.S. Importer: This is important information if you have no previous experience with the wine itself or its shipper. Importers usually are consistent in their choice of product. The same buyers taste all the wines in the line, and the same palate biases govern those chosen.

Mouton-Cadet and *Grande Marque* (see page 130)

These are also regional wines, but the region in question is larger—Bordeaux itself rather than the township of Margaux. This does not necessarily mean that these wines have less quality than those of Margaux. It simply means that they were made under less specific regulations.

Trade Name: Both appear under a trade name rather than that of a producer/shipper. In both cases, however, the shipper is the producer. Some observers might feel that Mouton-Cadet is so named to give (falsely) the impression of being a château-bottled wine. Granted, the word château does not appear on the label; but in France many estate-bottled wines are marketed under hyphenated vineyard names. Thus, it is not exactly inconceivable that some people who do not know very much about French wine might assume that Mouton-Cadet is in that category; they might also confuse the name with that of Château Mouton-Rothschild, rated among *deuxièmes crus* (second growths) in the 1855 official classification of Médoc wines, subsequently upgraded officially to *premier cru* (first growth) along with Châteaux Lafite-Rothschild, Margaux, Latour, and Haut-Brion. This wine is not in that league—nor is its price.

Producer/Shipper: In the case of Mouton-Cadet, this is Baron Philippe de Rothschild, located in the township of Pauillac in Gironde and the same Baron Philippe de Rothschild who produces Château Mouton-Rothschild, the *premier cru classé.* His name at the top of the bottle might further encourage the wine novice to confuse this regional wine with the *premier cru.*

In the case of Grande Marque, the producer/shipper is Dourthe Frères, a long established and widely respected Bordeaux shipper. So why does he hide his name near the bottom of the label? Well, he's probably stressing the trade name because he thinks the consumer he hopes to reach won't recognize his corporate name.

Controlled Name: If you know nothing else about either wine, this is the important item on the label. The Bordeaux appellation is not as restrictive as those of smaller geographic units (township, district), but the wine still meets (or purports to meet) the requirements of the appellation regulations.

Mis-en-Bouteilles: Mis en bouteilles par Dourthe Frères identifies this as a regional wine, bottled by the shipper. It is not to be confused with *mis en bouteilles au château,* which identifies a château-bottled wine.

Now let's look at the Mouton-Cadet label: *mis en bouteilles dans nos chais.* Since it's safe to assume the wine wasn't bottled in his attic, we might wonder why Baron Philippe is telling us it was bottled in his cellars. And we don't think it's too cynical to speculate that he wants novices to confuse this with an estate-bottled (*au château*) wine. None of this means that Mouton-Cadet is necessarily a bad or dishonest wine. As a matter of fact, many people like it very much. But the terms on the label can be confusing to people who don't know wine terminology.

Even more confusing is the phrase used by some French shippers, *mis en bouteilles du château.* Note *du* versus *au.* Wines bottled *au château* are bottled at the château. Those bottled *du château* are simply put into bottles *of* the château—bottles owned by the château. It being unlikely that the château would put its wine into bottles owned by someone else, we can't help but suspect the phrase is employed to dupe the naïve. Our suspicions are reinforced by the fact that we have never seen the expression on the label of a bottle sold in a French-speaking country.

Richebourg (see page 130)

Even more confusing than the labeling of Bordeaux is that of Burgundy. Here the château system gives way to a vineyard system, each vineyard being divided among a number of grape growers. If the grower makes his own wine and bottles it, the wine is termed estate-bottled. There are four common French phrases for this, and they may be used interchangeably: *Mis au domaine*, *Mis du domaine*, *Mis en bouteilles par le propriétaire*, and *Mis en bouteilles à la propriété*. In Burgundy the four phrases legitimately identify an estate-bottled wine, including the *du domaine* (not so for the *du château* in Bordeaux).

Those not bottled by the grower are bottled by shippers, and, as in Bordeaux, *appellation controlée* laws describe the area from which the blended wines are chosen. The smaller the area represented, the more precise the laws. The smallest area is the vineyard itself, then the commune, then the district, then the region. For example: Richebourg, commune of Vosne-Romanée, district of Côte de Nuits, region of Burgundy. All this is on the Richebourg label, but not so prominently as its equivalent would be on the Bordeaux label.

Producer: French wine-industry propagandists will disagree with us on this, but we say the producer's name—buried here at the bottom of the label—is the most important thing. The propagandists will say that the vineyard, Richebourg, is most important, because all growers on the vineyard are bound by the same appellation laws. We say laws are made to be broken and usually are. Moreover, some people are simply better or more fastidious winemakers than others. So, prized though the Richebourg label is, the grower's name is more important.

Incidentally, if Louis Gros had not bottled his own wine, the shipper would still be entitled to use the Richebourg label provided that all the wine came from that vineyard. If it did not, the shipper would have to use the

commune label, Vosne-Romanée. If the wine did not all come from this commune, the district label, Côte de Nuits, would apply. And if the wine did not all come from within the Côte de Nuits, we would be left with the regional label, Burgundy.

Controlled Name: In Bordeaux, the use of *appellation controlée* without a geographic term in the middle suggests that the wine is regional—that is, a blend of wines from all over Bordeaux. Not so in Burgundy. Each top-ranked vineyard has its own controlled name. So *appellation controlée* here means that the laws pertaining to Richebourg, not merely Burgundy, were observed.

Ranked vineyards, by the way, are classified as *grand cru,* the top of the line, or *premier cru,* actually the second growth. To compound the confusion, most producers entitled to use these terms on their label do not—the assumption apparently being that if you're sophisticated enough to appreciate the wine, you ought to know the vineyard's classification. Richebourg enjoys the classification of *grand cru.*

Shipper: There is none. Estate-bottled Burgundies often go directly from the grower to the importer.

Chablis (see page 133)

Two very similar labels point out both the similari-

ties and differences between classes of Chablis. The district of Chablis, named after the town in its center, comprises 4,700 acres of vineyards. Like other vineyards in the region of Burgundy, they may be rated *grand cru* (seven Chablis vineyards are) or *premier cru* (twenty-two vineyards are).

Regional Type: The name Chablis appears most prominently on both labels. This is not surprising. The quantity of *appellation controlée* wine produced in this district each year is quite small, and the producer apparently wants everyone to know he's in the game. This Chablis-produced wine, by the way, is not to be confused with wine marketed under the generic term Chablis and produced elsewhere in the world. The latter purports to duplicate the character of Chablis-produced wine.

Classification: Unlike the proprietors of the previously discussed Burgundian vineyards, this proprietor (Albert Pic, also the shipper) proclaims his *grand cru* classification. Apparently he does so because he believes the term will carry more weight with buyers than the name of the vineyard. This is not to say that Bougrots is a less prestigious vineyard than Richebourg, but simply that the proprietors, or their label designers, choose to approach the matter in different ways.

Controlled Name: Note that the *grand cru* appellation is more specific than the appellation of the regular Chablis. Beaujolais is another district—considerably larger than Chablis—of the region of Burgundy. Lower prices for its wines are a reflection of the increased production.

The name game in Beaujolais is even more complicated than elsewhere in France. There are nine areas classified *grand cru:* Fleurie, Moulin-à-Vent, Juliénas, Chénas, Morgon, Brouilly, Côte de Brouilly, Saint-Amour, and Chiroubles. Each of these areas has its own specific appellation regulations.

Elsewhere in the Beaujolais district are thirty-five communes, or townships, classified "Beaujolais-Villages." These share a series of appellation regulations less specific than in the *grand cru* areas but more specific than in the remainder of the Beaujolais district.

A wine meeting the appellation standards of one of the *grand cru* areas may—and almost invariably will—be marketed under the area name. One meeting the standards of the Beaujolais-Villages appellation normally will be marketed as a Beaujolais-Villages, regardless of the township or commune which produced it. All other wines produced in the Beaujolais district will be marketed under the simple Beaujolais appellation. Both the following wines are Beaujolais-Villages.

Marquisat (see page 133) and *Beaujolais-Villages Jadot*

Producer: Marquisat is a trade name for the producer/shipper, Pasquier Desvignes. Louis Jadot, producer of the other wine, labels it Beaujolais-Villages Jadot, a combination of the wine's regional name (also, therefore, the type of wine—a Beaujolais-Villages, as opposed to, say, a Saint-Emilion) and his own name. Marquisat carries the type/regional designation beneath the trade name.

None of this signifies anything about the quality of the wine. The differences merely indicate the producers' approaches to the wines' selling points.

Vintage: The Jadot carries its vintage designation on a neck label. Under French law and that of most other countries, a vintage date may be applied only if most or all of the wine was made in a given year (as opposed to its being a blend of older and younger wines). A vintage wine is not necessarily better or worse than a nonvintage wine.

Château des Tours and *Brouilly*

These wines, too, are Beaujolais; both are from one of the nine areas designated *grand cru*. Note that neither uses the name Beaujolais anywhere on the label. At first conjecture this would seem to be because the producers fear identification with the less expensive wines from the region. However, these wines are in the same price range as the Marquisat and Beaujolais-Villages Jadot.

Producer: Talk about chaos! The producer of one wine is Domaine des Tours, a shipper headquartered in the Burgundian city of Rhône. But the wine is marketed under the trade name, Château des Tours. Why Château instead of Domaine? Isn't it true that Domaine in Burgundy is the equivalent of Château in Bordeaux? And aren't we still in Burgundy? It is, and we are. And why Domaine des Tours has chosen to use nomenclature associated with the opposite coast of the country is something we cannot define. One conjecture might be that the firm wants to exploit the public's association of quality and high price with château-bottled wines. But this wine sells for the same price as a Beaujolais-Villages. So what's going on? Well, let's look again. The producer is indeed a Burgundian firm named Domaine des Tours. But this is a corporate name. The usual context in which "Domaine" is used in Burgundy is as the identification of a vineyard. We see nothing here about this domaine being a vineyard.

Now the Brouilly. It appears to be a regional wine, that is, a shipper's wine. Why else give greatest prominence to the regional name. But look below: *mise en bouteilles à la propriété.* It is indeed estate-bottled. The producer is Héritiers Jonnery, and the vineyard is Domaine de la Folie. This is no sleight-of-name trick like the *des Tours.* It's a bona fide vineyard. So why not emphasize this? We have no idea.

Estate-Bottled: There is no question that the Domaine de la Folie is a legitimate estate-bottled *grand cru* Beaujolais (assuming that the label is truthful). But we have our doubts about the claim to estate-bottling by Château des Tours. Granted, *mis en bouteilles au château*

is the legitimate way of saying estate-bottled. But in Bordeaux, not Burgundy. We've got a hunch that, though printed in France (and prominently identified as such), this label is only used on exported wines.

Vintage: The Domaine de la Folie reads *Récolte 1966.* We've not encountered the use of the word harvest often, but it's a legitimate way of identifying a vintage. Note that the Château des Tours is not vintage-dated.

Laurent Perrier and *Blanc de Blancs*

French law restricts the term Champagne to wines produced in the district of Champagne from grapes grown in the district. While there are differences in soil within the district, no one community or area is associated with grapes of a distinct character, as is true in Bordeaux and Burgundy. In fact, Champagne producers generally do not grow their own grapes. They buy them from vignerons throughout the district. Thus, the chief factor in the character and quality of the wine is the technique of the producer. Accordingly, most Champagne labels are considerably less complicated than those for French still wines.

Vintage: The grape crop in the district of Champagne varies considerably from year to year. This variance gives rise to the phenomenon of the "vintage year." Traditionally, if a producer considers a year prime, he dates the bottle with the year in which the grapes were grown. During other years, he blends wines from several years and sells the bottle without a vintage designation.

To determine whether a vintaged Champagne really is from a prime year—and whether the prime year is great or merely very good or good—consult a current vintage table. Incidentally, older Champagnes are notorious for traveling poorly—for losing much of their character as a result of being moved about during shipping.

Producer: This factor is even more important when buying Champagne than when buying a French still wine.

Laurent Perrier is one of the better known in the medium price range.

Degree of Sweetness: Most producers offer several degrees of sweetness. This is the result of a *dosage,* containing sugar and other ingredients, added at a late stage in the wine's production. The degrees are: Doux (Sweet) — 7 percent or more sweetening; Demi Sec (Medium Dry) — 5 to 7 percent sweetening; Sec (Dry) — 3 to 5 percent sweetening; Extra Sec (Extra Dry) — 1.5 to 3 percent sweetening; Brut 0.5 to 1.5 percent sweetening; and Natur — 0 to 1 percent sweetening.

To take these terms at face value would be misleading. Wines labeled *sec* are certainly not dry compared to most dry still wines. Indeed, very few French still wines contain even as much sugar as the *extra sec* Champagnes. The *demi sec* will seem very sweet to most drinkers of French still wines, and *doux* candy-sweet. To them, *extra sec* will be the sweetest desirable degree and *brut* or *natur* will be preferable under most circumstances. (A sweeter variety may be preferred to accompany a sweet dessert.)

Significantly, sweetening masks the properties of the base wine. Thus, more carefully made wines generally are used in the dryer Champagnes and this is reflected in the price. They cost about 20 percent more than the same producer's sweeter varieties.

Method of Production: This is something that is not on the label and we wish it were. An important consideration in predicting the character of a sparkling wine is whether it was produced under the *méthode Champenoise* (that is, second fermentation in the bottle in which it is offered for sale), the transfer method (second fermentation in another bottle or larger tank), or the *méthode Charmat* (second fermentation in a large tank). The *méthode Champenoise,* costlier and considerably more trouble, produces more and longer-lasting sparkle, among other characteristics deemed desirable in a sparkling wine. Actually, all sparkling wines from Champagne are produced under the *méthode Champenoise.* But not everyone is aware of this, so the information would be helpful on the label.

Size of Bottle: It is 13/16 quart (26 ounces) — half an ounce less than a fifth of a gallon. Some Champagne bottles which appear to be the same size contain only 1 pint 8 fluid ounces, or 24 ounces.

Alcohol Concentration: The Laurent Perrier is 13 percent, the *blanc de blancs* 12 percent. There are other sparkling wines of 11 percent alcohol or less. None of this testifies to the actual worth of the wine, but as a rule the lower alcohol concentrations are the result of *cuvée* blends involving less expensive base wines.

The only information on this label that wasn't on the previous one is the designation *blanc de blancs* (white of whites), which means that the wine was made exclusively of white grapes. Most Champagnes are made from white still wines, but these wines may have been made from red or white (that is to say, blue/black or yellow/green) grapes.

The fact that only white—more precisely, Chardonnay—grapes were used says nothing about the wine's quality. However, some drinkers find a *blanc de blancs* lighter. Also, some producers make a *blanc de blancs* a bit more carefully—with costlier base wines—than an ordinary Champagne, and many drinkers believe these differences worth the 20 to 30 percent more which *blanc de blancs* generally cost.

The home of this wine, Epernay, in the south of the Champagne district, produces most of the district's *blanc de blancs.* To the north, in Reims (home of the Laurent Perrier), *blanc de noirs* (white wines from dark or mixed grapes) prevail.

Germany

Traditionally, German wine labeling has been even more confusing than the French labeling. Such expressions as "estate wine" appeared on the label of wines that were not estate-bottled, and terms like *feine, feinste,* and *hochfeine* (fine, super-fine, and extra-fine) were frequently confused with official designations, when actually they were the producer's own characterization of his product. In addition, consumers were confronted with trade names, vineyard names, village names, county names, and regional names.

A law enacted in 1971 simplifies things somewhat—though far from entirely. The law divides wines into three broad categories: *Deutscher Tafelwein* (German table wine), *Qualitätswein bestimmter Anbaugebiete* (quality wine of designated regions, commonly abbreviated as "Q.b.A." or appearing simply as *Qualitätswein*), and *Qualitätswein mit Prädikat* (quality wine with special attributes).

Tafelwein is intended primarily for local consumption. Regulations governing its production are less strict than those for *Qualitätswein*, with or without *Prädikat*, and this is reflected in its price: about $1 (£0.60) a bottle. Still, the winemaker is subject to certain restrictions. Only six regions—Mosel, Rhein, Main, Neckar, Oberrhein Burgengau, and Oberrhein Roemertor—have been approved for grape growing, and only certain grape varieties may be grown in each region. Seventy-five percent of the grapes from which the wine was made must have been grown in one region. If the label specifies an individual community within that region, 75 percent of the grapes must have been grown within its borders. If a vintage year is specified, 75 percent of the grapes must have been picked that year. The name of the bottler must be plainly identified on the label (*abfüller*).

A distinguished collection of German wines. Though normally processed wines (tafelwein and qualitätswein) are priced competitively with those of other nations, the celebrated beerenauslese and trockenbeerenauslese can carry stratospheric tags.

Qualitätswein must be produced exclusively from grape varieties grown in one of eleven officially designated regions. It must contain a minimum of 7 percent natural alcohol (without addition of sugar before or during fermentation). The label must identify the region in which the wine was produced. It may also include the name of the collective vineyard (*grosslage*) or vineyard (*einzellage*), provided that 75 percent of the wine comes from grapes in the smallest named area. However, vineyards smaller than twenty-five acres cannot be named.

The label must also include the name of the community in which the wine was produced. If at least 75 percent of the grapes are of a single variety, the wine may be identified as a varietal (for example, Riesling and Gewürztraminer). The label must also identify the bottler and may identify the vintage. It must also carry an official certification number—through which, presumably, officials can hunt down the inspector who let a substandard bottle get past him.

Qualitätswein mit Prädikat must meet all the requirements of ordinary *Qualitätswein* and in addition must meet certain regional standards for minimum must-weight (*öchsle*) during fermentation and have a certain minimum alcohol concentration, depending on grape variety and region. A wine that achieves this is designated *Kabinett;* this is its *Prädikat,* or special attribute. Other *Prädikats* are *Spätlese, Auslese, Edelfaule, Beerenauslese, Trockenbeerenauslese,* and *Eiswein,* all discussed at the end of Chapter II.

Zeller Schwarze Katz (see page 141) and *Madrigal*

Zeller Schwarze Katz is not a brand wine (or a specific product of one producer, as is Château Margaux, in France). It is a type of wine; more precisely, it is a generic trade name for a blended still wine. At least 75 percent of its grapes come from the village of Zell in the

Mosel region.

Producer: Madrigal is a brand name of the shipper/bottler, Weinexport Hattenheim. On this colorful label, Zeller Schwarze Katz appears in the place traditionally reserved for the wine type. The shipper/bottler of the other Zeller Schwarze Katz, H. Sichel Söhne, gives the wine type top billing but with considerably more prominence for its own name than Weinexport Hattenheim does, probably because the Sichel family has an international reputation as shippers of German and French wines. Among its better-known German products is the Liebfraumilch, Blue Nun, with which it establishes identification on the neck label.

Alcohol Concentration: Note that it is considerably less than in most wines from other countries.

Size of Bottle: The Sichel bottle is only "1 pint, 7 ounces" (23 ounces) and the Madrigal "¾ quart," or 24 ounces.

Subregion Designation: Both wines are designated "Mosel-Saar-Ruwer," a region which covers the whole Mosel area. It might also be noted that neither label contains a *grosslage* or *enzellage* designation. Thus, the two Zeller Schwarze Katzen are regional wines, not the product of a given vineyard.

Varietal Name: Neither wine carries one. Most Mosel-produced wines supposedly are Rieslings; but the label doesn't state this, and it would be interesting to know if this is really true.

Greece

Greek wine labeling is relatively uncomplicated. Fairly uniform soil and climate conditions in the country's grape-growing regions make regional designations rather unimportant. Thus, the label does its job when it provides the name of the producer, type of wine, alcohol concentration, size of bottle, and whether the wine has been treated with pine resin (if so, it will be labeled *Retsina*).

Demestica

Producer: Achaia Clauss is one of the larger private bottling firms, headquartered at Patras, on the Peloponnesus peninsula, Greece's main wine-producing region.

Wine Type: "Demestica" does not mean domestic, as some readers might speculate. It is a generic trade name for this particular type of light wine—much as Liebfraumilch identifies a wine type in Germany.

Vintage: The wine is not vintaged. Greek wines tend to peak very quickly, especially the whites that have not been resinated. Accordingly, a vintage date would be useful. Actually, a bottling date appears on the label, in the lower right-hand corner in very small type.

Grape Variety: It will seldom if ever be identified on a Greek wine label, mainly because very few varieties are grown. Dry white wines are almost invariably a blend of Aghiorghitico and Phileri.

Hungary

Hungarian wine labels are models of simplicity. The name of the wine is always the name of the grape-growing region, followed by the wine's varietal or generic name. Thus, Hajósi Cabernet is a Cabernet from Hajós, and Egri Bikavér is a Bikavér (generic name for a traditional wine type) from Eger.

Hajósi Cabernet and Egri Bikavér

As in France, Hungarian vineyards are qualitatively classified by official agencies. In Hungary, there are nineteen "first great growths" and several dozen merely "great growths." The "first great growths" are subject to more stringent regulations. Contrary to procedures in France, however, none of this information appears on the wine label. The buyer must know independently which vineyards are which.

Producer: All wine exported from Hungary goes through the state's shipper, Export Monimpex, which monitors all shipments for quality. This, in theory at least, is the only protection the consumer needs. Accordingly, the producer's name appears rarely or without any prominence.

In the Egri Bikavér the producer is identified only by a trademark. In the Hajósi Cabernet no producer is identified. (The line at the bottom of the label, "Magyar Allami Exportpincegazdásag, Budafok," is the exporter's guarantee of the wine's territorial and varietal authenticity. The Bikavér, not being a varietal, does not carry such a guarantee.)

Wine Type: The Cabernet is, in fact, a Cabernet Sauvignon, the grape usually described in Hungary as Médoc Noir. The Bikavér is a blend of Kadarka (the principal grape of many Hungarian red wines), Médoc Noir, and Burgundi (Hungarian name for Pinot Noir).

A collector's choice of vini Italiani. *Italy is both the world's largest producer of wine and its largest consumer. Yet, with higher per capita consumption of alcohol than anywhere else, alcoholism is virtually nonexistent. There's a lesson here.*

Italy

Italian wine labels are almost as chaotic as the French. In addition to brand names, producers' names, shippers' names, and place names, they usually contain commercial messages, mottos or slogans, and not infrequently representations of various medals the wine has won over the years in various fairs and/or international expositions.

Italy has *denominazione di origine controllata* laws patterned after the *appellation-controlée* laws of France, but they are ignored by some of the country's most prestigious producers. Producers also widely ignore trade-association designations which purport to guarantee the wine's regional or varietal character.

The tiny community of Chianti, for example, in the hills of northern Italy's Tuscany region, has long been known for a dry red still wine made predominantly from the Sangiovese grape. In medieval times, travelers began referring to the wine by its regional name (writers as far away as Calabria made mention of having drunk *Chianti*), and as the wine's fame spread, so did the boundaries of the area which described its wine as Chianti. Eventually, Chiantis were being produced as far away as Rome.

Wine industry lobbyists went to work—and a law was passed, defining the boundaries of the Chianti region (though named after a tiny town, the region actually took in the entire area south of Florence and north of Siena). Lobbyists then went to work for producers whose operations bordered the region, and a compromise was struck. Thereafter there would be two Chianti regions: a general one, extending as far west as Arezzo, north to Pistoia, east almost to the Tyrrhenian Sea, and south almost to Grosseto; and a special, narrow subregion, between Florence and Siena, which would be entitled to describe its red wine as "Chianti Classico."

The Classico producers apparently felt that this did not go quite far enough. They formed their own association, the Consorzio Vino Chianti Classico, and established as a trademark the Gallo Nero, or black rooster. They decreed it would be awarded only to wines made from grapes grown no lower than two hundred meters above sea level and no higher than six hundred meters above sea level. Moreover, the wine must have an alcohol concentration of at least 12 percent. If it is to be called a Classico Riserva, it must have 12.5 percent and be aged a minimum of three years in oak casks. In either case, it must be approved by the association's tasters.

Having excluded perhaps nine out of ten producers who previously had been marketing Chianti, the Consorzio members presumably felt they had the field pretty much to themselves. But the absence of the Gallo Nero, or even the governmental Classico designation, has not deterred people from buying the "lesser" Chiantis. The nation's largest exporter of Chianti, Ruffino—Italy's most important winemaker—for many years did not use the Gallo Nero. Likewise a smaller but prestigious producer, Frescobaldi, instead of labeling his wine Classico—which he legitimately may on batches produced from vineyards he owns within the Classico zone—chooses to issue all his Chianti as "Chianti superiore," the adjective being a commercial message rather than an official designation. Marchese Vittorio Frescobaldi, head of the firm, told an interviewer why he uses neither the Gallo Nero, the *denominazione* designation, nor the familiar circular red seal which the government awards to Chianti Classici. "Our wines do not bear any seal other than our name. That is the only seal they need," explained the Marchese. *Frescobaldi, Bessi,* and *Villa Antinori* (see page 148)

Producer: Frescobaldi means it when he says his name is what he considers important. Apart from the marvelous Giottoesque drawing, there's little else on the label.

"Castello di Nipozzano" is simply the name of his estate.

Antinori and Bessi follow the same pattern. "Villa Antinori" is the trade name of the Antinori family. "Gran vino" is a commercial message, not an official designation. Bessi calls his wine "Chianti superiore," again not an official designation. Rufina is the town in which he is headquartered; the name has no connection with the larger producer, Ruffino, whose headquarters is at Pontassieve. Bessi's three stars must have been awarded by himself. They are not part of an official designation.

All three labels are for Italian distribution. If the wines were exported to the United States, the label would also have to reveal the size of the bottle, alcohol concentration, and similar information.

Brolio Riserva and *Nozzole* (see page 151)

These are two Chianti Classici, produced and labeled under *denominazione di origine controllata* regulations. Note that the Nozzole carries the *denominazione* designation, while the Brolio omits it. Yet Brolio observes standard procedure regarding labeling the wine *riserva*, an official designation for Chianti wines with at least 12.5 percent alcohol. The Nozzole reports exactly 12.5 percent, the Brolio 13, which does not necessarily mean the latter is better, just more potent.

Producer/Shipper: Some of the confusion of Italian wine labels is revealed in the various producers' and shippers' designations on these labels. Brolio combines his name with Riserva to form a trade name. Nozzole uses its name straight and treats *riserva* almost as a throwaway.

Brolio's shipper is clearly identified as Barone Ricasoli of Florence (*casa vinicola*—wine house—frequently is used to designate a shipper). The label also

Rows of vines besiege the ancient walls of Brolio Castle in the region of Chianti. It is here that Brolio's Chianti Classico earns the designation imbottigliato al castello (bottled at the castle).

states that the wine was "bottled at the castle" (on the estate) of Brolio in Chianti (that is, in the region of Chianti, not the town). So one might assume that this is, in fact, an estate-bottled Chianti which was trucked down the Tuscan hills to Florence for shipment.

But the Nozzole label says nothing about a shipper. Beneath the *riserva* designation we see "Letizia Rimediotti Mattioli," then "Tenuta di Nozzole-Greve (Firenze)." One of the producer's brochures speaks of the wine as being matured in the Rimediotti-Mattioli cellars. So is Rimediotti-Mattioli the shipper? If so, who is Letizia? The name translates as "joy." (This not seeming relevant, we are inclined to assume that Letizia is a proper name.) But what is the relationship of Letizia to Rimediotti and Mattioli? As for the line below, it says that the Estate (*Tenuta*) of Nozzole is at Greve, in the province of Firenze. But on neither of the labels is the corporate name of either the producer or the shipper explicitly given.

None of this should be construed as a complaint about the wine. We've been long-time fans of both wines, and we regard them as unusual values as well. But the label doesn't give us nearly enough information. However, we do have something of a recommendation on the label. We know both Browne Vintners and Kobrand as importers of some of our favorite wines. (Kobrand, being apprised of our complaint, tells us that the Nozzole label will be clarified.)

Size of Bottle: Note that each is only 24 ounces.
Mirafiore Barolo and *Marchesi di Barolo* (see page 151)

More confusion. The wine type is Barolo, one of the world's most celebrated. It is made predominantly or exclusively from grapes of the Nebbiolo variety. So far, so good. But what's this about Serralunga d'Alba?

Well, both Barolo and Serralunga d'Alba are towns in Italy's Piemonte (Piedmont) region, west of Milano. *Tenimenti* means both holdings and estates. So Mirafiore

of Canelli, Italy, whom we happen to know as a reputable shipper (his Bardolino is, in our opinion, twice as good as any available in the U.S., and an extraordinary value) apparently has holdings or estates at both Barolo and Serralunga d'Alba. But from which, if either, did this Barolo come? For all we can deduce from the label, Mirafiore may very well have bottled the wine in his cellars at Canelli, using grapes other than the traditional Nebbiolo.

The underline of the other label, "Gia'Opera Pia Barolo," could mean many things. We interpret it as an indication that the company's founder was named Pia Barolo. In any case, neither this nor anything else on the label tells us anything about the wine, apart from the fact that it is a Barolo (and therefore, if traditionally made, a product of the Nebbiolo grape).

The medals, by the way, are not identified as having been won by this wine. Nor would it be important if they were, for the winery could very well have changed hands (and/or standards and/or techniques) dozens of times in the interim.

Our producer interestingly provides us with a picture of a building labeled Barolo and another of a castle labeled Serralunga d'Alba, but he does not say which, if either, of these places was the source of his grapes.

Asti Gancia

Italian sparkling wine is marketed as *spumante*. The best-known source of this wine is the Piedmont community of Asti. Hence, the wine known as Asti spumante.

On this wine—quite simply and undeceitfully labeled—Gancia is the producer, and not Asti, as some people might think.

One thing not on the label would interest us: the method of fermentation (in this bottle, transfer method, or bulk). When one of the first two is not specified, we're inclined to suspect the latter.

Lambrusco

This handsome label calls for a pair of sharp eyes. Lambrusco is a generic name, and without an adjective it doesn't tell you an awful lot. There is a wine called Lambrusco Salamino, produced from the grape of the same name, popular in the northern Italian region of Reggio Emilia. It is dry, subtly astringent, and effervescent. (The effervescence results from a brief second fermentation, not quite enough to produce an out-and-out spumante, but enough to make the wine a bit more bubbly than an ordinary still wine.)

There is also a Lambrusco di Sorbara, popular in the nearby city of Modena, made predominantly from the Lambrusco grape (a parent of the Lambrusco Salamino, but somewhat different in character). It is dry, fresh, and very frothy. A third Lambrusco—Lambrusco Grappa Rossa—is similar to the Lambrusco di Sorbara, but a bit darker and thinner.

The wine described on the label above does not seem to be either of these. Rather, it is a Lambrusco-type wine, produced and bottled by a shipper in Trento. All well and good. But you have to read the label alertly to know what you're getting.

Alcohol Concentration: Note that it is only 10 percent. This is consistent with the original *lambruschi*, which usually have about 11 percent.

Effervescence: This wine is inexpensive—and it's unlikely that a naturally effervescent wine would sell at a low price. We suspect carbonation has been introduced; in other words, that this is sort of a cross between a still wine and a pop wine. Nothing wrong with that, of course. But you might not realize it at first reading of the label.

Vintage: Note that none of the labels in the above series carries a vintage date. When Italian wines are vintaged, it usually is noted on a neck label.

Japan

Japan imports almost all the grape-based wines its citizens consume. It exports very few. (The only one we've ever seen is a light red still wine marketed by the Takara Shuzo Company in California.) However, Japan exports a great deal of sake (pronounced saki), a rice-based wine of about 17.5 percent alcohol concentration.

Kiko Masamune Sake

As with most nongrape wines, the sake's character seems to be more a result of the producer's techniques than the ingredients on which he employs them (relatively few nongrape wines are available for comparison). Accordingly, the only item of significance on the nongrape wine's label, apart from such mechanical matters as size of bottle and alcohol concentration, is the producer's name.

Luxembourg

In Luxembourg, as in Germany, wine is produced and bottled under strict government control. In fact, Luxembourg was doing it long before Germany. In 1935, the *Marque Nationale* was created by the state to identify wines which have been produced and bottled under specified conditions. The marque appears on the neck of each exported bottle.

Rivaner

The Luxembourg wine label is a model of simplicity and accuracy. There seems to be only one thing missing: the name of a producer. That is until you realize that "Vin de la Moselle Luxembourgeoisie" is the name of a coöperative and the producer of the wine.

Regional Designation: The Luxembourg Mosel re-

Below: A distillery in Lisbon.
Distillation of wine produces brandy, which
can be used to stop fermentation in some fortified
wines and to add alcoholic strength to
others. Portugal produces some of the world's
most esteemed fortified wines.

ferred to here is the portion of the river that skirts Luxembourg on its way from Germany. The regional designation is superfluous; the duchy has only one wine region.

Alcohol Concentration: Only 10.5 percent.

Philippines
Sevilla's Duhat (see page 152)
Wine in the Philippines is made from various fruits, principally the duhat (also called Java plum). Labels are simple and to the point.

Portugal
Labeling in Portugal sticks pretty much to essentials and has done so for many years, as a comparison of these labels from the same producer reveals.

Trade Name: Lancers is a trade name of the producer, J. M. da Fonseca. It is used for rosé and white wines. The label shown is of a white wine (branco).
Lancers and Setúbal
Wine Types: Moscatel is a grape; Setúbal (pronounced SCHTOO-bal) is a port near the Portuguese vineyards where Moscatel is most widely grown. Traditionally Portuguese wines have taken their names from the ports where they were shipped rather than the places where the grapes were grown. Setúbal became so well known for wines from the Moscatel grape (in English, Muscatel) that this particular style of Muscatel came to be known as Moscatel da Setúbal.

The vinho branco almost certainly is a blend, and we'd like to know which grape varieties went into it.

South Africa

South African wine labels are exemplary, revealing almost everything you want to know about the wine you are going to sample.

Paarl Late Vintage

Producer: The Cooperative Wine Growers Association of South Africa, usually abbreviated in Afrikaans as K.W.V., is the main producer of the nation's exported wines and enjoys the status of a semiofficial governmental agency. Lacking competition from other South African exporters, it all but buries its own name on the label and stresses instead the wine's regional name.

Regional Name: The Paarl Valley is at the center of the Cape's grape-growing region. K.W.V. exports all wines from this region under the name, Paarl. There is a Paarl Cabernet, a Paarl Riesling, Paarl sherries, and Paarl Ports. "Late vintage" here is the equivalent of the German *Spätlese*, the vinification process is described in detail on the back label.

Grape: Note the helpful information on the back label. Paarl also has a normally harvested Steen varietal on the market.

U.S. Importer: As always, the importer's reputation can vouch for an unfamiliar producer's wines. Crosse and Blackwell offers one of the most distinguished lines available in the U.S., with special strength in Italian wines.

Spain

Labeling for Spanish wines is far from uniform. Some producers go the route of reproducing medals and using commercial messages that sound like official designations. Others simply identify the producer and his location.

Vineyard in the western hills of the canton of Véaud, above Lake Geneva in Switzerland. Bottom: Three well-aged sherries reflect the afternoon sun—(from left) a cream, a fino, and an amontillado. In background, winery at Jerez de la Frontera, Spain.

Marques de Riscal

Producer/Shipper: The firm is identified as "Heirs of the Marques de Riscal." The wine generally is spoken of simply as "Marques de Riscal."

Producer/Shipper's Location: Elciego is a community in Alava, which is one of the better-known wine-producing districts in Rioja. Rioja, in turn, is the most highly regarded (among wine men) region of Spain for production of still wines. But the designation doesn't mean an awful lot, because the wine is not identified as estate-bottled. "Elciego (Alava)/Rioja" on the label doesn't necessarily mean that the wine came from there, but only that the producer/shipper is headquartered there.

Wine Description: That Marques de Riscal is a red wine, we do not dispute. We do question the adjective "light." As a matter of fact, Marques de Riscal is one of the heaviest still wines we know. This is not a complaint; we like it that way! But someone who prefers light wines would probably be very unhappy with this one.

Vintage: Spanish vintage regulations are very loose. Indeed, in studying the vintages of shipments of Spanish wine coming into North America, you might get the impression Spain markets only two or three vintages per decade, and always in the years known as prime in France. (We have seen Spanish jug wines selling in New York in 1974 for less than $5 (£2) a gallon that carry a 1959 date. Probably the producer is labeling as vintage X a brand containing a relatively small amount of that year's wine. Perhaps he's even blending by way of a solera system established in that year. We are not referring specifically to Marques de Riscal on this point, but it is not out of the question that he employs this procedure too.)

Controlled Name: A trademark identifies the wine as conforming to the place and name laws of the Rioja district. But again this does not mean all the wine in the bottle

came from Rioja, or smaller named areas within Rioja.

Duff Gordon Pinta

Producer: Sherries traditionally are produced and shipped by English firms with headquarters in the wine-growing region of Jerez de la Frontera, Spain (owing to the historically great demand for sherry in England).

Trade Name for Wine Type: Most producers offer an assortment of sherries, ranging from very dry to very sweet. These are traditionally given trade names like "Pinta," after one of Columbus' ships (Duff Gordon also offers a Niña and a Santa Maria). To newcomers to the wine, much more important than the trade name is the description just beneath it: "very pale—very dry."

Switzerland

Swiss labeling is pretty much a catch-as-catch-can affair, with the wine man emphasizing what he deems his strongest selling points. There are no official designations for wine-producing regions or other standards established by the government.

Neuchâtel

Type of Wine: Neuchâtel is a grape-growing region named after the lake on whose shores it is located. Its vintners traditionally plant Chasselas, from which they make an effervescent wine—very similar to Champagne and Chablis wines. These wines bear the generic name Neuchâtel. As with all wines named generically, the producer's name is the important consideration.

Producer/Shipper: Meier-Charles, a small firm of high repute at La Coudre. Significantly, this wine is estate-bottled, but the label does not say so.

Commercial Message: Grappe d'Or (golden grape) is not an official designation; it is a phrase Charles employs to designate batches of wine he regards as the best of a given vintage.

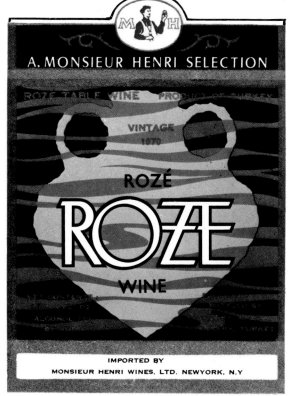

A. MONSIEUR HENRI SELECTION

ROZÉ TABLE WINE

VINTAGE 1970

ROZÉ

ROZE

WINE

IMPORTED BY
MONSIEUR HENRI WINES, LTD. NEW YORK, N.Y

Turkey
Roze

Some Turkish wines are produced by a state-owned firm, others by private enterprise. There are five grape-growing regions, but soil and climate do not differ significantly among them. Accordingly, producer and grape variety are the main considerations in choosing among wines. Wines not marketed as varietals are labeled red, white, or *roze*.

United States

In the United States, labeling is controlled by federal law and in major wine-producing states by state laws as well. The result is a great deal of useless or redundant information and, in many cases, a prohibition of certain designations that would be very useful. For example, in some

states wine cannot be named varietally unless it is made 100 percent from the named grape. In others, a vintage cannot be designated unless 100 percent of the wine is from grapes grown that year (California recently reduced this to 90 percent).

Producer: In the U.S., there are no shippers per se. The producer is the shipper. He may grow his own grapes, buy them from other growers, or do both.

A producer may term a wine "estate-bottled" if the grapes came from his own vineyard or from one which, in the language of California law, he "controls" (supervises for another owner), providing it is "in the vicinity of the winery." Most California wineries may legally describe their wines this way, but few bother. There is no restriction on the estate-bottled designation in other U.S. states.

The main reason estate-bottled is an important designation in France and Germany is that shippers blend wines from different winemakers. Estate-bottled means, in effect, that one winemaker made all the wine in the bottle. In the U.S., the winemaker almost always makes all the wine in the bottle, though in many cases he may not exercise as tight control over the grape growing as did the French or German winemaker. In either case, the matter of estate-bottling is largely academic. If the bottler, be he a shipper or winemaker, observes certain standards, his wine will reflect it.

Sebastiani Pinot Noir and *Gamay Beaujolais, Widmer Vergennes* (see pages 158 and 160)

Vintage: In California, a vintage date on the bottle means that at least 90 percent of the wine was made from

grapes grown and crushed that year. Some winemakers consider the law detrimental to optimum wines. They claim that blending small quantities (but more than 5 percent) of younger wines is a superior technique. They also point out that in most of Europe, only 51 to 75 percent of the wines in a vintage bottle must be made from grapes grown and crushed that year. Accordingly, several wineries give a bottling date rather than a vintage date.

In these labels, Sebastiani vintages his Gamay Beaujolais and also lists the bottling date and the dates of the harvest, but he gives only the bottling date of the Pinot Noir. Widmer neither vintages nor identifies the bottling date of his Vergennes. However, the date of the bottle's manufacture is stamped in the glass on the bottom of all bottles used in the U.S.

Regional Designation: In California, wines may obtain a regional designation if at least 75 percent of the volume of the wine was derived from grapes grown in that location (and all grapes must be grown in California). There is no comparable law in other wine-producing states, and a few winemakers during sparse years include bulk-purchased California wines in their blends.

"North Coast Counties" refers to the counties of Napa, Sonoma, and Mendocino. Had Sebastiani limited himself to grapes from one of these counties, he could use its designation. He could also use a "valley" designation, such as Alexander Valley or Russian River Valley, if 75 percent of his grapes had come from there.

Recent bottlings of wines from particular areas suggest that there are substantial differences between wine from different areas, and California wine men have begun to exploit them. Many observers believe that within two decades the individual regions of California will be as distinct in their types of wine as comparably sized districts in France, Italy, and Germany.

GOLD SEAL

NEW YORK STATE CHAMPAGNE

Charles Fournier

BLANC de BLANCS

FERMENTED IN THE BOTTLE

PRODUCED & BOTTLED BY **GOLD SEAL VINEYARDS, INC.**, HAMMONDSPORT, NEW YORK
CONTENTS ⅘ QUART   ESTABLISHED 1865   ALCOHOL 12% BY VOLUME

WIDMER NAPLES VALLEY
VERGENNES

The Naples Valley—heart of the Finger Lakes Wine Country of New York State. Here the rewarding combination of climate and soil, annually yield a precious harvest of grape varieties unique to the native American vineyard. Rich fruit is transformed into subtle, distinctive wines of surpassing quality and character.

VERGENNES (a varietal wine)

Pale, brilliantly clear—this wine presents a refreshing dryness. Delicate in flavor, Vergennes offers a finesse equal to the finest white wines available today.
SERVE CHILLED.

WIDMER

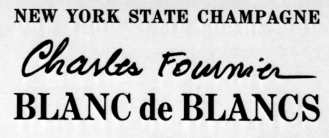

FINE WINES SINCE 1888

NAPLES VALLEY

VERGENNES

PRODUCED AND BOTTLED BY
WIDMER'S WINE CELLARS, INC.
ALCOHOL 12% BY VOLUME   •   NAPLES, NEW YORK STATE

Hanns Kornell

THIRD GENERATION CHAMPAGNE MASTER

Connoisseurs throughout the world recognize Hanns Kornell Champagnes as among the finest. In the heart of the beautiful wine-growing area of St. Helena, Napa County, California, Hanns Kornell eschews modern mass-production methods in favor of time-honored traditional practices developed more than two centuries ago in the Champagne district of France—using techniques taught him by his father and his grandfather before him, he converts the finest wines into superior champagnes.

A wine-yeast-sugar blend was placed in "THIS" same bottle and has been hand-tended by skilled workers through the years of fermentation, clearing and aging, under the personal supervision of Hanns Kornell. His signature on this label is your assurance of outstanding champagne quality.

Hanns Kornell

THIRD GENERATION

CALIFORNIA

Champagne

Produced from Muscadelle du Bordelais Grapes.
MUSCADELLE DU BORDELAIS

PRODUCED & BOTTLED BY **HANNS KORNELL CELLARS** ST. HELENA, CALIFORNIA
BONDED WINE CELLAR 605
ALCOHOL 12% BY VOLUME - CONTENTS 4/5 QUART

NATURALLY FERMENTED IN THIS BOTTLE

In New York, regional differences do not appear to be as pronounced.

Grape Variety: The Sebastiani, the Gamay and the Widmer are all varietals.

In California a wine may be given a varietal name if 51 percent of it came from grapes of that variety, and if the wine's visual, olfactory, and gustatory properties are deemed characteristic of the variety.

Kornell Champagne and Gold Seal Blanc de Blancs

White sparkling wines produced in the U.S. and marketed under the generic name Champagne always carry a qualifying adjective (California Champagne, New York State Champagne).

Grape Variety: Kornell helpfully indicates the grapes he used in this Champagne. The Gold Seal winemaker, Charles Fournier, does not. Unless we know, the *blanc de blancs* designation is not significant.

Fermentation Designation: Apart from the producer's name, this is the most important thing on the label. The Kornell underwent its second fermentation in this bottle and thus was produced under the costlier *méthode Champenoise.* The Gold Seal was produced by the transfer method—fermented in *the* bottle, not in *this* bottle.

Yugoslavia

Yugoslav labels, like those of Hungary, use the grape and the region of production as the name of the wine: for example, the Sipon grape (pronounced shee-PONE) from the Slovenian town of Maribor. As in the United States, wineries use both their own grapes and those provided by independent growers; thus, the shipper is the producer.

Conclusion

Complex though wine labeling is, knowing what to look for on the label is the only way to predict your reaction to the wine. A synopsis of things to look for:

Producer: Most important consideration of all. His reputation is the only sure guarantee of the wine's character, no matter how stringent the governmental regulations in the producing area.

Shipper: An important consideration when you don't know the producer. In Europe, shippers are the producers of regional wines. In any case, the shipper's reputation attaches to the products he ships.

Importer: His reputation can guarantee the wines of an unfamiliar shipper.

Varietal/Generic/Regional Type: The name of the wine usually tells you only its general character; the important consideration is who made it—and how.

Vintage: Not all years are good years, much less great years, but the vintage designation is one way to keep track of the wine's age.

Alcohol Concentration: It may be as low as 7 percent or as high as 14 percent.

Size of Bottle: A very important consideration, especially when comparing high-priced bottles. Some European bottles contain as little as 23 or 24 ounces, others up to a quart (32 ounces). The typical U.S. bottle is four-fifths of a quart (25.6 ounces).

6.

6.
SERVING WINE

here is, of course, no "correct" or "proper" time, place, or circumstance for serving wine. At the same time, many experienced wine drinkers find that there are certain circumstances and techniques of service that enhance the overall enjoyment of wine. With the emphatic *caveat* that they are suggestions rather than prescriptions, we offer here the precepts for wine drinking that have served us best over the years.

Red wine with "red" foods, white wine with "white" foods, rosé or sparkling wine with anything, right? Well, not quite.

Think for a moment of a meal that begins with pie and ice cream, then goes to cheese, a meat course, pasta, soup, and ends with grapefruit. Doesn't work, does it? Certainly not for our palate. The sweetness of the pie and ice cream, coming first, would kill our appetite for everything else, yet we would be by no means "full." But if we ate the dishes in the order in which most people would serve them, we'd have appetite enough to welcome each dish in its turn.

Fact is, sweet-tasting things tend to kill the appetite, even in small quantities, whereas dry-tasting things stimulate it. Hence, Precept Number One: Dry wines when you want to stimulate the appetite, sweet ones when you want to dampen it. This is by no means an inflexible rule; there are exceptions, and we'll go into them shortly. But the basic precept is valid for nonmealtime as well as mealtime drinking.

For most of us the day begins with breakfast, which usually does not include wine, though it could if that were our preference.

If we chose to drink a wine with breakfast, we would want one to stimulate the appetite. A very dry (*brut* or *nature*) white sparkling wine appeals to us. It might appear as an apéritif, or it would go very nicely mixed half-and-half with orange juice—in which case we would want it slightly less dry.

A glass of sherry might also go well as an apéritif, but it would have to be very dry—and very light. Which brings us to Precept Number Two: Match the body of the wine with the time of day. The earlier the time, the lighter-bodied the wine. There are exceptions to this, too, but not very many.

Let's assume that we have had our first breakfast course—juice and/or fruit. If cereal with milk were on the menu, we would not serve wine, even as an apéritif. Milk and wine, to our taste, are like oil and water. After that, we have eggs and toast. Eggs always create a problem for wine. All that protein calls for something equally strong to offset it. The standard rule book (not our own) says white with white things, but most white wines would die with eggs. The standard rule book also says that sparkling whites go with anything, but we don't see our apéritif/ orange juice choice holding up here, either—especially if the eggs are served with bacon or sausage. These high-fat meats are crude and rugged. They demand a wine of comparable character, perhaps a Zinfandel or Gamay. This violates the white-with-white rule, but it works out very nicely for our palate.

The eggs done with, we turn to pastry and coffee or tea. No wine with tea or coffee—although if the coffee is espresso, we'd enjoy lacing it with anisette. However, after the coffee (assuming we didn't have the anisette), we'd enjoy a cream sherry. Sweet? Indeed. Now that the meal is over, we are happy to dampen the appetite. Heavy? A little. We're bending the precept about light wines early in the day. But we're not disregarding it completely—we're not serving a Malmsey or a ruby Port.

Question: Should we have broken out our best, costliest white sparkling wine for that orange juice-mixture, say a Dom Ruinart or Bollinger R. D. 1961? Answer: No. There's no question that the Ruinart or the Bollinger would hold up beautifully against the orange juice. But if you can get what you need from the less expensive product, why pay more? Precept Number Three: Don't waste the good stuff. By mixing wine with other drinks, you overpower the subtle refinements that make expensive wines expensive.

Breakfast being over and some time having been spent relaxing and digesting it, we are ready for a midmorning drink. We set up lawn chairs beneath a shady tree (it is a very hot day), leaf through the newspaper, and sip some—what? Sherry again? Yes, a *fino* (very dry) would go nicely. Perhaps an *amontillado* (less dry, more full-bodied) instead? Not quite. Were this the afternoon, we'd probably lean toward it, but not during the morning. A glass of still wine? Definitely. Though the standard rule book restricts still wines to mealtime, we find them enjoyable almost anytime (before breakfast is the one exception which readily leaps to mind). We'd like a white wine with a slight bite—say Cordon d'Alsace, the Alsatian, predominantly Sylvaner blend produced by A. Willm, or an Antinori Bianco (but not Bianco della Costa Toscana—too bland), or Paul Masson's Emerald Dry Riesling (but not a Johannisberger Riesling—too authoritative for this time of day), or a very cold glass of Widmer's Lake Niagara.

We would not be in the mood for a Chardonnay, no matter how carefully made, even though this is the one white wine we'd take to a desert isle if told we could take but one. For midmorning sipping, the Chardonnay strikes us as a bit too vigorous. Paradoxically, a delicate Traminer, like Inglenook's, which we love under certain circumstances, would be too bland. How about a red? Say a

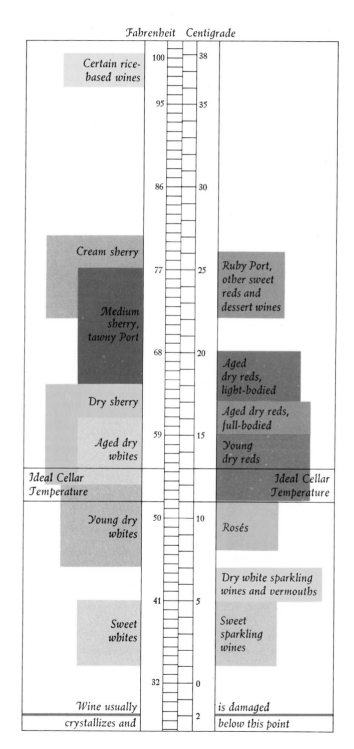

Fahrenheit Centigrade

Certain rice-based wines	100 / 38	
	95 / 35	
	86 / 30	
Cream sherry	77 / 25	Ruby Port, other sweet reds and dessert wines
Medium sherry, tawny Port	68 / 20	Aged dry reds, light-bodied
Dry sherry		Aged dry reds, full-bodied
Aged dry whites	59 / 15	Young dry reds
Ideal Cellar Temperature		Ideal Cellar Temperature
Young dry whites	50 / 10	Rosés
	41 / 5	Dry white sparkling wines and vermouths
Sweet whites		Sweet sparkling wines
	32 / 0	
Wine usually crystallizes and	2	is damaged below this point

Zinfandel or Gamay? No. They're lighter than most reds, but not quite light enough for our summer morn mood. But we could enjoy a red-wine punch, like sangria.

How about a sparkling wine? Most definitely—and preferably in the same sweetness range as the orange-juice sparkler. Anything drier would be too formal. Anything sweeter would diminish the enjoyment of anticipating lunch.

This, we stress, is the summer morn regimen. In colder weather, we would be attracted to more robust wines. The *amontillado* we declined earlier could not be more welcome than on a brisk autumn morning. In winter we'd lean toward a tawny Port for indoor drinking; outdoors—especially on the ski slopes—we'd want the most vulgar red wine we could find, say a Bilibio (Rioja) or a Hernandez Burgella, or a home-blended combination of equal parts Gallo Hearty Burgundy and Great Western Baco Noir (the Gallo for the body, the Great Western for the bite). In late spring, our fancy would turn to something more perfumy, like Christian Brothers' Chenin Blanc, Château-Gai Johannisberger Riesling (considerably more perfumy and less assertive than any other producer's version of this varietal), or Almadén Dry Sémillon. Another precept: The colder the weather, the more full-bodied the wine.

Now to lunch. If we had had no midmorning drink, a natural white sparkling wine would really be perfect as an apéritif. We could also enjoy a *brut*, provided it contained no more than 1 percent sweetening. But if we'd had a midmorning drink, this sweetness level would be too low; the memory of the sweeter wines would mar our enjoyment of something drier. Precept Number Five: Follow wines with others no less sweet or tangy.

It is true that the actual gastronomic/olfactory memory of the midmorning wines would be long gone by apéritif time, particularly if a piece of cheese, bread, or fruit, or a glass of water had been consumed in the interim. But for us, the psychological memory would carry over, and the drier sparkling wines would suffer.

The choice of the table wines for lunch would depend on the food—or perhaps the food would depend on the wines. Almost inevitably, wine and food writers build the meal around the food, but there's no reason it can't be done the other way. In fact, there are times when both G-1 and G-2 think it should be.

Not long ago, a friend brought to us from Italy a bottle of Cirò, the tangy and full-bodied red wine of Calabria. Had we followed the usual procedure of matching the wine to the food, we probably would have put it on a shelf in reserve for the next meal of *pasta con polpetti* or some similar red-sauced dish. Nothing is wrong with that combination, but there are better uses for the Cirò. A more vulgar (in the original sense) wine is probably not made anywhere, and this vulgarity would not be complemented—it would merely be tolerated—by the *spaghetti con polpetti*. The Cirò demanded *trippa Calabrese*, the boiled stomach linings of cattle, simmered for a day in a crude tomato sauce. They could be served, of course, only with huge chunks of homemade bread, dipped in the sauce as we ate it. For a first course, something white (but tangy) for color balance: *pasta con piselli*. To accompany it, a Corvo—geographic and gustatory kin to the Cirò but somewhat better-mannered (we must not distract from the star of the meal). After the tripe, a lusty lettuce and tomato salad, smothered in olive oil, accompanied by some sharp cheese—perhaps a good aged *provolone*, or, better still, hard chunks of *romano*. And with this, more Cirò.

A French gastronome once remarked that he could never find a wine that held up against vinegar, so he stopped eating salad. He should try Cirò—or salad without

Top: Assortment of French wine glasses. Burgundy bowls are at extreme left and right, claret glasses front, white wine glasses rear. Below: Italian corkscrew. Turning top lever imbeds screw in cork, turning bottom one extracts cork.

vinegar. Actually, even Cirò doesn't hold up well against vinegar. But by slotting the salad between the main course and the cheese, G-1 and G-2 never combine the wine and vinegar. There is always a piece of cheese to clear the palate. Even then, most wines would not hold up. But zestier ones, like Zinfandel and Gamay could, provided the salad maker did not go overboard on the vinegar.

We can't help wondering if perhaps the North American propensity to start meals with salad might not in some way be responsible for the absence of wine from so many North American tables. True, bread will clear the palate—it will remove the actual physical memory of the vinegar. But what of the psychological memory? Very, very few wines can hold up against the gustatory/olfactory onslaught of a vinegary salad dressing.

In any case—to return to the Cirò—we'll advance the proposition that we could not possibly have created a dining experience of such unique Calabrian vulgarity had we simply put the bottle in the cellar and fetched it the next time we served something that *it* matched. The secret was matching the food to the wine.

How does one determine which foods match which wines? In our opinion, it's mostly a matter of matching the strength of one with the strength of the other. A gently steamed bass, for example, would be well served by a Chardonnay or dry Sémillon. But the same wines would be lost against steak or roast beef. These call for something with more bite. A Cabernet Sauvignon perhaps, or, better still with steak, a Pinot Noir. The precept is, the more delicate and subtle the taste of the food, the more delicate and subtle the wine.

You may notice that this is consistent with the standard rule book edict about white-with-white and red-with-red. It is not without reason that the edict came into being. Red wines and red foods generally do measure in at

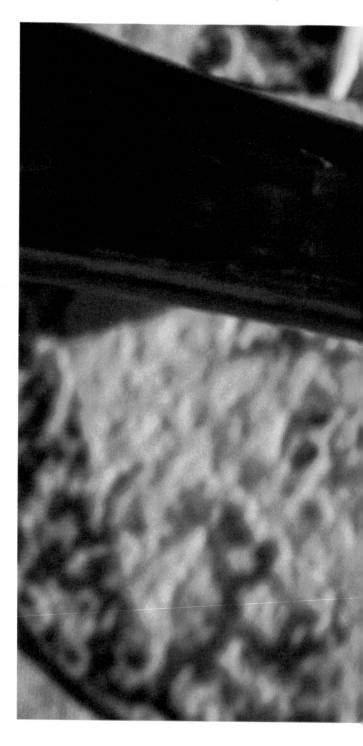

about the same olfactory/gustatory strength, as do white wines and white foods. But that "generally" is very important. There are many exceptions, and even food and wine experts differ in their choices on some of the more difficult combinations.

And that brings us to a point often overlooked. There is not necessarily—or even usually—only *one* felicitous food-wine combination. Each diner will find several wines that go splendidly with a certain dish, some that are just compatible, and others that are merely tolerable. If you think about the strength of flavor in one and try to balance it with the strength of flavor in the other, you'll very likely come up with a combination that both you and most your guests will find not merely acceptable but downright delightful.

For readers who prefer more specific counsel, some trade agencies within the wine industry offer recommendations. For whatever interest they may be, here are two—from the French and the Portuguese.

French

Serve with seafood, shellfish, or goat's cheese: Graves, Muscadet, Pouilly-Fumé, Chablis, Macon, Alsace-Sylvaner, Sancerre, Loire white.

Serve with fried fish and cold chicken: Alsace Riesling, white Burgundy, white Jura, white Côtes de Provence, white Côtes du Rhône.

Serve with hors d'oeuvres, cold meats, entrées, roast chicken, and Gruyère cheese: Anjou rosé, Jura rosé, Côtes de Provence rosé, Côtes du Rhône rosé, Burgundy and Macon rosé, Corbières rosé.

Serve with fish in sauce, foie gras, desserts: Sauternes, Barsac, Gewürztztraminer, Côteaux du Layon.

Serve with grilled meats, roast meats, Camembert, Brie, delicatessen meats, and egg dishes: Beaujolais, Loire

*Imaginative combinations of
food and wine can turn an ordinary meal
into a gastronomic experience. Diners here
match Portuguese white wine with
quiche (French), zucchini (Italian), and
Spanish-style fruit-and-cheese platter.*

red, Macon red, Bordeaux red, Médoc, Saint-Julien, Margaux, Saint-Estèphe, Côtes de Beaune, Côtes du Rhône red, Pauillac, Pomerol, Corbières, Minervois, Bergerac red.

Serve with game, poultry in sauce, red meat in sauce, strong and sharp cheese: Côtes de Nuits, Saint-Emilion, Pomerol, Hermitage red, Châteauneuf-du-Pape, Pommard, Corton, Jura red, Provence red, Côte Rôtie.

Portuguese

As apéritifs: *generosos* (strong sweet wines, particularly Port, Madeira, Carcavelos, and Moscatel de Setúbal); natural sparkling wines.

With fish and shellfish boiled with butter or white sauces: rosé or sweet white still wines.

With fish and shellfish grilled or roasted: dry white still wines.

With fish or shellfish stewed or *bouillabaisse*: dry white or red still wines.

With entrées: dry red still wines.

With roasts and game: dry red still wines, particularly old ones, or sparkling wines.

With desserts and fruits: *generosos*, sweet white or rosé still wines, or sparkling wines.

With cheese: if served before sweets and fruits, dry red still wines, preferably old ones; if with or after sweets and fruits, *generosos*.

Well, back to G-1 and G-2's summer day. After having matched our luncheon wines and foods, we would cap things off with a medium sherry. (In spring, autumn, or winter, it would be a cream sherry, a Tokay, or a *generoso*.)

For afternoon drinking, we'd want to go back to a sparkling wine (not too dry) or a punch, or we might continue with one of the luncheon still wines. One of the wines mentioned for morning drinking could also be en-

joyable. If we interrupted our drinking for some vigorous exercise, that would nullify the sweetness of the previous wines, and we'd be ready to start in at any level of dryness again. However, we'd still hold off on the natural sparkling wine until cocktail hour. For us, this wine is rather like a tuxedo: There's no law that you can't wear one earlier in the day, but you just don't.

During colder seasons, we'd tend toward fortified wines, medium-sweet—*amontillado* or thereabouts; we'd especially enjoy a glass or two of Dos Cortados. In winter we could very much enjoy a glass or two—but no more than two—of Beaulieu's Muscat de Frontignan. But that's for indoor drinking. On the ski slopes, we'd stay with vulgar reds of the sort you wouldn't feel badly about putting into a *bota* (the pitch-lined Spanish wine bag of untanned goatskin, which annihilates the subtleties).

We'd definitely want a break before cocktail hour, and we'd want enough exercise in it to overcome the psychological as well as physical carryover of the sweet wines. Then, after a nice hot shower, we'd be very much in the mood for a natural like Korbel's, which we rate the top sparkling-wine value in the world, at around $6 at bottle (£2.40), or Sonoma Vineyards Brut at about a dollar more than the Korbel, but still a tremendous bargain at today's prices.

We would select our dinner wines and food together, as at lunch; but we'd tend toward heavier wines for dinner (Precept Number Two) and older ones. This leads to another Precept: Older wines after younger. This applies most pointedly when they are served in the same meal, because the older wines, more complex and sophisticated in bouquet, are the climax of the meal's wine choices. But it also applies, at least for G-1 and G-2, with respect to the day as a whole. We'd find it very hard to be interested in a young Zinfandel for dinner if we had had a forty-

year-old Cabernet Sauvignon that afternoon for lunch. For reasons we'd just as soon not theorize about, we also favor our oldest wines during colder weather. Somehow, a noble, aged Cabernet or Pinot seems too dignified to be brought out during the summertime. But on a bitter winter's eve. . . . We can only sigh as we contemplate it.

If dinner ended with cheese rather than a pastry, we might very well continue to drink our table wine as a recreational drink for the evening—continuing, indeed, to nibble on cheese and nuts along with it. We know few pleasures more exquisite than an evening of cheese, nuts, very old Cabernet Sauvignon or Pinot Noir, and good company.

If the final dinner course was pastry or fruit, we would accompany it with a semidry sparkling wine or a sweet fortified wine, like Château-Gai Cream Canadian Sherry (one of the great sherry bargains anywhere), Dow's 1960 or 1963 Vintage Port, Harveys Bristol Cream or Gold Cap Port, or Duff Gordon Santa Maria Cream Sherry. We could enjoy a second glass of any of these, but a third would be a bit much.

In summer, we'd tone down the sweetness and heaviness of this postprandial regimen, possibly returning to sangria or some other punch for the rest of the evening. We could also enjoy a semidry sparkling wine, but on very hot nights we would want more liquid volume than we could comfortably consume at the alcohol concentration of undiluted wine, so we almost certainly would opt for the punch.

Speaking of comfortably consuming alcohol, we're well aware that few mortals could consume nearly the quantity involved in the G-1 and G-2's mythical day of wine drinking. Our presentation was aimed—obviously, we would hope—merely at demonstrating the drinking possibilities at various times of day.

There is one precept yet to be covered. We respond most enthusiastically to wine-food combinations with geographic kinship. We speak now not merely of geographic wine types (a California Burgundy, for example), but of wine that actually comes from the same place the food does. Thus the Baroli of Piemonte harmonize much more smoothly with the *cucina Torinese* than with the *cucina Fiorentina;* conversely, Tuscan wines like Chianti blend much more felicitously with Florentine than with Torinese dishes. And we've yet to find a European wine, or even a Californian, that goes as well with that native American bird, turkey—especially roast turkey with raisin-walnut-breadcrumb stuffing—as the native American Labrusca wines, particularly those with a Niagara, Isabella, or Delaware base. At the same time, we don't care at all for these Labrusca wines with French food and find them simply undrinkable with Italian dishes.

Those are our precepts. We don't always observe them, but over the long haul they have served us rather well. Hopefully, any that you choose to adopt will serve you at least as well.

How to Serve Wine

There is no question that the temperature of wine at the time of serving is an important consideration. The tang, zest, and sprightliness of Riesling or Gewürztraminer is lost—in our opinion—at room temperature. (Americans feel comfortable at a room temperature of about 70 degrees Fahrenheit (21°C); the British and North Europeans, little conditioned by central heating, are comfortable in room temperatures five to ten degrees lower. This is the range covered by the term "room temperature.") Conversely, served too cold, these wines lose most of their taste. Serve a world-famous thirty-year-old Cabernet Sauvignon, like Beaulieu's celebrated 1941 vintage or a 1945

Château Latour of Bordeaux, at 41 degrees Fahrenheit (5°C)—a good temperature for sparkling wines—and you may as well be serving a jug wine. The complexity and sophistication of an aged Cabernet simply do not come through when served below room temperature. And Chinese rice-based wines and Japanese sake seem to be most enjoyable at body temperature (98.6 degrees Fahrenheit or 37°C).

The diagram on page 167 shows the temperature serving range the winemakers themselves generally recommend for their wines. Naturally, your palate may dictate a different temperature. But we find these temperatures most to our taste, and most wine drinkers we know feel the same way.

To cool a wine, most wine men recommend immersing the bottle in a bucket of ice cubes for fifteen minutes to half an hour before serving. If this is inconvenient, put it in the refrigerator for two to two and a half hours before serving. Don't store a dry white in a refrigerator with a temperature of less than 45 degrees Fahrenheit (7.2°C), and don't store a sweet white below 33.8 degrees Fahrenheit (1°C). The cold can damage the wine.

If a bottle has been stored at a temperature colder than that at which the wine will be served—an aged dry red in a 56-degree cellar (13.3°C), for example—bring it up to room temperature by letting it sit in the room where it will be served. Don't try to warm it quickly by putting it into an oven or dipping the bottle in hot water. Sudden heat is death to a wine.

If poured wine is too cold, an easy way to bring it to desired temperature is to cup the bowl of the drinking glass in both hands. If the wine is not cold enough, we recommend pouring it back into the bottle and putting the bottle in ice. Some people serve wine over ice (on-the-rocks), but the dilution will kill the subtleties and most

Strawberries and apples, accompanied by a bottle of Concannon Vineyards Moselle—a delightful midafternoon refreshment. Though frequently described as "table" wines, still wines need not be restricted to mealtime.

other desired properties of a carefully made wine. Aromatized and pop wines may be strongly enough flavored to stand up against ice, but we don't know any others that can. Some people regularly serve sherry on-the-rocks, and one producer, Williams & Humbert, recommends serving Dry Sack this way. We prefer Dry Sack—and all other wines—straight.

Most wine drinkers don't like to open a bottle of white wine until very shortly before they drink it, because most white wines lose some of their character through aeration. Red wines, on the other hand, seem to benefit from airing, especially those varieties that profit most from bottle aging, like Cabernet Sauvignon and Pinot Noir. A handy (though by no means inviolable) rule of thumb is, the older the bottle, the less air it needs.

A wine that is fifteen or more years old usually will contain a quantity of sediment. There are certain techniques for pouring wine without getting sediment into your glass.

If you know in advance the wine you are going to serve, take the bottle from its storage place two or three days before. Place it standing up (wines are best stored on their side, to keep the cork moist and thus prevent air from entering the bottle) in the room where it will be served. During these two or three days, the sediment will sink to the bottom of the bottle. Then, just before you are ready to serve the wine, decant it. This means, simply, pouring the wine into another container. But there's a special way to do it. Place a lighted candle on the surface where the decanting will be done. Hold the decanter at an angle alongside the candle, and pour with the neck of the bottle over the flame. As you pour, watch the neck of the bottle. The moment sediment appears, stop pouring. Then serve the wine in the decanter, and put the bottle aside. (Most wine men will tell you to forget about the little wine that remains in the bottle, but some people will want to pour it into cheesecloth and perhaps squeeze an extra ounce out of it for drinking on a less genteel occasion. It's also great for cooking—unstrained.)

If your choice of wine is made more or less at the time of serving, carry the bottle from its storage place in the position in which it was stored. Some restaurants use a wicker basket for this, others simply have the sommelier carry the bottle by hand. Whichever you do at home, be very careful not to jostle the bottle as you carry it to the serving room. Once there, decant as above.

If the wine is younger than five years, don't wait until immediately before serving to decant. Do so two or three hours before serving. This will aerate the wine and bring out its character. Five years is an arbitrary cutoff point. Some younger wines will be better decanted immediately before being served. Some older wines will profit from decanting an hour or more before. There's obviously an element of personal taste in this. If you have no previous experience in decanting a particular producer's wine, we suggest contacting the producer or his importer for decanting recommendations. (Most producers and importers will be all too happy to help you get maximum enjoyment from their wines.)

Whether one does or does not decant, opening the bottle is an important—though not difficult—operation. The first step is to cut away the lead or foil wrapper covering the neck and top. G-1 and G-2 like to remove the entire wrapper, although some wine men prefer to cut away only to a point about a half-inch below the bulge in the neck.

When the wrapper is removed, there may be some mold or other accumulated growth at the mouth of the bottle—especially if the bottle is old. Wipe this with a cloth —a damp cloth if the material is stubborn. Next, draw the cork with a corkscrew. We prefer the jackknife type, but the type really doesn't matter so long as the corkscrew gets the cork out without mangling it or, in the case of old wine, shaking up the sediment in the bottle.

More important than the type of corkscrew is the construction of the screw. The construction that is cheaper and easier to make has a solid core. The costlier, more difficult one has a hollow core. You could insert a drinking straw through it. The one with the solid core displaces more of the cork than the one with the hollow core. This will mangle an older cork, possibly getting quite a bit of it into the wine.

When inserting the screw, one aims to get as much thread as possible into the cork without going through the bottom. One also aims dead center on the cork. All this may sound pretty finicky, if not downright esoteric. But corks are pretty fragile things, and the older they are, the more fragile they tend to be. It won't ruin the wine if you get cork in it, but one's enjoyment of the wine might be dampened somewhat if he has to fish cork out of his glass.

The cork having been removed, the mouth of the bottle is again wiped, and the wine is either decanted or poured directly into one's glass. At table, tradition calls for guests to be served first, but when serving wine the host pours his own glass first. This custom probably dates to the Middle Ages, when a common way of getting rid of one's enemies was to invite them over to the castle for dinner, then poison their wine. The host would sip the wine himself to put everyone else at ease. The host-first custom serves the secondary purpose of getting chips of cork and other debris, if there is any, into the host's glass instead of those of his guests. In a restaurant, the host sips his wine before any is poured for guests—to make sure it has not gone bad. Some hosts will do this for home entertaining also, while others will simply pour. (G-1 and G-2 prefer to taste the wine before pouring for guests.)

When more than one wine is served at a meal, some hosts like to bring them out a bottle at a time while others prefer to display them all together at the beginning of the meal. Whatever your preference, we suggest opening all red wines no later than the start of the meal, even if they will not be served until the cheese course, so the wines can aerate. (This, in the phrase wine men like, is "letting them breathe.") However, the wines are not poured at the same time. They stay in their bottles or decanters until it is time for them to be served.

Each wine should have its own glass, with the glasses arranged in a format convenient to the order of service. In recent years many hosts have taken to using the same type of glass for all types of wine, but we prefer the old-school approach of different-shaped glasses for different wine types. Whatever your preference, most experienced drinkers agree that the bowl of the glass should be large (absolute minimum of six ounces, preferably eight or more) and taller than it is wide. A notable exception is the classic Burgundy bowl, which is approximately spherical. Many people serve sparkling wines in a flat, saucer-shaped glass, a custom wine men abhor. The preferred glass for sparkling wines is even narrower than that for still wines, and usually is fluted or tulip shaped. This permits maximum development of bubbles and nose.

Whenever possible, we prefer to serve a different wine with each course of a meal. This, of course, is impractical—and would be fiendishly expensive—for a couple dining in a restaurant where the smallest available bottle is 23 ounces. But when there are more diners, and/or when half bottles are available, it's possible to share a variety of wines for not much more than it would cost to drink the same quantity of a single wine.

Here are two of our favorite multicourse national menus with accompanying wines.

Canada

Niagara Falls/Château-Gai Brut Champagne
Islington/Château Cartier Riesling
      Cold Garnish Salmon Pie Frontenac
Niagara Falls/Bright's Manor St. Davids Sauterne
      Cape Breton Chowder
Niagara Falls/Château-Gai Canadian Claret
      Boneless Breast of Brome Lake Duckling
      with Wild Rice and Mountain Cranberries
      Fiddlehead Salad
Niagara Falls/Château-Gai Haut Sauternes
      Apple Fritters with Maple Syrup

Greece

Patras/Achaia St. Helena
      Dolmadakia (Small Stuffed Grapevine Leaves)
      Spanakopetes (Spinach-Cheese Triangles)
      Taramasalata (Fish Roe Spread)
      Kalamata Olives (Marinated Dark Olives)
      Anchovies
      Feta Cheese (Goat's Milk Cheese)
      Soupe Avgolemono (Chicken Soup with
      Egg-Lemon Sauce)
Patras/Achaia Clauss Demestica Aspro (White)
      Psari Mayoneza (Fish with Mayonnaise Sauce)
Patras/Castel Daniels (Red)
      Arni Psito Me Anginares (Roast Lamb
      with Artichokes)
      Pastichio (Baked Macaroni with Cream Sauce)
      Salata Horyiatiki (Greek Country Salad)
Patras/Achaia Clauss Mavrodaphne
      Galato Boureko (Custard Strudel)
      Fraoules (Strawberries)
Greek Coffee/Metaxa Brandy
(Note: In Mediterranean countries, a social period sepa-

Left: At Rocca Bernarda winery in Friuli, northern Italy, a winter's eve is passed playing cards, sipping wine, and nibbling cheese. Right: Tumblers of wine raised in toast at wedding feast in Monserrato, on the Italian island of Sardinia.

rates the after-dinner wine—here, Mavrodaphne—and dessert. In many countries, dessert and coffee are not available at the restaurant; instead, after a salad, cheese, or fruit course, the diners adjourn to a bar for dessert, coffee, and brandy.)

Cooking With Wine

Most foods will benefit from cooking with wine. Originally, we suspect, cooks began using wine as a substitute for water during the plagues of the Middle Ages. Water frequently was polluted, but wine, because of its fermentation, was known to be pure. They rapidly found that wine imparts its own taste to foods, especially if an additional quantity is added shortly before serving. Wine soon became the staple of French and Italian cuisine, and other Mediterranean countries promptly followed suit.

The cost of wine today will, for most people, rule out using it as a water substitute. But small quantities added immediately before serving can give most foods a previously unrealized zestiness and tang.

Here is a quick guide to types and quantities of wine to add to standard dishes. For soups: per serving, 1 teaspoon of still wine or sherry. In sauces: per cup, 1 teaspoon of sherry or still wine (for dessert sauces, use Port). Use red wine with beef, white wine with veal and lamb. Port is excellent for basting ham, and sherry will enhance the flavor of kidneys and tongue; use ¼ to ½ cup per pound. Chicken dishes will develop nicely with either red or white still wine; duck asks for red, as does venison. For pheasant, sherry or white or red still wine will do. Port, sherry, and rosé work well with fruit dishes. Use about 1 teaspoon per serving.

Remember, the characteristics that make wines expensive will be lost in cooking, so there is no point in using expensive wines. We advise cooking with the least expen-

sive available wine you like (flavor, not nose, is the important thing for cooking wines).

The red still wine may be a Labrusca or Vinifera, dry or sweet—although, as noted, there are not many sweet red wines around. With white wines, most cooks prefer medium sweets; this would include such varietals as Chenin Blanc, Sauvignon Blanc, or Sémillon, or any generic Sauternes; however, generically labeled Chablis, Rhines, and other inexpensive wines—Labrusca or Vinefera—might also be used. The usual choice in sherry is *amontillado*.

Sangria and Other Punches

Ever since the Spanish tourist boom took hold in the 1960's, one of the favorite punches of the Western world has been sangria. On a night not long ago in one of the *mesones* near Madrid's Plaza Mayor, G-1 discussed its popularity with a wine man. "How do you suppose it was invented?" the Madrileño asked.

As G-1 has been known to do on such occasions, he promptly spun out a few theories. The one he finally settled on had it that the Spaniards, wanting something thirst-quenching but not too alcoholic for hot summer nights, approached the problem with their characteristic artistry and devised this delicious, fruit-filled punch as a modification on the old European summertime practice of diluting wine with mineral water.

The Madrileño was pleased with G-1's assessment of the Spanish artistic character. "But," he said, "I think you are ascribing the motherhood of invention to Beauty rather than Necessity. I confess that I have no facts to support me on this, but I am firmly convinced that we began putting all that citrus fruit in our wine to mask its taste once it had gone bad."

We know many Iberophiles—and sangriaphiles—who wouldn't accept that explanation, even if incontro-

vertible facts could be marshalled in support of it. But we have to admit that it's plausible. Which brings us to a very brief consideration of the purposes of punches and the erroneous self-serving advice many wine men give about them. Generally, the advice is: Don't scrimp on ingredients in a punch. Don't go with a cheap wine. Go with the very best you can afford, because it will give the punch character.

If that is true, it takes a more sensitive palate than ours to discern it. In fact, the fruit presence in most punches overpowers the wine to such an extent that the same effect often can be achieved with vodka and grape juice.

So why bother to use wine in punches at all? Because, quite frankly, it's cheaper than vodka and grape juice. And a well-made punch does indeed serve artistic as well as economic ends. On a hot day, few things are as refreshing to the eye, the taste, or the touch as an ice-cold, fruit-bedecked, wine-based punch.

Here follow what seem to us to be the three secrets of punch making.

First, do all you can to make the punch visually attractive. Serve from the most elegant punchbowl you can find, and give full rein to your artistic impulses when it comes to things like carving orange peels and garnishing glasses. The better the punch looks, both in the bowl and in the glass, the more enjoyable it will be.

Use lots of ice. The colder a punch is, the more refreshing it will be.

Go light on the alcohol. There are numerous punch recipes that call for hefty portions of distilled spirits, but if you wanted to knock your guests out it would be a lot simpler to hit them over the head with a hammer. The *raison d'être* of a punch is refreshment and conviviality, not inebriation.

Cacahuates (peanuts), bread sticks, and a tray of cold cuts accompany a carafe of lusty red Mexican wine. As a rule, the stronger the tastes in the food, the less point in serving an expensive wine— because its subtleties will be lost.

Here are a few of our favorite recipes:

Sangria: grapefruit, 1 gallon dry red still wine (the more tannic, the better), 1 gallon apple juice, 1 lemon, 1 orange, 1 apple, and 1 pear.

Cut grapefruit into eighths and combine with wine and apple juice. Cover and let stand in refrigerator for 16 to 32 hours (depending on how eager you are to serve it). Dice lemon, orange, apple and pear; add to mixture and let stand for another 8 to 16 hours. (Serves 12 thirsty or 24 to 42 light-sipping guests.)

Regarding the choice of wine, our preference for many years was Gallo Zimbardella—a blend of Zinfandel and Barbera. Gallo no longer makes Zimbardella, and neither, to our knowledge, does anyone else. So we now use Hernandez Burgella from Wine Imports of America, Hawthorne, New Jersey. We'd get equally good results, we're sure, by blending on our own equal portions of any two reputable winemakers' Zinfandel and Barbera, but it would cost about three times as much.

Port and Tonic: 1 cup Port wine, 2 cups quinine water, crushed ice, and lemon wedges for garnish.

For each person, mix ¼ cup wine and ½ cup quinine water over crushed ice. Stir, serve garnished with lemon wedge.

Wine-Herb Cooler: ½ cup rosé wine, 2 teaspoons tarragon-flavored wine vinegar, 2 sprigs fresh oregano, 1 cup apricot syrup, 4/5 quart chilled rosé wine, 1 quart chilled carbonated water, herb sprigs for garnish, and ice.

Make a syrup combining ½ cup wine, vinegar, and 2 sprigs oregano. Heat to simmering, covered. Cool. Discard herbs. Add apricot syrup. Store in refrigerator for at least 3 hours. When ready to serve, put 3 tablespoons herb syrup in tall glass, add three ice cubes. Fill glass to half with rosé wine, add carbonated water to fill glass. Garnish with fresh sprigs of herbs.

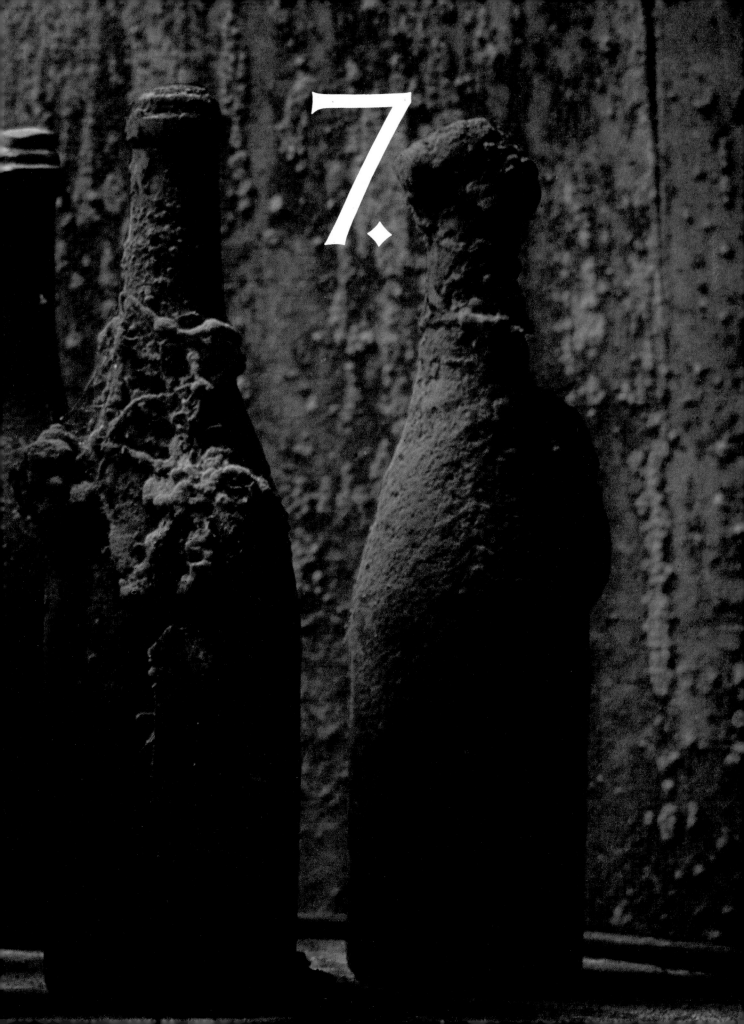

7.

7.

THE VALUE OF WINES

Opening pages: Bottles in cellar of Italian wine man Antonio Vallana date from 1874 (center) to 1912. Sold at auctions, such as those conducted by Christie's in London and Heublein in U.S., single bottles may command $1,000 and more. Left: Merchant carries his barrel of wine to market.

ines have no par value. Like stocks, they are worth whatever the buyer is willing to pay for them. Sometimes this willingness will be a matter of personal idiosyncrasy: A Greek billionaire, with his yacht moored off Biarritz, is just a stone's throw from the Bordeaux wine region, where he can buy some of the world's most celebrated wines for $10 or $15 a bottle. Instead, he pays thousands of dollars to have flown to him some resinated Patras wine which in Greece would cost him $2 a case.

More frequently, the cost of wine will relate to the demand for it. If 24 ounces of Château Latour 1948 costs $60, the going price in New York City in 1974, it is because there are people willing to buy it at that price.

Politics also can affect a wine's price, as is demonstrated by the tax (more than $3 per gallon) which is imposed on sparkling wine in North America. At times, bizarre geographical combinations of supply, demand, taxation, and other elements come into play. A Château Pétrus 1970, selling in the Liquor Control Board of Ontario Rare Wines and Spirits Shop (all wines and spirits in Canada are sold by a government monopoly) for $73.45 per bottle, was selling on the same day in New York for $56, in London for £14 ($36), and in Paris for 100 francs ($22). In the same Canadian store, a 1971 Meursault-Charmes, not estate-bottled, was selling at $24. Just across the border in Niagara Falls, New York, it could be had for $10 a bottle.

At first thought, one might be inclined to attribute the lower London price to that city's relative propinquity to France. But it doesn't cost $20 more to ship a bottle of wine from Bordeaux to New York than from Bordeaux to London—nor does it cost $14 more Bordeaux-to-London than Bordeaux-to-Paris. The per-bottle shipping costs

amount to only a few cents—which explains why Australian and Chilean wines can be sold in New York at $2 and Spanish wines at 80 cents.

In this connection, it is interesting to compare London, New York, and Stockholm retail prices for the same Bordeaux wines on a given day in 1974. Bear in mind that Bordeaux-Stockholm shipping rates are within a cent a bottle of Bordeaux-New York shipping rates; London rates are less than 2 cents a bottle cheaper than those of Stockholm.

	London	New York	Stockholm
Beychevelle 1967	£4.54 ($13.50)	$20.00	$ 9.50
Lafite-Rothschild 1967	£13.09 ($33.00)	$55.00	$18.00
Margaux 1962	£14 ($35.00)	$45.00	$20.00
Mouton-Rothschild 1949	£28 ($70.00)	$150.00	$60.00

All this relates to the price of wine, not to its value. And that brings us to one of our favorite wine concepts: the value/price index of a wine.

First, a bit of background. Some wines are, it will be remembered, costlier to make than others. It costs more to produce a wine from grapes that yield three tons per acre than from grapes that yield nine tons per acre. It costs more to age wine in 50-gallon barrels than in 100,000-gallon tanks (the barrels cost more, they take up more warehouse space, and you have to pay the people who fill them, check them, and ultimately empty them). And, finally, it costs more to age wine for five years than to age it for one.

Generally, one costly procedure begets another. There's no point using an expensive, low-yield grape like the Cabernet Sauvignon if you're going to bottle the wine a week after it stops fermenting. Likewise, there's no

International assortment of bottle
shapes and sizes includes elegant Chianti
half-gallon (top left), squat Portuguese fifth
(top center), Spanish gallon in basket (top right).
Despite handsome containers, none of these
wines retails above $4 (£1.5) a fifth.

point in aging the wine from a high-yield grape like the Concord for three years in Limousin oak. So the wines from inexpensive grapes tend to be produced inexpensively, and the wines from expensive grapes tend to be produced expensively. The producer's own cost for the wines covers a very broad range—a much broader range, to be sure, than that required for the production of whiskeys, beers, or other beverages.

And this is only a start. Grapes do not grow equally well everywhere in the world. Cabernet Sauvignon, grown on the banks of the Gironde River north of Bordeaux, produces a substantially different wine from that made by identical methods when the grape is grown on the banks of the Bío-Bío River in Chile. Indeed, the Cabernet grown along the Gironde north of Bordeaux produces a substantially different wine from that made by identical methods when the grape is grown along the same Gironde, but south of Bordeaux. Some experienced wine drinkers perceive significant differences when the grape is grown in the township of Saint-Julien rather than the adjacent township of Pauillac, both on the west bank of the Gironde north of Bordeaux, and some drinkers say they perceive a difference from vineyard to vineyard—although differences in winemakers' techniques probably explain most such claims. In any case, the price of real estate goes up in districts traditionally associated with the wines that are most in demand, and this, too, affects the producer's own cost of wine.

There are other costs, many which the wine drinker never considers. A four-color label costs about six times as much as a plain black-and-white label. A lead capsule (hood) for the mouth and neck of the bottle is more expensive than one made of plastic. In California's Livermore Valley, Concannon Vineyards uses corks that cost 6 cents each; other corks are available at 4 cents, but

Concannon feels that the thicker, 6-cent corks provide added safety against oxidation for wines intended to be laid away for twenty years. Then there is insurance, advertising, promotion, shipping. Not all of these factors affect the character of the wine, but all are taken into account when the producer and his colleagues, the shipper and importer for foreign wines, the distributor, wholesaler and retailer on all wines, calculate the price you ultimately pay.

However, the variation in purveyors' costs is not nearly proportionate to the variation in ultimate retail costs. It may very well cost the purveyors of the current year's Château Lafite-Rothschild more to put a bottle on your retailer's shelf than it costs the purveyors of the same year's Château Beychevelle, made in the adjacent Bordeaux township. The Château Beychevelle, in turn, may also cost more to purvey than the Château Kirwan, produced a few kilometers down the road at Cantenac. But the retail prices of the 1967 vintage of these three wines in New York City at this writing are respectively $55, $24, and $12! It does not cost the Lafite purveyors more than double the costs of the Beychevelle purveyors and more than quadruple the costs of the Kirwan purveyors! Likewise, the cost of a 24-ounce bottle of Château Léoville-Barton, 1961, a prime year, is $9.30. The same vintage is not available in the Pennsylvania Liquor Control Board's monopoly retail outlets (run by the state), but a bottle of the 1970 is listed at $28.02. It does not cost that much more to ship the wine to Pennsylvania than to ship it to New York.

The Pennsylvania price of the Léoville-Barton can possibly be explained by the incompetence of those who run the state liquor stores. But how do we explain the difference in New York prices among the Lafite, the Beychevelle, and the Kirwan? The only explanation is that Lafite and Beychevelle find their wines in proportionately greater demand and are charging what they believe the traffic will bear.

This is not to say that the Kirwan, the Beychevelle, and the Lafite are of equal quality. That's a subjective decision, obviously enough. But if you enjoy the Kirwan as much as the Lafite, it's pretty silly to pay the extra $45 for the Lafite, isn't it?

Let's take this a step farther. Let's say you don't enjoy the Kirwan quite as much as the Lafite, but you do enjoy it almost as much. So to your palate the Lafite is definitely worth more. But $45 more?

G-2's approach to questions of this sort is to match the wines against each other in a blind tasting. He rates them on his 20-point scorecard (discussed in an earlier chapter), then divides the number of points into the price of the wine. The resulting figure is the wine's price per point of quality.

Let's say, for example, that the Lafite is rated at 19 points and the Kirwan 13. The cost of the Lafite is $2.89 per point, that of the Kirwan 77 cents.

We are not saying that the lower its price per point, the more attractive the wine. A 5-point wine selling at $1 per bottle would work out to only 20 cents per point—but a 5-point wine, you'll recall, is rated undrinkable! All the same, the point-value approach provides a useful basis for comparison.

For instance, let's take that 1967 Lafite rated at 19 points, the Kirwan at 13, a 1966 Mirassou Cabernet Sauvignon at 17, a 1967 Concannon Cabernet Sauvignon at 18, a Louis Martini Merlot at 16, a Villa Antinori Chianti 1969 at 14, and a Gallo Hearty Burgundy at 12. Here are the retail prices for 24 ounces of each wine on the same day in New York City, followed by G-2's per-point value rating.

	Price	Per Point		Price	Per Point
Lafite-Rothschild	$55.00	$2.89	Martini	$3.50	$ .22
Kirwan	10.00	.77	Antinori	3.98	.28
Mirassou	5.25	.30	Gallo	1.49	.12
Concannon	9.00	.50			

There is no question that the Lafite, with 19 points, is the "best" wine in the group—for this particular rater's palate. Assuming he was being offered his choice of the seven wines at no cost, we might safely predict that he would select the Lafite—provided that he was in the mood for a Bordeaux-type Cabernet Sauvignon blend.

Now let's take away the assumption that our rater was being offered one wine free. If he were buying and wanted a Cabernet, he might very well take the Concannon or the Mirassou. No question that the Mirassou, at 30 cents a point, is the best buy of the three. But one point makes quite a bit of difference to a consistent rater —particularly at the upper end of the scale, where, indeed, one point separates a wine of "high excellence" from one of "outstanding excellence." Occasionally he might very well feel like paying $3.75 more for the better (to him) wine. Likewise, though $46, or an average of $2.49 per point, separates the Concannon from the Lafite, on certain occasions he might very well be willing to spend the extra money for a wine he considers to be "outstanding."

Now let us compare the Concannon and the Kirwan: 5 points—a very substantial margin—separate them. And the Concannon is $1 less, as well as a better value by 27 cents per point. Would anyone, knowing this, ever buy the Kirwan—except, perhaps, in the interest of impressing a wine snob who would recognize the latter as a *troisième cru* in the Médoc official classification of 1855? Well, perhaps. There are distinct differences between the Kirwan and the Concannon, owing to, among

other things, the soil, drainage, and climatic conditions in the respective parts of the world where they were made. Conceivably a person who rates the Concannon 5 points higher overall than the Kirwan might nonetheless, on one occasion or another, simply be in the mood for the lesser (to him) wine. But he could find better buys than the Kirwan among "unclassified" (the French refer to them as *petits*) châteaux.

Viewing the list as a whole, there is no question that the Gallo is the best buy, then the Martini. And assuming that our rater has less than unlimited funds, we might safely predict that he will choose one of them much more often than he chooses the other five combined— unless he happens to have a strong attraction to Cabernet Sauvignon, in which case, budget permitting, he will move up to the Mirassou.

All told, then, the per-point value ratings are only a starting point, not a sole determinant of which wine to buy. But they offer a means of reducing wine values to numbers which can be compared.

It is interesting to speculate about how other people might compare the wines in the above list. The aspiring wine snob, whose sole criterion for judgment is what he has read in wine books and magazines, would almost certainly put the Lafite-Rothschild in a class by itself. Not only would he proudly pay $55 for a bottle of the 1967, which professionals regard as only a fair year; he would think of himself as getting a real bargain when he found a 1968 Lafite selling for $24 a bottle. Actually, 1968 was a pretty horrible year for Lafite, which accounts for the $24 price. On the average professional rater's 20-point scale, this wine would be lucky to garner 14 points. That makes it a better per-point buy than the 1967. But it still is not a good buy. In fact, stacked up against the Concannon, the Mirassou, and even the

Left: Two of the world's most
expensive wines, Château Haut-Brion of Pessac,
Graves, and Château Lafite-Rothschild, of
Pauillac, Médoc. Right: Tasting in a
British wineshop. Royal appointment
is proclaimed on window.

Kirwan, the 1968 Lafite is a pretty awful buy.

An aspiring wine snob would probably be very impressed with the Kirwan's status as a *troisième cru*, and would have a hard time figuring out why it was selling at $10 when *cinquièmes crus* like Beychevelle are drawing $24 a bottle. He probably would assume that the liquor store had made a mistake and would buy a few cases to lay by.

True, Kirwan was rated *troisième cru* category in 1855, but a few things have happened since then. In 1880, the vineyard became the property of the city of Bordeaux, and in 1924 it was sold to the shipping firm of Schröder and Schyler. The wine is now bottled not *au château*, but in the Schröder and Schyler cellars. Thus, its illustrious past notwithstanding, Château Kirwan has become a ship-

per's wine. But for its pedigree, it probably would sell for no more than $5 or $6 a bottle.

Continuing down the list, our aspiring wine snob would dismiss the California wines out-of-hand, with the exception of the Gallo, which he would know to have been written up in a number of wine magazines as an excellent buy. He would also sneer slightly at the Antinori, which, being Italian, would not, in his opinion, merit serious consideration.

A confirmed rather than a merely aspiring wine snob might recognize the value of the Concannon and the Mirassou; but even if he knew the Kirwan as a shipper's wine, he probably would esteem it higher than either. He would, of course, hail the Lafite as the wine of wines, thereby continuing to support its inflated price.

Ultimately, in our opinion, the only way to judge wines is to taste them. Moreover, the tasting should be blind—because that is the only way to insure that the wine's reputation won't influence one's reaction to it. If a group of wine-loving friends shares the cost of the tasted wines, it will permit inclusion of some that individual tasters might hesitate to buy.

The wines should be tasted against others of the same basic type, and the bottles should be wrapped or otherwise disguised until each wine has been rated. When ratings have been made and discussed, the cost per quality point of each wine can be computed.

You may be one of those whose palate is right in line with professional raters. Or you may find that you're just as well pleased, if not more so, with wines costing much less than the ones the experts (whether on the wine-industry payroll or not) are touting. In either case, you'll know what each wine is worth to you—which is a lot more important than knowing what it's worth to the general wine-buying public.

In setting up tastings, we recommend limiting each to four or five wines, all of the same type. Newcomers to wine might profit from including a wide price range in a first tasting, then a narrower range in subsequent tastings of the same wine type.

If the wine is vintaged, scorecards should note this as well as its other vital statistics. And speaking of vintage: There's no such thing as an all-round "very good" or "great" year. Frequently the better years in Germany are bad in France, and vice versa. Likewise, a superb year in Burgundy may be so-so in Bordeaux. And individual districts, townships, and vineyards have ups and downs which don't necessarily coincide with those of their neighbors.

Moreover, the appraisal by professional wine men of a given vintage often will vary from time for time. For example, in 1959, Bordeaux wine men believed they had the vintage of the century, as promised by the weather, the sugar-acid balance noted at harvest time, and other factors. Subsequent tastings proved this enthusiasm unwarranted. The 1959's still are regarded as good (most professionals give the year an overall 16 of 20 points), but they have been overshadowed by the 1961's. At this writing, the 1959's are considered to have reached their prime, whereas the 1961's are believed capable of improving for another twenty years or longer.

Regional vintage charts abound, and they are a useful reference point for newcomers to a given wine. Any good wine merchant will have one on hand for customers to consult. But there's no substitute for sampling the wine yourself before you buy more than one bottle of it. If it's a costly wine, you still may be hesitant without a recommendation. And that brings us back to the subject of your wine merchant.

There are two kinds of wine merchant: the good wine merchant, who is in the business primarily because he enjoys wine, and the hustler, who is in it primarily to make money. The former may, in the long run, make a lot more money than the latter, but he goes about it in an entirely different way.

The good wine merchant thinks of himself as his customer's representative. He identifies his mission as getting you the best possible wines he can for the price. He usually will have available, for customers who insist on them, the most highly regarded vintages of the most celebrated wines. But he'll also have less well-known wines that he considers of equal or almost equal quality, and at a much lower price.

When he makes your acquaintance, he will appraise your wine likes and dislikes on the basis of the purchases you make. If he has even the slightest suspicion that you're seriously interested in wine, he probably will try to get a discussion going about your preferences. If not immediately, he certainly will, by your third or fourth visit, decide that he has something in stock that you will like at a price he considers very good. He'll recommend it, you'll buy it, and the two of you will talk about it the next time you stop in.

As your relationship matures, he will investigate your interests thoroughly. Some merchants will keep a record of every purchase a customer makes and will note his reactions to various wines. The longer you buy from him, the better he will come to know your wine-buying personality, and the more diligently he will search for the best wine for you—at the best price.

Because of his sound counsel, you probably will become more enthusiastic about wines than you previously were. You therefore will buy more of them, and you will buy them from him. As you continue to do business with him, he will prosper, and while he might not make as much per sale as the hustler, he should make at least as much in the long run—and feel better about it.

Now for the hustler. His aim is to separate you from as much money as possible as quickly as possible. He does not consider himself your representative; he considers himself your adversary. If you express interest in a wine that is not a high-profit item, he will promptly try to tout you onto one that is more profitable. Sometimes this will involve a larger dollar amount, sometimes it won't.

You might, for example, express interest in a Château Duhart-Milon, a Pauillac rated midway down the list of *quatrièmes crus* in 1855. He paid $18 per bottle and is selling it at the usual 50 percent markup, or $27. He points out to you that he has available a Château Lynch-Moussas, another Pauillac, at only $21.

"Now, granted, this Lynch-Moussas is only a fifth growth, not a fourth," he tells you. "But the vineyard is right in the same district as Château Lafite-Rothschild and only a few miles away from Château Latour; it gets the same sun exposure. I frankly think the Lynch-Moussas is a much better buy than the Duhart-Milon."

If you don't know a lot more about Bordeaux wines than the average layman, you'd probably be inclined to believe the merchant is doing you a very good turn. His sales pitch is especially appealing because he's saving you $6. And you're inclined to trust him because he not only was very open and above-board about the Lynch-Moussas being one class down from the Duhart-Milon in the 1855 ratings, but he actually insisted on showing you the 1855 list to prove his point.

What he hasn't told you is that Bordeaux wine men have elevated the Duhart-Milon to a *troisième cru*, while downgrading the Lynch-Moussas to a *cru bourgeois*. So three steps, not one, separate the wines. The 1855 list won't reflect this.

Chances are our hustler got a very good buy on the Lynch-Moussas. Possibly he paid no more than $5 or $6 a bottle for it. So he can make 400 percent profit selling it to you at $21. So much for the big favor he is doing you.

Hustlers, if they choose, can pull all sorts of tricks like these. If he thinks you are easily fooled, he might offer you a great buy on a Château Lafitte—only $14 a bottle, special this week.

Your eyebrows shoot up. Fourteen bucks!? What vintage?

"Well," he says, "I won't try to kid you, it's only a 1965, and as you probably know they're rated 12 out of 20. It's certainly not a '61. Obviously, I couldn't sell a '61 at that price."

Well, obviously. But how bad could the 1965's be if they're rated 12 out of 20? That's more than half. (The hustler promptly produces a vintage chart to show you he's telling the truth.) So you buy the Château Lafitte, which you never expected to get at that price, and you walk out feeling as though you've stolen the store.

But look again at the label. It says Château Lafitte, all right. But with two t's, not one. The *premier grand cru classé* wine that everybody talks about but few people have ever drunk—that one is spelled Lafite, with one t. Furthermore, while it is listed in the 1855 classification as "Château Lafite," its name subsequently was changed to "Château Lafite-Rothschild." The Château Lafitte that you bought for $14 is a Bordeaux wine, but it's not a classified growth or even a shipper's wine produced under *appellation Pauillac controlée* regulations. It's

a *vin du pays*, or "country wine," that the hustler could profitably sell at $2.50 because he paid only $1.25 for it.

Assuming that he doesn't consider you enough of a hick to fall for Château Lafitte, the hustling wine merchant can still jostle you around with château names. For example, there are fully half a dozen legitimate classified growths of Bordeaux that have "Latour" as a hyphenated part of their names—but none of them is the top-ranked Château Latour of Pauillac. There are easily a dozen legitimate classified growths that have Haut-Brion in their names—but none of them is the top-ranked Château Haut-Brion of Pessac, Graves. As a matter of fact, there's a classified growth of Talence, Graves, that bears the name—fully legitimate—of "Château Latour-Haut-Brion." It's a much-respected wine, but it isn't Château Latour *or* Château Haut-Brion.

Over in Burgundy, the confusion is even greater. Communities frequently take as a second half of their name that of the most celebrated vineyard therein. Thus, the village that used to be simply Gevrey, home of the celebrated Chambertin vineyard, is now Gevrey-Chambertin. A dozen legitimate classified growths now come from there carrying "Chambertin" as part of their names—"Griotte-Chambertin," "Charmes-Chambertin," "Chapelle-Chambertin." None of them is *the* Chambertin. Moreover, any shipper's wine that conforms to appellation regulations for the community can legitimately be sold as "Gevrey-Chambertin." *The* Chambertin they are not.

Unless you know the wines of the individual regions extremely well, it's easy to fall victim to an unscrupulous wine merchant's sleight of hand. And that's all the more reason not to buy wines you don't know from someone who has not yet earned your trust.

How does one find a good wine merchant? We wish it were easier than it is. A knowledgeable friend can, of course, steer you to one. But without such a recommendation you pretty much have to go on external signs. Here are a few we deem worth looking for—and a few tests to which to subject any wine merchant before putting your trust in him:

1. What's the emphasis of the store? Does the merchant present himself primarily as a seller of wines or a seller of whiskey and other spirits? You can usually gauge his main selling thrust by the signs in his windows, the various items being offered as specials, etc. If he's running what is primarily a liquor store instead of a wineshop, it doesn't necessarily mean that he's not knowledgeable about wines or that he is incapable of offering you good buys. But we presume him out of the ball game until he gives us reason to think otherwise.

2. How extensive is his wine selection? It isn't necessarily true that the bigger the selection the better the merchant, but those who care about wine usually try hard to stock a considerable variety. This variety, by the way, should extend in several directions. First, it should cover a full gamut of prices. If the merchant has almost all low-priced wines, it's a good bet he doesn't sell many high-priced ones and doesn't take the trouble to keep himself informed about them. If he stocks almost all high-priced wines, it's a good bet he's a hustler. A merchant who is sincerely interested in providing full service for his customers stocks low-priced wines for their everyday consumption as well as high-priced ones for special occasions. There should be price variety even in a store that caters only to the very rich. The rich, too, sometimes get a yen for earthy, lower-priced wines.

The range of wine-producing nations should also be well represented. In France, Italy, and Germany, except for cities very close to the national boundaries, it is extremely unusual to see other than local wines. But

in North America, England, and Japan, most good wine stores have wines from the major wine-exporting nations. If a store limits itself to wines of only one or two nations, and they are mostly expensive, be suspicious.

There should be a fairly broad range of wine types and prices within each exporting nation's wines. Naturally the range will be broader for French wines, many of which are priced astronomically, than for those of Italy and Spain, which generally stay under $10. But there should be a range even in Italian and Spanish wines. If the store offers only $2 and $3 bottles, it isn't covering the field.

3. How extensive is his local wine selection? It naturally costs more to ship a wine halfway across the world than to ship it within your own country. Hustlers capitalize on this, limiting sharply the number of local wines they offer so that they can induce customers to buy higher-priced imports. Unless a minimum of 25 percent of the store's display space is given over to local wines, we suspect a hustle.

4. How well does he treat his wines? Corked bottles should be stored on their sides, and no bottle should be exposed to strong light. The most damaging light is daylight, the next most damaging, fluorescent. If full wine bottles are displayed in an unshaded window (a dark green shade is best, but amber provides some protection), or under fluorescent light, you may be confident that this merchant doesn't care very much about the condition of the wines he sells. In any case, never buy a corked bottle that you see displayed upright, or in strong light.

5. Is he willing to let you browse? On our first visit to a wineshop, we like to look the whole place over, stem to stern. Most good wine merchants know—and appreciate—that many wine lovers want to do this before making a purchase. Accordingly, they let you alone until you approach them. Or if they think you may be having a problem, they inquire politely if they may be of help, then vanish when you say you'd like to browse for a while. But the hustler doesn't like people to browse. He wants to move in, make the sale, and get you on your way. Accordingly, when you say that you'd like to browse, he asks if there is a particular type of wine you are looking for, or if perhaps he may make some recommendations. No surer sign of a hustler than the attempted hard sell.

6. Will he sell you a bottle that he shouldn't? We've got an acid test for wine merchants, and it never has let us down. We give the merchant an opportunity to give us bad advice. We begin by saying that we are planning an important dinner party at which there will be several guests who are very knowledgeable about wines. We add that we would like to offer these guests a wine they will both appreciate and which will earn us their respect for selecting it. We then say that someone has recommended wine X—which inevitably is a very high-priced wine of a superior vintage which we have seen in the merchant's store—but which is too young to be served! For example, the *premier cru* 1961 Bordeaux—Châteaux Lafite-Rothschild, Margaux, Latour, Haut-Brion, and Mouton-Rothschild—are widely regarded as the most extraordinary wines of the mid-twentieth century. But they are still maturing. They will not reach their peak until somewhere between 1990 and 2010, if then. (A guest of restaurateur George Carros at the Monaco Room in Scranton, Pennsylvania, asked him why there were none of these celebrated 61's on his wine list along with lesser recent years of these wines. "Because I don't believe in infanticide," Carros replied. "I have them in my cellar, but I won't sell them until they're ready to be drunk.") If the merchant encourages us to buy for immediate consumption a too-young wine (on which, at 50 percent

markup, he'll make $30 to $50 per bottle), we know we've found ourselves a hustler. If, on the other hand, he encourages us to buy these wines only for laying away (cellar-storing until they mature), and recommends a currently ready vintage for our mythical dinner party, we know we've found ourselves a good wine shop.

7. What does he recommend for $10? A second test: Tell the merchant that you are planning an important dinner party at which you'll be serving roast beef. Add that you've budgeted $10 for a bottle of wine, and ask what he recommends. If he suggests a California Cabernet Sauvignon or Pinot Noir selling for $7 to $12, or an Italian or Spanish red selling for $5 to $10 (very few Italian or Spanish reds cost more than $10), it's a good bet you've got yourself a good man. If he questions you about the menu and then suggests two bottles of wine totaling $10—one for an earlier course, the other for the entrée—that's an even better sign. If he suggests a $5 to $15 French wine, be alert. He may be recommending something like Château Cos d'Estournel, a highly esteemed $12 wine from the district of Saint-Estèphe in Bordeaux. But he also may be trying to unload a high-profit shipper's wine that is nowhere near the value, in terms of its purveyors' combined costs, of the wines of other nations.

Some Notable Wines

There is no question that a wine like Gallo Hearty Burgundy, rated at 12 points and costing 12 cents per quality point, is a better dollar value than a wine costing 35, 50, 75 cents or even $1 per quality point. But dollar value isn't the wine drinker's only concern. If it were, he'd drink water. Most drinkers will want one or two—or five or six—high-value, low-priced wines for everyday drinking, and they will also want to move up every now and then to costlier, more sophisticated wines, even if the extra few

points they would rate these wines cost a great deal more than the points of the everyday wines.

G-1 and G-2 have divided wines into four price categories: under $2 per bottle (we call these everyday wines), $2 to $5 per bottle (we call these once-a-week wines), $5.01 to $10 per bottle (we call these special-occasion wines), and over $10 per bottle (we call these extra-special-occasion wines). Our prices are based on New York City retail in selected stores as of February, 1974, at which time wine professionals calculated that a recent inflationary wave had halted and prices had become relatively stabilized. Barring other such extreme inflationary waves, which most wine men we know deem highly unlikely for the next two or three decades, these prices should not have increased more than 7 percent per year since February, 1974. The New York prices, by the way, are typical of those in most states where wine is sold by private enterprise. In states with government-operated stores, prices may be substantially higher.

All our prices assume single-case purchases. When selling by the case, retailers almost invariably allow a 10 percent discount from the individual bottle list price. In other words, a case of twelve $1 bottles would sell for not $12 but $10.80. Once you've sampled the wine, we deem case purchases the only prudent course. Many retailers will allow an additional 3 to 6 percent discount on purchases of three, five, or six cases of the same wine.

These recommendations are offered not as endorsements but as suggested starting points for the wine newcomer. As always, the only test is in the tasting. The names of certain recommended wines are preceded by a number (1 to 5) and a symbol. The dots denote our (naturally subjective) appraisal of the wine's quality, and the triangles denote our appraisal of its dollar value (the higher the number, the greater the value).

Everyday Wines

G1	Ratings	G2	Producer, Marketing Name	Origin
			Still Wines	
2● △		3● △	Adriatica, Cabernet (R)	Yugoslavia/Maribor
●		2●	Almadén, Mountain Red Burgundy (R)	Cal./Paicines
2●		2●	Bilibio (R)	Spain/Rioja
3● △		4● △	Château-Gai, Claret (R)	Ont./Niagara Falls
●		● △	Château-Gai, Haut White (W)	Ont./Niagara Falls
●		●	Château-Gai, Rosé (P)	Ont./Niagara Falls
●		●	Château-Gai, Sauterne (W)	Ont./Niagara Falls
●		●	Château-Gai, Dry White (W)	Ont./Niagara Falls
●			Gallo Vineyards, Hearty Burgundy (R)	Cal./Modesto
2● △		2● △	Gallo Vineyards, Chablis Blanc (W)	Cal./Modesto
2● △		3● 2△	Gallo Vineyards, Rhine (W)	Cal./Modesto
●			Gold Seal, Rhine (W)	New York/Hammondsport
●			Gomez Crusado, Spanish Chablis (W)	Spain/Rioja
●			Great Western, Isabella Rosé (P)	New York/Hammondsport
●		● △	Great Western, Dutchess Rhine (W)	New York/Hammondsport
2●		2●	Juan Hernandez, Burgella (R)	Spain/Valencia
2●		3●	Juan Hernandez, Claret (R)	Spain/Valencia
●			Italian Swiss Colony, Grenache Rosé (P)	Cal./Asti
●			Italian Swiss Colony, Rhineskeller (W)	Cal./Asti
●			M. La Mont, Rosé (P)	Cal./La Mont
● △			M. La Mont, Sémillon (W)	Cal./La Mont
●			M. La Mont, Grenache Rosé (P)	Cal./La Mont
● △		●	M. La Mont, French Colombard (W)	Cal./La Mont
2● △		3● 2△	Primavera, Vinho Verde (W)	Portugal/Penefiel
● △		●	Louis M. Martini, Mountain Rhine (W)	Cal./St. Helena
● △		●	Louis M. Martini, Mountain Dry Sauterne (W)	Cal./St. Helena
● △		●	Louis M. Martini, Mountain Chianti (R)	Cal./St. Helena
●			Paul Masson, Chablis (W)	Cal./Saratoga
●			Paul Masson, Vin Rosé (P)	Cal./Saratoga
●			Winemasters, Pink Chablis (P)	Cal./Lodi
			Fortified	
●		● △	Almadén, Solera Cream Sherry (W)	Cal./Paicines
5● 2△		5● 3△	Beaulieu Vineyard, Muscat de Frontignan (W)	Cal./Napa Valley
●		●	Château-Gai, Old Niagara (W)	Ont./Niagara Falls
●			Gallo Vineyards, Very Dry Sherry (W)	Cal./Modesto
2● △		3● 2△	Merrydown, Mead (W)	Heathfield/Sussex
●		3● △	Winemasters, Cream Sherry (W)	Cal./Lodi

Once-a-Week Wines

G1	Ratings	G2	Producer, Marketing Name	Origin
			Still Wines	
●		● △	Achaia-Clauss, Demestica Red (R)	Greece/Patras
		● △	Achaia-Clauss, Sta. Helena (W)	Greece/Patras
2● 2△		3● 3△	Almadén, Pinot Blanc (W)	Cal./Paicines
● △		2● 2△	Almadén, Cabernet Sauvignon (R)	Cal./Paicines
2● 2△		4● 3△	Almadén, Grey Riesling (W)	Cal./Paicines
● △		2● 2△	Alsace Willm, Cordon d' Alsace (W)	Alsace/Barr
△		● 2△	Alsace Willm, Riesling (W)	Alsace/Barr
3△		3△	Beaulieu Vineyard, Beaumont Pinot Noir (R)	Cal./Napa Valle
2△		3△	Beaulieu Vineyard, Pinot Chardonnay (W)	Cal./Napa Valle
3● 2△		3● 2△	Beaulieu Vineyard, Chablis (W)	Cal./Napa Valle
● △		● 2△	Beringer, Grignolino (R)	Cal./Napa Valle
△		● △	Beringer, Barenblut (R)	Cal./Napa Valle
△		● △	Beringer, Chenin Blanc (W)	Cal./Napa Valle
△		● △	Beringer, Fumé Blanc (W)	Cal./Napa Valle
2● 2△		2● 2△	Beringer, Pinot Chardonnay (W) -	Cal./Napa Valle
2△		● 2△	Beringer, Pinot Noir (R)	Cal./Napa Valle
△		△	Blue Nun (Sichel), Liebfraumilch (W)	Germany/Rhein
● △		3● 3△	Buena Vista, Green Hungarian (W)	Cal./Sonoma Val
4● 3△		4● 4△	Buena Vista, Zinfandel (R)	Cal./Sonoma Val
△		2△	Casal Garcia, Vinho Verde (W)	Portugal/Penefie
△		△	Château des Ravatys, Beaujolais (R)	Burgundy/Beaujolais
△		● △	Château-Gai, Johannisberg Riesling (W)	Ont./Niagara Fa
△		● △	Château-Gai, Gamay Beaujolais (R)	Ont./Niagara Fa
△		2△	Château Ste. Roseline (P)	France/Côte de Proven
2● 3△		2● 3△	Christian Brothers, Cabernet Sauvignon (R)	Cal./Napa Valley
2● 3△		2● 3△	Christian Brothers, Pinot Noir (R)	Cal./Napa Valley
3● 3△		2● 3△	Christian Brothers, Chenin Blanc (W)	Cal./Napa Valley
3● 2△		3● 3△	Christian Brothers, Chablis (W)	Cal./Napa Valley
● 3△		2● 4△	Christian Brothers, Pinot Chardonnay (W)	Cal./Napa Valley
△		△	Concannon, Zinfandel Rosé (P)	Cal./Livermore Vall
2△		2● 3△	Concannon, Petite Sirah (R)	Cal./Livermore Vall
2● 2△		3● 2△	Concha y Toro, Cabernet Sauvignon (R)	Chile
● △			Cresta Blanca, Green Hungarian (W)	Cal./San Francis

● = quality △ = dollar value Color of the wine R=Red W=White P=Pink Y=Yellow B=Brown

G1 Ratings	G2	Producer, Marketing Name	Origin
●2△	△	Cresta Blanca, Pinot Chardonnay (W)	Cal./San Francisco
△	●2△	Cresta Blanca, Petite Sirah (R)	Cal./San Francisco
△	● △	Deinhard, Bereich Bernkastel (W)	Mosel-Saar-Ruwer/ Bernkastel
●		Giacobazzi, Lambrusco (R)	Italy/Nonantola
△	△	Ginestet, Graves Extra (W)	Bordeaux/Graves
△	●2△	Gold Seal, Chablis Natur (W)	New York/ Hammondsport
△		Grand Marque, Claret (R)	Bordeaux
△	● △	Great Western, Delaware Moselle (W)	New York/ Hammondsport
●2△	4●3△	Great Western, Baco Noir (R)	New York/ Hammondsport
△		Monimpex, Hajosi Cabernet (R)	Hungary/Hajos
△		Hanns Christof, Liebfraumilch (W)	Rhein/Koblenz
△	● △	Inglenook, Beaujolais (R)	Cal./Napa Valley
●2△	3●3△	Inglenook, Dry Sémillon (W)	Cal./Napa Valley
2△	2△	Inglenook, Pinot Noir (R)	Cal./Napa Valley
3△	3△	Inglenook, Charbono (R)	Cal./Napa Valley
△		Inglenook, Gamay (R)	Cal./Napa Valley
2△	3△	Louis Jadot, Beaujolais-Villages (R)	France/Côte d'Or
3△	3△	Hanns Kornell, Gamay Special Selection (R)	Cal./St. Helena
2△	3△	Hanns Kornell, Franken Riesling (W)	Cal./St. Helena
2△	3△	Charles Krug, Pinot Chardonnay (W)	Cal./St. Helena
3△	2△	Charles Krug, Cabernet Sauvignon (R)	Cal./St. Helena
3△	3△	Charles Krug, Pouilly Fumé (W)	Cal./St. Helena
2△	2△	Charles Krug, Chenin Blanc (W)	Cal./St. Helena
● △	2●2△	Jean Leon, Cabernet Sauvignon (R)	Spain/ Pla. del Panadés
●3△	2△	Llords & Elwood, Cabernet Sauvignon (R)	Cal./San José
●2△	2△	Llords & Elwood, Johannisberg Riesling (W)	Cal./San José
3△	●2△	Madrigal, Johannisberger Riesling (W)	Germany/ Johannisberg
2△	2●2△	Marques de Riscal (R)	Spain/Elciego
		Martel, Oeil de Perdrix (P)	Switzerland/ Neuchâtel
● △	●2△	Louis M. Martini, Cabernet Sauvignon (R)	Cal./St. Helena
△	△	Louis M. Martini, Mountain Zinfandel (R)	Cal./St. Helena
2△	2△	Louis M. Martini, Mountain Barbera (R)	Cal./St. Helena
2△	△	Paul Masson, Pinot Noir (R)	Cal./Saratoga
2△	△	Paul Masson, Pinot Chardonnay (W)	Cal./Saratoga

G1 Ratings	G2	Producer, Marketing Name	Origin
2△	△	Paul Masson, Cabernet Sauvignon (R)	Cal./Saratoga
	△	Merrydown, Riesling Sylvaner (W)	Heathfield/Sussex
3●3△	4●4△	Mirafiore, Bardolino (R)	Verona/Bardolino
● △	● △	Mirafiore, Valpolicella (R)	Verona/Valpolicella
● △	●2△	Mirafiore, Soave (W)	Verona/Soave
△	2△	Mirassou, White Burgundy (W)	Cal./San José
2△	2△	Mirassou, Chenin Blanc (W)	Cal./San José
2△	2△	Mirassou, Gamay Beaujolais (R)	Cal./San José
3△	3△	Mirassou, Monterey Riesling (W)	Cal./San José
2△	△	Robert Mondavi, Johannisberg Riesling (W)	Cal./Oakville
3△	△	Robert Mondavi, Fumé Blanc (W)	Cal./Oakville
2△	2△	Robert Mondavi, Petite Sirah (R)	Cal./Oakville
2△	△	Robert Mondavi, Gamay Rosé (P)	Cal./Oakville
	△	Monimpex, Egri Bikaver (R)	Hungary/Eger
△	2△	Monopole Le Château, Mercurey Burgundy (R)	Burgundy/Beaune
	2△	New Dynasty, Shao-Hsing (Y)	China/Taiwan
● △	△	New Dynasty, Plum (B)	China/Taiwan
	2△	New Dynasty, Tien-Sho (W)	China/Taiwan
	△	Oakville, French Colombard (W)	Cal./Napa Valley
△	2△	Jean Olivier, Château d'Aqueria Tavel Rosé (P)	France/Tavel
△	△	Ruffino, Chianti (R)	Italy/Pontassieve
	△	Ruffino, Soave (W)	Verona/Soave
2△	△	Ruffino, Bardolino (R)	Verona/Negrar
△	△	Ruffino, Valpolicella (R)	Verona/Valpolicella
△	● △	Ruffino, Orvieto (W)	Italy/Pontassieve
2△	2●2△	Sebastiani, Johannisberg Riesling (W)	Cal./Sonoma Valley
●2△	2●3△	Sebastiani, Pinot Noir (R)	Cal./Sonoma Valley
2△	2●3△	Sebastiani, Nouveau Beaujolais (R)	Cal./Sonoma Valley
△	△	Sichel, Entre-Deux-Mers (W)	Bordeaux
	△	Sichel, Blanc de Blancs (W)	Bordeaux
△	2△	Sichel, Pinot Chardonnay (W)	Bordeaux
△	△	Sichel, Moselblümchen (W)	Mosel-Saar-Ruwer
△	2△	Sichel, Cabernet Merlot	Bordeaux
△	△	Sichel, Wan Fu (W)	Bordeaux
△	● △	Sichel, Rüdesheimer Riesling (W)	Rheingau/ Rüdesheim
●2△	2●3△	Sichel, Pinot Noir Gamay (R)	Burgundy
△	2△	Simi, Cabernet Sauvignon (R)	Cal./Russian River Valley
2△	3△	Simi, Pinot Chardonnay (W)	Cal./Russian River Valley
2△	●3△	Souverain, Mountain Zinfandel (R)	Cal./Napa Valley
	△	Souverain, Pineau Souverain (W)	Cal./Napa Valley

G1 Ratings	G2	Producer, Marketing Name	Origin
△	● △	Steinberger, Bernkasteler Riesling (W)	Germany/Moselle
3●3△	4●3△	Travaglini, Spanna (R)	Italy/Piedmont
2●3△	3●4△	Vignes de l'Etat, Ruländer (W)	Luxembourg
2●3△	3●4△	Vignes de l'Etat, Riesling (W)	Luxembourg
3△	3△	Wente, Pinot Noir (R)	Cal./Livermore Valley
2△	3△	Wente, Pinot Chardonnay (W)	Cal./Livermore Valley
2△	2△	Wente, Petite Sirah (R)	Cal./Livermore Valley
2●2△	2●2△	Widmer, Moore's Diamond (W)	New York/Naples Valley
●2△	2●2△	Widmer, Vergennes (W)	New York/Naples Valley

Fortified

G1 Ratings	G2	Producer, Marketing Name	Origin
△	△	Achaia-Clauss, Mavrodaphne (B)	Greece/Patras
△	2△	Beaulieu Vineyard, Cream Sherry (W)	Cal./Napa Valley
2△	△	Beringer, Malvasia Bianca (W)	Cal./Napa Valley
△	2△	Château-Gai, Solera Sherry (W)	Ont./Niagara Falls
4●△	3●△	Château-Gai, Cream Sherry (W)	Ont./Niagara Falls
●△	●△	Cresta Blanca, Triple Cream Sherry (W)	Cal./San Francisco
△	△	Duff Gordon, Pinta Sherry (W)	Andalusia/Puerto de Santa Maria
△	△	Duff Gordon, El Cid Sherry (W)	Andalusia/Puerto de Santa Maria
△	△	Duff Gordon, No. 28 Sherry (W)	Andalusia/Puerto de Santa Maria
△	△	Duff Gordon, Niña Sherry (W)	Andalusia/Puerto de Santa Maria
3△	4△	Harveys, Amontillado (W)	England/Bristol
2△	2△	Harveys, Bristol Cream Sherry (W)	England/Bristol
2△	2△	Harveys, Gold Cap Ruby Port (R)	England/Bristol
2△	4△	Harveys, Tico Sherry (W)	England/Bristol
2△	△	Hanns Kornell, Pale Dry Sherry (W)	Cal./Asti
2△	2△	Hanns Kornell, Muscatel (W)	Cal./St. Helena
△	△	Charles Krug, Tinta Madeira Port (B)	Cal./St. Helena
4△	3△	Llords & Elwood, The Judge's Secret Cream Sherry (W)	Cal./San José
3△	3△	Llords & Elwood, Dry Wit Sherry (W)	Cal./San José
4△	3△	Llords & Elwood, Ancient Proverb Port (R)	Cal./San José
4△	3△	Llords & Elwood, Great Day Dr-ry Sherry (W)	Cal./San José
2●△	2●△	Savory & James, Amontillado (W)	Spain/Jerez

G1 Ratings	G2	Producer, Marketing Name	Origin
●△	●2△	Sevilla, Santol (W)	Philippines/Nueva Ecija
●△	●2△	Sevilla, Duhat (W)	Philippines/Nueva Ecija
●2△	3●3△	Widmer, Special Selection Sherry (W)	New York/Naples Valley
3△	4△	Williams & Humbert, Pando (W)	Spain/Jerez

Sparkling

G1 Ratings	G2	Producer, Marketing Name	Origin
●△	●2△	Blue Nun, Sekt (W)	Germany/Rhein
●	●	Château-Gai, Crackling White Cordon Blanc (W)	Ont./Niagara Falls
4●△	4●△	Gallo, Champagne (W)	Cal./Modesto
2●△	2●△	Gancia, Asti Spumante (W)	Piedmont/Asti
●△	2●△	Gold Seal, Champagne (W)	New York/Hammondsport
3●△	●△	Llords & Elwood, Superb Extra Dry Cuvée (W)	Cal./San José
●2△	2●2△	Mirassou, Champagne (W)	Cal./San José

Special-Occasion Wines

Still Wines

G1 Ratings	G2	Producer, Marketing Name	Origin
●4△	2●4△	Borgogno, Barolo (R)	Italy/Piedmont
2△	●3△	Château Monbousquet (R)	Bordeaux/Saint-Emilion
3△	3△	Freemark Abbey, Cabernet Sauvignon (R)	Cal./Napa Valley
2△	2△	Freemark Abbey, Pinot Noir (R)	Cal./Napa Valley
2△	2△	Ginestet, Saint-Emilion (R)	Bordeaux
3△	4△	Louis Jadot, Chevalier-Montrachet (W)	Côte d'Or/Beaune
2△	2△	L'Héritier-Guyot, Clos Blanc de Vougeot (W)	Côte d'Or
4△	5△	Mayacamas, Cabernet Sauvignon (R)	Cal./Napa Valley
2△	2△	Mayacamas, Zinfandel (R)	Cal./Napa Valley
3△	3△	Robert Mondavi, Cabernet Sauvignon (R)	Cal./Napa Valley
3△	2△	Robert Mondavi, Pinot Noir (R)	Cal./Napa Valley
3△	3△	Robert Mondavi, Chardonnay (W)	Cal./Napa Valley
4△	4△	Souverain, Cabernet Sauvignon (R)	Cal./Napa Valley
△	2△	Reine Pédauque, Nuits-Saint-Georges (R)	Burgundy/Nuits-Saint-Georges

Sparkling

G1 Ratings	G2	Producer, Marketing Name	Origin
2●3△	3●3△	Almadén, Blanc de Blancs Champagne (W)	Cal./Napa Valley
●2△	●2△	Beaulieu Vineyard, Champagne (W)	Cal./Napa Valley
2△	2△	Beringer, Champagne (W)	Ont./Niagara Falls
△	△	Cinzano, Asti Spumante (W)	Piedmont/Asti
△	△	Gold Seal, Blanc de Blancs Champagne (W)	New York/Hammondsport

● = quality   △ = dollar value   Color of the wine   R=Red   W=White   P=Pink   Y=Yellow   B=Brown

G1 Ratings G2		Producer, Marketing Name	Origin
●4△	5●4△	Korbel, Champagne Natural (W)	Cal./Russian River Valley
●4△	3●3△	Hanns Kornell, Sehr Trocken (W)	Cal./St. Helena
●3△	3●3△	Hanns Kornell, Muscadelle du Bordelais (W)	Cal./St. Helena
●4△	3●4△	Hanns Kornell, Champagne (W)	Cal./St. Helena
●5△	3●4△	Schramsberg, Blanc de Blancs Champagne (W)	Cal./Napa Valley
●4△	2●3△	Schramsberg, Blanc de Noir Champagne (W)	Cal./Napa Valley
●4△	3●4△	Sonoma Vineyards, Champagne (W)	Cal./Sonoma Valley

Fortified

3△	3△	Duff Gordon, Santa Maria Cream Sherry (W)	Andalusia/Puerto de Santa Maria
4△	4△	Williams & Humbert, Dos Cortados (W)	Spain/Jerez

Extra-Special-Occasion Wines

Still Wines

4△	4△	Château Ausone (R)	Bordeaux/Saint-Emilion
4△	4△	Château Cos-d'Estournel (R)	Bordeaux/Saint-Estèphe
●4△	4△	Château Duhart-Milon (R)	Bordeaux/Pauillac
3△	4△	Château Figeac (R)	Bordeaux/Saint-Emilion
3△	4△	Château Gazin (R)	Bordeaux/Pomerol
3△	3△	Château Giscours (R)	Bordeaux/Margaux
2△	3△	Château Haut-Bailly (R)	Bordeaux/Léognan
5△	5△	Château Haut-Brion (R)	Bordeaux/Pessac, Graves
4△	5△	Château Lafite-Rothschild (R)	Bordeaux/Pauillac
3△	4△	Château Lafleur (R)	Bordeaux/Pomerol
3△	3△	Château Lafleur-Pétrus (R)	Bordeaux/Pomerol
3△	4△	Château La Lagune (R)	Bordeaux/Ludon
3△	4△	Château Lascombes (R)	Bordeaux/Margaux
5△	5△	Château Latour (R)	Bordeaux/Pauillac
4△	5△	Château Léoville-Barton (R)	Bordeaux/Saint-Julien
4△	4△	Château Léoville-Las-Cases (R)	Bordeaux/Saint-Julien
4△	5△	Château Lynch-Bages (R)	Bordeaux/Pauillac
5△	5△	Château Margaux (R)	Bordeaux/Margaux
3△	4△	Château Montrose (R)	Bordeaux/Saint-Estèphe
4△	4△	Château Mouton-Rothschild (R)	Bordeaux/Pauillac
4△	4△	Château Palmer (R)	Bordeaux/Cantenac-Margaux
3△	4△	Château Pavie (R)	Bordeaux/Saint-Emilion
4△	5△	Château Pétrus (R)	Bordeaux/Pomerol
4△	5△	Château Pichon-Lalande (R)	Bordeaux/Pauillac
5△	5△	Château Pontet-Canet (R)	Bordeaux/Pauillac
3△	4△	Château Talbot (R)	Bordeaux/Saint-Julien
2△	2△	Château Teyssier (R)	Bordeaux/Saint-Emilion
4△	5△	Domaine Bart, Chambertin (R)	Burgundy/Gevrey-Chambertin
3△	4△	Domaine Caron, Beaune Cent Vignes (R)	Burgundy/Beaune
3△	4△	Domaine de Chevalier, Léognan (R)	Bordeaux/Léognan
3△	3△	Domaine du Clos du Roi, Châteauneuf-du-Pape (R)	Burgundy/Aloxe-Corton
3△	4△	Domaine Dufouleur, Musigny (R)	Burgundy/Chambolle-Musigny
4△	4△	Domaine Gaunoux, Pommard-Epenots (R)	Burgundy/Pommard
3△	4△	Domaine Grivot, Vosne-Romanée (R)	Burgundy/Vosne-Romanée
5△	5△	Domaine Gros, Richebourg (R)	Burgundy/Vosne-Romanée
3△	4△	Domaine Mugneret, Echezeaux (R)	Burgundy/Flagey-Echezeaux
3△	4△	Domaine G. Roumier, Chambolle-Musigny (R)	Burgundy/Musigny
3△	4△	Domaine Voarick, Corton-Bressandes (R)	Burgundy/Aloxe-Corton
4△	5△	Fürst von Metternich, Schloss Johannisberger (W)	Rheingau
4△	4△	Graf Matuschka-Greiffenclau, Schloss Vollrads Spätlese (W)	Rheingau
4△	4△	Graf Matuschka-Greiffenclau, Schloss Vollrads Auslese (W)	Rheingau
3△	4△	Guigone de Salins, Hospice de Beaune (R)	Burgundy/Beaune
4△	4△	Landgraf von Hessen, Winkeler Dachsberg Beerenaulese (W)	Rheingau
4△	4△	L'Héritier-Guyot, Clos de Vougeot (R)	Burgundy/Vougeot
4△	4△	O. Tobias, Piesporter Goldtröpfchen Spätlese (W)	Mosel Valley/Piesporter
4△	4△	Reichsgraf von Kesselstadt, Piesporter Goldtröpfchen Auslese (W)	Mosel Valley/Piesporter

Sparkling Wines

5△	5△	Dom Ruinart, Champagne (W)	Champagne/Rheims
4△	4△	Moët et Chandon, Champagne (W)	Champagne/Epernay
5△	5△	Taittinger, Comtes de Champagne, Blanc de Blancs (W)	Champagne/Rheims

8.
WINE IN RESTAURANTS

A restaurateur can be the wine-lover's best friend or worst enemy. In most of North America, unfortunately—and, equally unfortunately, in many of the more renowned restaurants elsewhere in the world—he chooses to be the wine-lover's enemy.

The restaurateur buys wine at wholesale prices. In free-enterprise states, like Illinois, New York, and California, he usually pays about 40 percent under the usual retail price. In government monopoly states like Pennsylvania, his usual price is 15 percent below retail (thus, he pays $3.40 for a bottle the retailer sells for $4). Having bought the bottle, what does he do with it to warrant charging more than the retailer does? Well, he stores it in (hopefully!) a cool, dark, dry place until he is ready to serve it—but the retailer does that, also. He maintains an inventory, which involves tying up capital that could be appreciating elsewhere—but that's part of the retailer's burden also. Really, the only thing the restaurateur does that the retailer does not is serve the wine—he opens the bottle and pours it into glasses.

The difference between his price and the retailer's price is wholly the result of this one act. Now, granted, there are costs incurred in serving wine. Glasses must be bought, kept in inventory, and from time to time be replaced. Someone must be paid to wash them. Someone else must be paid to serve the wine (although in most restaurants this is part of the duties of the captain or waiter, who is paid the same whether or not his table drinks wine). A white wine must be chilled, preferably by placing the bottle in crushed ice or in a refrigerator before it is served. And a wine list must be printed, or at least committed to writing by typewriter or hand, so that patrons know which wines are available and at what price. But beyond that we can't think of any service the restaurateur performs that the retailer does not.

Now how much should he be paid for performing these services: $1, $5, or maybe even $10 a bottle? Fact is, some restaurateurs take that much and more.

On the current wine list of a leading restaurant in midtown Manhattan, a bottle of Lancers rosé, which sells retail at under $4, is listed at $14. Now what are they doing with the bottle of Lancers that makes it cost 350 percent more in their establishment than it would in a retail outlet a few doors down the street? (Remember that the restaurateur, like the retailer, profits also from the markup between wholesale and retail.)

The good restaurateur, of course, is mainly interested in giving you the best bottle of wine he can at the best possible price, and is himself interested in and knowledgeable about wine. Let's look briefly at the way a good restaurateur works.

First, he puts together a selection of wines suitable for his cuisine. If he features food of predominantly one national type, he probably will focus on wines of that national type. In any case, he will try to offer as wide a selection as possible consistent with the size of his restaurant, and he will try to represent all price levels within each wine type.

His genius lies in his ability to ferret out bargain wines. Anybody can find out that the highest priced wine in Bordeaux is Château Lafite-Rothschild. Because of its name, most *haute cuisine* restaurants will want it on their list. But the good restaurateur will hunt down a few other Pauillacs which, to his taste, rate right alongside Lafite, or only a point or two below it. Because these wines have little recognition, they will be available at considerably less than Lafite, and the savings can be passed on to the customers.

Two esteemed crus, one from Bordeaux and one from Burgundy, are being guarded by stuffed fox in the famous Blue Fox cellars at San Francisco. Aging bottles are horizontal to keep corks moist. Chianti, usually served young, can be stored vertically.

The good restaurateur will also achieve vintage depth. He will keep informed of vintage conditions from year to year, and will make substantial purchases of years he considers prime. He then will cellar these wines until he deems them ready to serve. Because of his skill in buying, he will have some of the most in-demand vintages long after they have disappeared from retailers' shelves and are available only at auction. Because he bought these wines young, he will be able to sell them at a price which, although it reflects his investment (both in dollars and in expertise), will be considerably less than the retail price. For example, at the Four Seasons in New York City, which has one of North America's best and most fairly priced French wine lists, a bottle of Château Latour 1959 was priced in February, 1974, at $60. The very same wine was selling retail that month at almost double this price—$115.

The good restaurateur usually will stock a broad range of local wines—mainly because these are available to him (and can likewise be made available to you) at prices substantially lower than those of imported wines of comparable esteem. Finally, he will see to it that all wines, local or foreign, famed or unknown, costly or inexpensive, are served at the optimum temperature, at the desired point in the meal, and in a suitable glass. How will he compute his price? Based on discussions with some good restaurateurs and some professional wine men, G-1 and G-2 have come up with their own formula: To the wholesale price he pays for the bottle, the restaurateur adds 60 percent. This is the amount the retailer normally marks up a bottle that is sold individually (rather than as part of a case), and it takes into account such normal overhead items as storage space, handling, insurance, and tie-up of capital. It also, of course, leaves plenty of room for profit.

In addition, the restaurateur is entitled to some-

thing extra for serving the wine. This is what would be called a ''corkage'' charge in restaurants which allow you to bring your own bottle. (This was frequently done until restaurateurs decided they could make more money inventorying and selling their own wine. In some localities the practice is now prohibited by law—following lobbying by restaurateurs who didn't want the competition.) The corkage charge should reflect the restaurant's own cost of serving the wine, but not an additional profit—the restaurateur already took his profit when he marked the bottle up 60 percent. In a small restaurant with casual service and only a few items on the wine list, the corkage charge might be as low as 25 or 50 cents. In more elegant surroundings it could be as high as $2—but certainly no more than that, because wine simply does not cost that much to serve.

We allow the restaurateur an additional 10 percent markup over the corkage price, and think of this as a ''headache'' charge—compensation beyond actual costs for going through the trouble of offering wine service.

And that, for a routinely available wine—one you can buy at most liquor stores—is the very most the restaurateur should charge. Let's take a look at what this charge does to the price of four different wines:

First, an expensive wine, like the famed Bernkasteler Doctor U. Graben Auslese Eiswein Christwein 1970 of the German producer, Dr. Thanisch. A New York restaurateur, like a New York retailer, pays $600 for a case of twelve 23-ounce bottles. His per-unit cost thus is $50 per bottle, which he marks up another $30 (60 percent). Adding a corkage charge of $2 and a headache charge of $8, we arrive at a total of $90—a lot of money for a bottle of wine, but then this is not your everyday garden-variety bargain-basement Liebfraumilch.

Next, a Marques de Riscal Riserva 1952, for which

a New York restaurateur pays $180 a case or $15 a bottle. A case of the current year's Marques de Riscal would cost him $27.80, or $2.50 per bottle. The 1952 riserva is a specially selected quantity of wine held back by the winery for additional aging, and its additional price is what its purveyors feel they deserve for the twenty-two years they gave it special treatment. Fair enough, as we see it. Allowing himself a 60 percent markup, our restaurateur boosts the price to $24, adds a maximum corkage charge of $2 and a headache charge of $2.60, and lists the wine at $28.60—still not a cheap bottle, but then we're talking about a 1952 wine.

Next, a Freemark Abbey Cabernet Sauvignon 1967, for which our restaurateur pays $60.45 a case, or $5.04 per bottle. A 60 percent markup raises the price to $8; with the $2 corkage and a $1 headache charge, the final price is $11.

Finally, there is a Planella Riesling, which costs our restaurateur $11.95 a case, or $1 a bottle. A 60 percent markup raises the price to $1.60 (recommended retail price in a store is $1.49); with the $2 corkage charge and a headache charge, it is boosted to $4.

The customer of this restaurant enjoys considerable flexibility. If he wants and can pay for an extraordinary wine, it's available for not an awful lot more than he would pay in a liquor store—the Bernkasteler Doctor would retail at $80, the Marques de Riscal at $24. But he also can enjoy a bottle of wine for $4, and while it may not be a celebrated wine, it will be a decent buy.

The good restaurateur will see to it that you have a reasonably broad selection in each price range. Granted, there is not as much difference in wines that retail under $2 as among those $10 and up. But there should be enough cheap wines on the list so the customer doesn't feel miserly when he orders one.

We want to stress that the above wine-pricing formula is the *most* the good restaurateur will charge. There are very few restaurants with the kind of service that would warrant a $2 corkage charge. Usually, $1 per bottle is more than enough to cover all costs of service.

So much for the readily available wines. Naturally, the restaurateur deserves something extra for his efforts to obtain rare prime vintages. We feel he should be compensated for tying up his capital during the period the wines are aging, and for risking loss through breakage and spoilage. The effort and energy he invested in obtaining the wines in the first place should also be rewarded. For tying up his capital, we think he should get 10 percent simple interest per year; 10 percent more for storage space and insurance; and for his expertise we allocate another 5 percent: in sum, 25 percent simple interest per year on his purchase price for the wine for every year he has cellared it.

This may seem like a lot of money, especially for wines that have been cellared ten to twenty years. But your cost would not be significantly less if you were to drink the wines from your own cellar. In any case, the total cost of the wine after adding 25 percent annual simple interest should be less than a comparable wine would cost at retail if held back for special aging by the producer or distributor.

For example, in 1952 our restaurateur would have paid 80 cents a bottle for the 1952 Marques de Riscal Riserva we mentioned earlier. In 1972, marking it up 500 percent, he would value it at $4.80. Adding his 60 percent profit markup (on the original, not the adjusted price), we get another 48 cents, bringing the price to $5.30. With a corkage of $2 and a headache charge of 10 percent, the wine would sell for about $8.

This is an extreme example. Not all wines were sold as inexpensively in 1952 as Marques de Riscal. But few, if any, sold anywhere near their current prices, and that's why a restaurant like the Four Seasons can sell a 1959 Château Latour for $55 less than your neighborhood retailer's price.

So much for good restaurateurs. Let's turn now to the bad ones. Their interest is solely in making as much money as they can with as little effort as possible.

The best way to do this, they have calculated (correctly), is to fill the list with unfamiliar names. If you saw Italian Swiss Colony Chablis priced at $9 a fifth, you immediately would be suspicious because you bought a bottle just the other day for $1.19. If you see Gomez Crusado Spanish Chablis 1971 at $9 a fifth, you may be less suspicious—although in retail stores the Gomez Crusado is even cheaper: 98 cents a bottle.

The super-hustler among restaurateurs selects as headline items for his list the well-known names of Chateaux Margaux, Latour, Lafite-Rothschild, and Haut-Brion. He buys them by the single bottle and marks them up 100 percent. Very few people will order them at that price; meanwhile, they dress up the list. If he sells one, he takes his 100 percent profit and sends out for a replacement bottle. If he doesn't sell any, all the better: He keeps the wine in his cellar, and with every year it becomes more valuable (or so believe his patrons—actually, all wines eventually start downhill).

As for the rest of the list—well, this is where he makes his money. It's not hard to find a French wine with the word "château" in the name for under $5—especially if you stay away from the prime townships of the Haut-Médoc. A Château Falfas, for example, from a non-Médoc area of Bordeaux, is selling in New York at this writing at $4.59 retail. It's not Château Margaux, nor does it purport to be, but it's a good wine for its price.

The hustling restaurateur will place some Falfas and some similar *petits châteaux* (preferably those with names that might be confused with more famous wines) on the list next to the more famous wines, but at prices substantially lower. Château Falfas at $24 sounds pretty good next to Château Pétrus at $85 and Château Margaux at $120. Likewise, a shipper-bottled Nuits-Saint-Georges at $18 sounds like a real bargain next to a Nuits-Saints-Georges Les Saint-Georges, Domaine Maurice Chevillon 1971, at $45.

We repeat, it's hard to get away with this kind of thing if your list abounds in local wines with whose prices customers are familiar. And that's why hustling restaurateurs stay away from better-known names—or at least rarely stock more than two or three such wines, priced relatively high and buried somewhere near the back of the list in a manner designed to make anyone who orders them feel uncomfortable.

How does one evaluate the honesty of a restaurant list? G-1 and G-2 have a few simple rules.

1. We like to see a substantial representation of local wines. By local, we mean wines of the region in which we happen to be—or, if we are not in a wine-producing region, wines from the nation itself, assuming it is a significant wine producer. By substantial, we mean that at least half of the wines on the list should be local and beyond that one local wine for every three foreign ones. Our only exception is an ethnic specialty restaurant, where we'll look respectfully on a list with only one local wine in four (assuming that the remaining wines are principally of the restaurant's ethnic specialty).

2. Producers' names should be provided along with the name of the wines—for example, Sichel Corbières as opposed to merely Corbières. Naturally, you can't assess the wine unless you know the producer's name.

3. We like to see familiar names of inexpensive wines, as well as those of celebrated wines like Château Lafite-Rothschild.

4. There should be a substantial representation of inexpensive wines—around 30 percent of the list priced less than the average entrée.

5. In restaurants with entrées priced at less than $5, we suspect a hustle if a house wine—a jug wine served by the carafe—is not available. Ideally, this house wine should be priced under $2 a fifth or $3 a liter, and its producer should be identified on the menu.

Let's now look at some wine lists and see what they reveal, good and bad, about the restaurateurs who are offering them.

The first list comes from one of the most celebrated restaurants in one of the largest cities in the United States (it appears at the top of page 216). It is a ghastly list, and the restaurateur should be ashamed to offer it.

1. This is untrue; not all sparkling wines are superb at any time with any food. If the restaurateur believes his customers need advice about which ones to serve with which foods, he should at least provide sound advice. We'd be very surprised to find someone who would consider Meier's Cold Duck a superb accompaniment to steak or roast beef.

2. These sparkling wines are generally marked up 250 percent over the price the restaurateur paid for them. What is he doing for that 250 percent other than chilling the wine and pouring it?

3. Rosés are not excellent with any food.

4. "Tavel" is a generic name for rosé, not a producer. Without knowing *whose* Tavel rosé this is, we can't make a judgment about its value. But most rosé wines from France retail at under $4, so there's at least 100 percent

In traditional restaurant service, sommelier (top left) removes foil hood from bottle, wipes top of cork clean with napkin, then extracts cork. After feeling it for moisture and sniffing for off-odors, he offers it for customer to examine.

Wine List (Anonymous)

Champagnes and Sparkling Wines
(1) Superb at Any Time and with Any Food. Served Chilled.

	half bottle	bottle
Great Western, Extra Dry, *New York*	$5.50	$10.00
Almadén Blanc De Blancs, *California*		13.00
Mumm's Extra Dry, *France*	9.50	18.00
Dom Pérignon, *France* **(2)**		35.00
Cold Duck, Meier's, *Ohio*		8.50
Taylor Sparkling Burgundy, *New York*	5.50	10.00

Rosé Dinner Wines
(3) Excellent with Any Food. Served Chilled.

	half bottle	bottle
Mateus, Still, *Portugal*		7.50
(4) Tavel, Dry, *France*	4.50	8.00
Taylor, *New York*	3.00	5.50
Mateus Sparkling, *Portugal*		8.50
(5) B. V. Beaurosé, *California*		5.50
Lancers, *Portugal*		8.50
Costa Do Sol, *Portugal*		6.50

Red Dinner Wines
To Enjoy with Red Meats, Fowl and Game.

Served Room Temperature.

	half bottle	bottle
(6) Nuits-Saint-Georges, *France*	7.00	13.50
Médoc, Bordeaux, *France* **(7)**		6.50
Beaujolais, *France*	4.00	7.50
(8) Burgundy, *California*	3.00	5.50

White Dinner Wines
To Complement Fish and Poultry. Served Chilled.

	half bottle	bottle
Lancers Vinho Branco, *Portugal* **(9)**		8.00
Bernkasteler Riesling, *Moselle, Germany*		8.00
Moselblümchen, *Moselle, Germany*		7.50
Piesporter, *Moselle, Germany*	4.50	8.50
Johannisberg Riesling, *California*		7.50
Blue Nun Liebfraumilch, *Rhine, Germany*	4.50	8.50
Little Rhine Bear, Liebfraumilch, *Germany*		7.00
Chablis, *France* **(11)**		11.00
Gewürztraminer, *Alsace, France* **(12)**		7.50
Meursault, *Burgundy, France*	5.75	11.00
Pouilly-Fumé, *Loire, France*		8.50
Muscadet, Dry, *Loire, France*	4.00	7.50
Beaujolais, Blanc, *France*	4.50	8.50
Verdicchio, *Italy*		7.50
Soave Bolla, *Italy*		7.50
Château Olivier, *Bordeaux* **(14)**		8.50
Pinot Chardonnay, *France*		7.00
Taylor Sauterne, *New York*	2.75	5.00
Meier's Sauterne, *Ohio*	2.75	5.00
Chablis, *California*	3.50	6.50
Pouilly-Fuissé, *Burgundy, France*	5.75	11.00
Chenin Blanc, *California* **(15)**		6.00

(**10** marks the Bernkasteler through Johannisberg group; **13** marks the Meursault through Verdicchio group)

Pompei's Grotto

Red Wines

	small	large
(1) Paul Masson Pinot Noir	$2.50	$4.25
Louis Martini Cabernet Sauvignon	3.75	5.85

Rosé Wine

	small	large
Almadén Grenache Rosé	2.25	3.85

White Wines

	small	large
Paul Masson Pinot Chardonnay	2.75	5.00
Emerald Dry Riesling	2.50	4.50
Almadén Pinot Chardonnay	2.75	5.00
(2) Wente Grey Riesling	2.50	4.50
B. V. Chablis	2.25	3.85
Charles Krug Chenin Blanc	2.25	4.00
Johannisberg Riesling	2.75	5.00

White Wines (cont.)

	small	large
Christian Brothers Sauvignon Blanc	$2.50	$4.25
	3.75	5.85

Sparkling Wine

	small	large
Almadén Brut Champagne **(3)**	4.50	8.00
Lancers Crackling Rosé **(4)**	3.95	7.00

Imported White

	small	large
Louis Jadot V Pouilly Fuissé	4.00	7.75
Beaujolais Blanc **(5)**	4.00	7.75

House Wine

	small	large
Carafe (*White, Red or Rosé*)	1.90	3.40
Wine by the Glass (*White, Red or Rosé*) **(6)**		.70

*Below: Aboard cruise ship
of the Italian Line, sommelier
carefully samples a Bardolino before
pouring the wine out to be tasted.
The guest will then taste the wine before
deciding to accept it.*

markup here. Actually, all the wines in this group are unreasonably priced. They're all readily available at any liquor store for less than half their prices here.

5. Here's a pretty good buy, comparatively speaking. "B.V." refers to Beaulieu Vineyard, one of California's most prestigious producers. The restaurateur probably doesn't know what he's selling, or he'd charge much more.

6. Nuits-Saint-Georges? That's a regional designation. The important consideration is the shipper. We should be told who he is.

7. Médoc? Beaujolais? Also regional designations. The producer/shipper should be identified.

8. If this is Gallo's California Burgundy, it's marked up 400 percent over retail and 600 percent over the restaurateur's purchase price. If it isn't Gallo's, whose is it?

9. The Lancers is marked up 250 percent. Why?

10. We're not being told enough. *Whose* regional wines are these?

11. A château price for a generically named wine that may have cost the restaurant $1 per bottle.

12. *Whose* Alsatian Gewürtztraminer? If it's Willm's Clos Gainsbrounnel (but we think it's not), this

would be the buy of the list—about the same as retail.

13. Whose?

14. The only wine listed with the word "château" in the title. But is it a legitimate château-bottled wine? Comparing its price to others on the list, we doubt it. We have never heard of this wine.

15. Whose? The Chenin Blanc, a varietal, is one of the best buys on the list. If we were dining at this restaurant, we'd be most interested in this one.

Pompei's Grotto on Fisherman's Wharf in San Francisco has a small list that could serve as a model for restaurants offering entrées averaging $4 to $5 (for the list see opposite). Note that, as a seafood house, it offers a preponderance of white wines. Note also the availability of a house wine either by the carafe or the glass. We'd like to know who the producer is of the house wine; but if he's up to the rest of the list, we have no worries—although we'd probably order a bottle from the rest of the list because the prices are so good.

1. These prime red varietals cost only $1 to $2 more than in a retail store.

2. It's a toss-up between these two as to which is the best buy on the list. We selected the B.V. Chablis.

3. A good price for a sparkling wine.

4. Slightly high-priced, but less than 100 percent markup over retail.

5. A reliable shipper whose wines retail in the $4 to $5 range. Note that the list identifies Jadot and not merely "Pouilly-Fuissé" or "Beaujolais Blanc," which by themselves would mean very little.

6. Unless it's a very large glass, this house wine in individual portions is overpriced. The bottled wines are such good buys that it would be ridiculous to buy a carafe here, much less an individual glass.

Another world-champion list—from the Connaught Grill and Restaurant in London (for list see pages 220-221). Note the broad range of prices as well as wines. It's rare to see this extensive an array of German wines outside Germany.

1. Legend, "bottled in France," is confusing, giving the impression that the other wines were bottled outside France. Actually, excepting a few shippers' wines like the Haut Pomerol, the wines were not only bottled in France but on the estate of the grape grower *(au château)*.

2. Prices for prime-vintage *premier cru* Bordeaux are more than reasonable. The 1960 Haut-Brion, for example, would cost over $75 in most U.S. restaurants (and many retail establishments).

3. Note that the Connaught is keeping the super-prime vintages, like 1961 Margaux, under wraps and offering only those wines that are ready to be drunk now.

4. Note shipper's name—essential information—on regional wines of Burgundy. This should also be provided for the Haut Pomerol—which, by the way, is a trade name, like Haute Sauternes, not a bona fide geographic designation like Haut-Médoc.

5. The German prices are the very soul of reasonableness. £8.00 for the Erbacher Auslese and Spätlese, 1959 and 1967, is unusually cheap.

6. Producers' names would be very helpful for the routine Alsatian wines as well as for the *Grands Reserves*.

7. The German sparkling wines are much better buys than the French. We think the list would be more useful if these great values were not buried toward the end of the list.

8. The rare Burgundies seem absolute steals at these prices. But we still want to know the producer!

9. We've never seen such a wide selection of Ports outside Oporto. They are a star attraction of the

Connaught Grill and Restaurant

	Bots. £.p	½-Bots. £.p
Bordeaux—Red		
Chât. Loudenne 1967	2.75	1.45
(St. Yzans) Château-Bottled		
Chât. Laujac N.V. ❶	2.75	1.45
Bottled in France		
Chât. Le Menaudat 1962	3.00	1.60
Domaine de la Fleur 1962	3.00	1.65
(Pomerol)		
Chât. Pavie-Macquin 1962	3.00	1.65
(St. Emilion)		
Chât. Cantemerle 1958		1.75
(Macau)		
Chât. Malescot-Margaux N.V.	3.50	
(Margaux)		
Chât. Pontet-Canet N.V.	4.65	2.45
(Pauillac) Bottled in France		
Chât. Les Ormes de Pez 1962	3.75	1.95
(St. Estèphe)		
Chât. du Vieux Sarpe 1961	4.75	2.50
(St. Emilion)		
Chât. de Pichon-Lalande 1964		2.50
(Pauillac)		
Haut-Pomerol 1967 ❹	5.00	
Chât. Paveil de Luze 1969	6.75	
(Médoc) Bottled in France		
Chât. Haut-Pourret 1962	3.75	
(St. Emilion)		
Chât. d'Issan 1962		2.45
(Cantenac) Bottled in France		
Chât. Lanessan 1966	4.75	2.45
(Médoc) Château-Bottled		
Chât. Marquis d'Alesme Becker 1964		2.45
(Margaux) Château-Bottled		
Chât. Bouscaut 1964	4.75	2.45
(Graves) Château-Bottled		
Chât. Calon St.-Georges 1961	5.50	
(St. Emilion) Château-Bottled		
Chât. Cantenac-Brown 1969	6.00	3.15
(Margaux) Château-Bottled		
Chât. Corbin-Michotte 1961	7.50	
(St. Emilion) Château-Bottled		
Chât. Gruaud-Larose 1962	7.75	
(St. Julien) Château-Bottled		
Chât. Talbot 1964	7.75	3.95
(St. Julien) Château-Bottled		
Chât. Cantemerle 1966	7.75	
(Macau) Château-Bottled		
Chât. Branaire-Ducru 1962	7.75	
(St. Julien) Château-Bottled		
Chât. La Mission Haut-Brion 1962	8.25	
(Graves-Pessac) Château-Bottled		
Chât. Calon-Ségur 1962	8.25	
(St. Estèphe) Château-Bottled		
Chât. Palmer 1964	9.25	
(Margaux) Château-Bottled		
Chât. de Sales 1959	10.50	
(Pomerol) Château-Bottled		
Chât. Cheval-Blanc 1962	14.50	
(St. Emilion) Château-Bottled		
Chât. Margaux 1959	18.00	
1964 ❸	15.50	
(Margaux) Château-Bottled		

	Bots. £.p	½-Bots. £.p
Chât. Latour 1962	18.00	
(Pauillac) Château-Bottled		
Chât. Pavie 1961	16.00	
(St. Emilion) Château-Bottled ❷		
Chât. Haut-Brion 1960	16.50	
(Graves-Pessac) Château-Bottled		
Burgundy—Red		
Marcilly-Beaujolais N.V.	2.50	
Beaujolais-Villages N.V. ❹	2.50	
Selected and Shipped by Louis Latour for the Connaught Hotel		
Brouilly 1970	2.50	
Bouchard Père et Fils		
Nuits Clos des Princes 1969	2.75	1.35
Chénas 1966	3.00	
Domaine des Côtes du Remont		
Fleurie 1972	3.00	2.30
Bottled in France Georges Duboeuf		
Morgon 1970	3.25	
Bottled in France Georges Duboeuf		
Clos de Conté 1969	3.25	1.70
Pierre Gerard et Cie		
Chassagne-Montrachet 1966	3.50	1.80
Clos St.-Jean Bottled in France P. de Marcilly Frères		
Moulin-à-Vent 1972	3.50	
Bottled in France Georges Duboeuf		
Chiroubles 1967	3.20	1.75
Bottled in France Sichel et Cie		
Chambolle-Musigny 1969	4.25	2.15
J. Belin		
Chambertin 1966		2.50
Bottled in France P. de Marcilly Frères		
Aloxe-Corton 1969	5.25	
Bottled in France Charles Viénot		
Clos de Tart 1967	5.75	
Bottled in France J. Mommessin		
Morgon 1970	5.75	
Tête de Cuvée Domaine-Bottled Louis Latour		
Gevrey-Chambertin 1970	5.75	3.00
Barault—Lucotte et Fils		
Nuits-Saint-Georges— Tastevinage 1966	6.50	
Clos de Forets St.-Georges Bottled in France J. Belin		
Corton 1969	8.25	
Bottled in France Charles Viénot		
Musigny 1964	7.25	
Bottled in France Pierre Ponnelle		
Vosne-Romanée 1970	7.25	
Bottled in France Charles Viénot		
Chât. Corton-Grancey 1955	6.75	
Domaine-Bottled Louis Latour		
Beaune 1964	7.75	
Clox des Avaux Bottled in France J. Thorin		
Savigny-les-Beaune 1969	7.75	
Domaine-Bottled Louis Latour		
Clos-Vougeot 1970	8.25	
Domaine-Bottled Robert Arnoux		
Nuits-Saint-Georges 1969	9.00	
Domaine-Bottled Louis Latour		

	Bots. £.p	½-Bots. £.p
Pommard Clos des Citeau 1964	9.00	
Domaine-Bottled Jean Monnier & Son Fils		
Romanée-Conti 1970	18.00	
Domaine-Bottled		
Chablis and White Burgundy		
Blanc de Blancs N.V.	2.25	1.20
Specially Selected for the Connaught Hotel		
Beaujolais Blanc 1970	2.75	
Château de Loyse		
Macon 1967	2.75	1.45
Bottled in France Jules Belin		
Chablis 1970	3.50	1.85
Gloire de Chablis J. Moreau et Fils		
Montagny 1970	3.50	
Georges Duboeuf		
Meursault-Santenots 1963	3.50	
Bottled in France Marquis d'Angerville		
Puligny-Montrachet 1971	3.75	2.00
Bouchard Père et Fils		
Batard-Montrachet 1970	5.75	3.00
Geisweiller et Fils		
Meursault-Perrierès 1971	4.25	2.25
Jules Belin		
Montagny 1970	4.25	2.25
Bottled in France Louis Latour		
Pouilly-Fuissé 1971	3.75	1.95
Morgan Furze & Co.		
Chablis 1970	3.95	2.55
Bottled in France J. Thorin		
Chassagne-Montrachet 1971	4.95	
Château-Bottled Marcel Picard		
Nuits-Saint-Georges 1970	5.25	
Clos de L'Arlot Domaine-Bottled Jules Belin		
Corton-Charlemagne 1969	5.75	
Domaine Bonneau du Martray		
Corton-Charlemagne 1963	6.25	
Domaine-Bottled Bouchard Père et Fils		
Corton-Charlemagne 1969	7.25	
Bottled in France Joseph Droubin		
Corton-Charlemagne 1970	8.50	
Domaine-Bottled Rapet Père et Fils		
Côtes du Rhône		
Gigondas (R) 1970	3.75	2.00
Bottled in France Edmond Chauvet		
Gigondas Rosé 1969	3.75	2.00
Bottled in France Edmond Chauvet		
Hermitage la Chapelle (W) 1971	2.95	
Paul Jaboulet Ainé		
Châteauneuf-du-Pape (R) 1970	3.75	2.00
Bottled in France Paul Jaboulet Ainé		
Châteauneuf-du-Pape (W) N.V.	2.95	
Bottled in France J. Mommessin		
Vins de Loire		
Muscadet 1971	3.00	
Bottled in France		
Blanc Fumé de Pouilly 1972	3.00	1.65
Bottled in France		

	Bots. £.p	½-Bots. £.p
Chât. de Sancerre 1972	4.25	2.25
Bottled in France Louis de Sancerre		
Pouilly-Fumé Chât. du Nozet 1970	3.50	1.85
Domaine-Bottled de Ladoucette Frères		

Graves and Sauternes

	Bots.	½-Bots.
Chât. Loudenne 1970	2.50	
(St. Yzans) Château-Bottled		
Agneau Blanc 1966	2.25	1.15
Graves Dry Superior *Rothschilds Selection*		
Graves N.V.	2.25	1.15
Dry Royal		
Chât. Doisy-Daëne 1966		1.50
Château-Bottled		
Chât. Latour-Blanche 1940	2.50	
Château-Bottled		
Agneau Blanc N.V.	3.50	1.85
Sauternes Rothschilds Selection		
Chât. Climens 1967	4.25	2.25
Barsac		
Chât. Suduiraut 1967	5.75	
Château-Bottled		
Chât. d'Yquem 1961	8.95	
Château-Bottled		

Moselle

	Bots.	½-Bots.
Bernkasteler Schwanen 1965	2.75	1.50
Zeltinger Riesling 1969	2.75	1.50
Kellerei Freiherr von *Schorlemer-Lieser*		
Waldracher Sonnenberg 1970	2.75	1.50
Bernkasteler Bratenhöfchen 1966	2.75	
Brauneberger Mandelgraben 1969	3.25	
Estate-Bottled Stephanus Freiherr *von Schorlemer-Lieser*		
Deinhard's Bernkasteler 1971	3.25	1.75
Green Label		
Piesporter Goldtröpfchen 1971	3.25	1.75
Deinhard's Bernkasteler 1970	3.75	2.00
Lilac Seal		
Graacher Himmelreich 1969	3.75	
Estate-Bottled *Freiherr von Schorlemer-Lieser*		
Erdener Treppchen Spätlese 1970	4.75	
Estate-Bottled Schwaab-Scherr		

Rhine Wine

	Bots.	½-Bots.
Dorf Johannisberger 1967	2.25	1.20
Liebfraumilch 1970	2.50	1.30
Crown of Crowns		
Deinhard's Liebfraumilch 1969	2.75	1.45
Hans Christof Wein		
Oppenheimer Goldberg Riesling 1957	2.75	1.45
Ostricher Gottestal Riesling 1967	2.75	1.45
Johannisberger Erntebringer 1967	2.75	1.45
Forster Neuberg Riesling 1964	2.75	
Niersteiner Domtal 1967	2.75	

	Bots. £.p	½-Bots. £.p
Hallgartener Schönhell Riesling Cabinet 1966	2.75	
Orig. Abf. Fürst v. Löwenstein		
Liebfraumilch Auslese 1969	3.25	1.70
Blue Nun Label		
Alsheimer Fischerpfad Spätlese 1953	3.25	
Estate-Bottling *Weingut Franz Bernard 3*		
Kiedricher Wasserros Riesling Cabinet 1969	3.25	
Estate-Bottling Dr. R. Weil		
Mittelheimer Honigberg Riesling Spätlese 1953	3.50	
Estate-Bottling *Weingut Hch. Franz Walter*		
Hallgartener Schönhell Riesling Auslese 1959	5.75	
Fürst. Löwenstein'sches Wgt. *Estate-Bottling*		
Eltviller Sonnenberg Riesling Spätlese 1969	5.75	
Estate-Bottling Schloss Eltz		
Steinberger Auslese Cabinet 1959	7.50	
Estate-Bottling—Staatsweingut		
Erbacher Markobrunn Auslese 1959	8.00	
Schloss Reinhartshausener Cabinet *Estate-Bottling*		
Erbacher Riesling Marcobrunn Spätlese 1967	8.00	
Schloss Reinhartshausener *Estate-Bottling*		

⑤

	Bots.	½-Bots.
Deidesheimer Hohenmorgen Riesling Beerenauslese 1959	9.50	
Estate-Bottling Dr. Burklin-Wolf		
Erbacher Honigberg Beerenauslese 1959	13.50	
Schloss Reinhartshausener Cabinet *Estate-Bottling*		
Niersteiner Kehr Riesling 1964	15.50	
St. Nikolaus-Wein *Estate-Bottling Weingut Seip*		

Franconia Wines

	Bots.	½-Bots.
Steinwein 1967	2.75	
Langenbach & Co.		

Vins de Provence

	Bots.	½-Bots.
Chât. de Selle Rosé 1968	3.75	1.95
Domaines Ott		

Vins d' Alsace ⑥

	Bots.	½-Bots.
Schoenenberg 1967	2.00	1.15
Traminer 1969	2.35	
1967		1.25
Riesling "Hügel" N.V.	2.50	
Gewürztraminer 1969	3.00	1.60
Riesling—Grand Reserve 1970	3.00	1.60
Bottled in Alsace Dopff		
Gewürztraminer— Grand Reserve 1970	3.25	1.75
Bottled in Alsace Dopff		

Portuguese Wines

	Bots.	½-Bots.
Mateus Rosé N.V.	2.20	1.20

Sparkling Wines ⑦

	Bots. £.p	½-Bots. £.p
Sparkling Hock-Langenbach N.V.	3.00	1.55
Langenbach Privat		
Sparkling Hock-Burgeff N.V.	3.00	1.55
Schloss Hochheim		
Deinhard Cabinet N.V.	3.00	1.55
Extra Dry		
Sparkling Red Burgundy N.V.	3.00	1.55

Fine Burgundy ⑧

	Bots.	
Pommard-Epenots 1928	14.50	
Chambolle-Musigny Charmes 1934	12.50	
Echezeaux 1934	12.50	

Vintage Port ⑨

	Bots.	
Warre's 1950	11.00	
Branded Cork		
Croft's 1950	11.00	
Branded Cork		
Cockburn's 1950	11.00	
Branded Cork		
Dow's 1948	13.00	
Branded Cork		
Taylor's 1948	13.00	
Branded Cork		
Graham's 1948	13.00	
Branded Cork		
Fonseca 1948	13.00	
Branded Cork		
Cockburn's 1947	14.00	
Branded Cork		
Tuke Holdsworth 1947	14.00	
Branded Cork		
Sandeman 1947	14.00	
Branded Cork		
Warre's 1947	14.00	
Branded Cork		
Martinez 1945	14.00	
Branded Cork		
Quinta de Noval 1945	14.00	
Branded Cork		
Cockburn's 1935	16.50	
Branded Cork		
Croft's 1935	16.50	
Branded Cork		
Sandeman 1935	16.50	
Branded Cork		
Taylor's 1935	16.50	
Branded Cork		
Warre's 1934	17.50	
Branded Cork		
Tuke Holdsworth 1934	17.50	
Branded Cork		
Martinez 1934	17.50	
Branded Cork		
Dow's 1934	17.50	
Branded Cork		
Martinez 1927		
Branded Cork		
Croft's 1924	17.50	
Branded Cork		
Sandeman 1920	17.50	
Branded Cork		
Kopke 1919	17.50	
Branded Cork		

Left: Sommelier chills white wine at Ernie's in San Francisco. Below: Old bottle of Burgundy is uncorked in straw basket. Basket permits carrying wine from cellar without disturbing sediment. Right: Wine served in classic Burgundy glass.

Connaught list, assuming one is ready to make the major expenditure required.

We have not reprinted here the Connaught's sound and extensive list of sparkling wines. Nor are the glass and carafe prices included; the bottles are better values.

The wine list of the Four Seasons restaurant in New York City is a world-champion list, with prices generally lower than in several other New York restaurants which don't approach the Four Seasons in quality or price of food. In fact, some wine-lovers feel that the wine bargains more than compensate for the Four Seasons' well-known high food prices. (For the list see pages 228-229.)

1. We like very much the idea of arranging wines by vintage. It steers the customer immediately to the type of wine experience he seeks.

2. Note not only the broad price range for the 1967 (or any other) group of Bordeaux, but also the depth —a large number of wines in each end, so that not only the affluent customer but also his budget-conscious counterpart has a wide choice. The Beychevelle is priced only a few dollars above retail.

3. Note the price difference for the same wine in different years. The inconsistencies (Latour costlier in 1967, Margaux in 1966) reflect the value appraisals by professional wine men of different years in different vineyards.

4. The Duplessis 1962 at $9.50 is a buy if ever there was one.

5. Note that the proprietor Paul Kovi is keeping his prime 1961's under wraps until they're ready. Only Latour of the Big Five of Bordeaux appears.

6. Now, in 1955, the Big Five start coming out in force. They're ready. The 1955 Château Margaux is one

*Ernie's in San Francisco has
one of the most extensive and reasonably
priced wine lists in the world. At the
tasting table in the restaurant's cellars,
candles illuminate prime vintages of Châteaux
Lafite-Rothschild, Ausone, Latour, and Pétrus.*

of our personal favorites. However, the '53 Château Margaux, at the same price, would be regarded by most wine professionals as a much better buy. Many professionals consider the 1953 Château Margaux the ideal wine to drink today to demonstrate the greatness of a *premier grand cru classé de Bordeaux.*

7. Note availability of a regional bottling at $5.50. We'd enjoy a bit more choice among shippers' wines, but with one available at $5.50, we won't complain too loudly.

8. A superb selection from Burgundy. Note that proprietors as well as vineyards are identified. With vineyards whose names require communal clarification, the village name appears first. This creates some confusion on what otherwise is an exemplarily clear list.

9. The selection is thin, but the most highly reputed châteaux are represented, and the prices are right. We'd like to see a Barsac along with the Sauternes and Graves, but we won't quibble. Note again the inexpensive regional bottling.

10. It's impossible to quarrel with either the range, depth, choices, or prices of these white Burgundies. That Chevalier-Montrachet by Louis Jadot, at $26.50, is, in our opinion, a much better buy than the better-known Thénard-Montrachet at $35.

11. This miscellaneous selection is very good, and the prices are in line.

The Four Seasons' list includes fortified wines, as well as wines from other countries than France. Though not reprinted here, they are well deserving of comment.

The lists for countries outside France are fairly limited—this probably because the restaurant's cuisine is predominantly French. In any case, most major wine types of the various countries are represented, and the Hungarian selection is much more extensive than normally will be found outside Hungary.

The American list represents the best general American selection we've seen anywhere and the best California selection we've seen outside California. Rarely seen items as Bully Hill's red and white from Lake Keuka (New York) and Dr. Konstantin Frank's Johannisberg Riesling from nearby Hammondsport are on the list. Also such prime vintages as the Simi 1935 Zinfandel and Cabernet, and the 1950 Beaulieu.

The sparkling wines are priced slightly higher than the still wines. The selection is excellent.

The fortified wines represent an outstanding selection, but in our view their prices are too high.

Ordering Wine in a Restaurant

Usually the man in charge of wine in better restaurants is a sommelier; he has overall responsibility for the cellar and for serving everyone in the restaurant. In some restaurants, the sommelier also is responsible for actually buying the wines. This, we think, is the ideal situation; unfortunately, it doesn't often prevail. More frequently, the wines will be bought by the proprietor, who doesn't know very much about them, and will be served by a captain or waiter, who knows less and cares still less.

When a knowledgeable sommelier is on the job, ordering can be an interesting and educational experience. A superior sommelier will bring you the wine list as soon as you've been seated, then will withdraw until you put the list aside or give some other signal that you've finished studying it. If the list is good, we like to take time with it; and if it contains provocative items, like some of those we've noted on the lists from the Connaught and the Four Seasons, we'll want to discuss them with the sommelier.

The good sommelier almost invariably will welcome such a discussion. He doesn't often get the opportunity to talk with someone who knows anything about

wine and he takes pride in his own knowledge of the subject. Naturally, he is eager to be helpful; he knows that if he does steer guests to a selection that pleases them, it will increase his tip.

On the other hand, there are sommeliers who aren't very knowledgeable and who welcome a discussion because it enhances their opportunities to sell you a high-profit wine. How can you tell the good guys from the villains? Most newcomers to wine can't, and we think it's pointless to try until you've acquired enough tasting experience to really know what you're talking about. A better bet, in our view, is simply to peruse the list, find a familiar wine at a good price, and order it.

When we say "familiar," we don't necessarily mean that you must have tasted it. It may simply be a wine you know by name, from reading or from friends' recommendations. If the price is right, a restaurant is an excellent place to become acquainted with such a wine; then, if you like it, you can buy a case or more for your own cellar.

How do you know if the price is right? That, for the newcomer, can be quite a problem. We know some people who actually carry a wine price list with them when they go to a restaurant, then compare it to the prices on the restaurant list. In places with state-operated stores, the official list usually is small enough that it can be carried conveniently and without attracting attention. If the res-

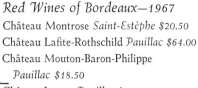

Red Wines of Bordeaux—1967

Château Montrose *Saint-Estèphe $20.50*
Château Lafite-Rothschild *Pauillac $64.00*
Château Mouton-Baron-Philippe
 Pauillac $18.50
Château Latour *Pauillac $62.00*
Château Margaux *Margaux $56.00*
Château Giscours *Margaux $15.50*
Château Malescot-Saint-Exupéry
 Margaux $18.50
Château Beychevelle *Saint-Julien $28.50*
Château Léoville-Poyferré
 Saint-Julien $22.50
Château Figeac *Saint-Emilion $18.50*
Château Monbousquet *Saint-Emilion $12.50*
Château Ausone *Saint-Emilion $48.00*
Château Trotanoy *Pomerol $19.50*
Château La Mission-Haut-Brion
 Graves $32 00
Château Bouscaut *Graves $14.50*

Red Wines of Bordeaux—1966

Château Mouton-Baron-Philippe
 Pauillac $24.00
Château Latour *Pauillac $58.00*
Château Margaux *Margaux $58.00*
Château Rausan-Ségla *Margaux $20.00*
Château Ausone *Saint-Emilion $48.00*
Château La Gaffelière *Saint-Emilion $17.50*
Château Roc-St.-Michel *Saint-Emilion $8.50*
Château La Mission-Haut-Brion
 Graves $30.00
Château Bouscaut *Graves $15.50*

Red Wines of Bordeaux—1964

Château Calon-Ségur *Saint-Estèphe $23.50*
Château Cos d'Estournel
 Saint-Estèphe $22.50
Château Lafite-Rothschild
 Pauillac $65.00
Château Latour *Pauillac $52.00*
Château Mouton-Rothschild *Pauillac $65.00*
Château Ducru-Beaucaillou
 Saint-Julien $10.50 half bottle
Château Margaux *Margaux $48.00*
Château Ausone *Saint-Emilion $44.00*
Château Cheval-Blanc *Saint-Emilion $48.00*
Château La Croix-de-Gay *Pomerol $9.50*
Château Haut-Brion *Graves $42.00*
Château Bouscaut *Graves $12.50*

Red Wines of Bordeaux—1962

Château Calon-Ségur *Saint-Estèphe $24.50*

Château Cos d'Estournel
 Saint-Estèphe $25.50
Château Latour *Pauillac $55.00*
Château Ausone *Saint-Emilion $57.00*
Château Duplessis *Saint-Emilion $9.50*
Château Cheval-Blanc *Saint-Emilion $52.00*
Château Haut-Brion *Graves $55.00*

Red Wines of Bordeaux—1961

Château Latour *Pauillac $60.00*
Château Pichonne-Longueville-Baron
 Pauillac $29.00
Château Pavie-Decesse *Saint-Emilion $13.50*
Château Ausone *Saint-Emilion $52.00*
Château La Mission-Haut-Brion
 Graves $49.00

Red Wines of Bordeaux—1960

Château Lafite-Rothschild *Pauillac $40.00*
Château Latour *Pauillac $32.00*
Château Pichon-Longueville-Baron
 Pauillac $24.00
Château Haut-Brion *Graves $28.50*

Red Wines of Bordeaux—1959

Château Cos d'Estournel
 Saint-Estèphe $35.00
Château Lafite-Rothschild *Pauillac $150.00*
Château Latour *Pauillac $80.00*
Château Cheval-Blanc *Saint-Emilion $75.00*
Château Bouscaut *Graves $22.50*

Red Wines of Bordeaux—1955

Château Montrose *Saint-Estèphe $36.00*
Château Lafite-Rothschild *Pauillac $120.00*
Château Latour *Pauillac $90.00*
Château Margaux *Margaux $90.00*
Château Léoville-Poyferré *Saint-Julien $25.00*
Château Ausone *Saint-Emilion $62.00*

Red Wines of Bordeaux—1953

Château Latour *Pauillac $90.00*
Château Margaux *Margaux $90.00*
Château La Mission-Haut-Brion
 Graves $48.00
Château Cheval-Blanc *Saint-Emilion $85.00*

Red Wines of Bordeaux—1952

Château Montrose *Saint-Estèphe $32.00*
Château Lafite-Rothschild *Pauillac $120.00*
Château Latour *Pauillac $82.00*
Château Margaux *Margaux $85.00*
Château Cheval-Blanc *Saint-Emilion $70.00*

Red Wines of Bordeaux—1949

Château Montrose *Saint-Estèphe $48.00*
Château Cheval-Blanc *Saint-Emilion $95.00*
Château Haut-Brion *Graves 90.00*

Red Wines of Bordeaux—1934

Château Pichon-Longueville-Baron
 Pauillac $52.00
Prince Noir *Barton & Guestier $5.50*
Mouton-Cadet Rouge
 Baron Philippe de Rothschild
 1969/70 *$7.50*

Red Wines of Burgundy

Côte de Nuits
Fixin, Clos de la Perrière, Pierre Olivier
 1969/71 *$16.50*
Gevrey-Chambertin, Clos St.-Jacques, Pernot
 1964/66 *$24.50*
Chambertin, Clos de Bèze 1969/71 *$28.50*
Morey, Clos de la Roche, A. Rousseau
 1969/70 *$19.50*
Bonnes Mares, Comte de Vogue
 1967/69 *$26.50*
Bonnes Mares, Roumier 1962 *$29.50*
Chambolle-Musigny Amoureuses,
 Domaine J. Bertheau 1964/66 *$19.50*
Musigny, Comte de Vogue 1967/69 *$29.50*
Clos de Vougeot, L'Héritier Guyot
 1971 *$18.50*
Vosne-Romanée, Grivot 1969 *$17.50*
Romanée-St.-Vivant, Thomas Frère
 1967/69 *$24.50*
Vosne-Romanée "Les Cheumes"
 1967/69 *$16.50*
Le Richebourg, P. Maufoux
 1969/70 *$44.00*
Nuits-Saint-Georges,
 Clos de la Maréchale, Faiveley
 1970 *$13.50*
Nuits-Saint-Georges, Clos des Corvées,
 Gilles 1966/69 *$19.50*
Nuits-Saint-Georges,
 "Les Boudots" Noellat 1967/69 *$18.50*
Hospices de Nuits Les St.-Georges,
 Sirgs de Vergy 1964/66 *$13.50*
Côte de Beaune
Corton-Bressandes, Paul Tollot 1969 *$19.50*
Aloxe-Corton, Domaine Senard
 1969/70 *$16.50*
Corton, Clos du Roi, Baron Thénard
 1969 *$18.50*
Corton-Pougets, Louis Jadot 1970 *$21.50*

Givry, Baron Thénard 1969/71 *$10.50*
Beaune, Clos des Couchereaux
   1970/71 *$14.50*
Pommard, Grand Clos Epenots, Courcel
   1969 *$22.50*
Pommard, Clos de la Commaraine,
   Jaboulet-Vercherre 1970/71 *$19.50*
Pommard, Epenots, J. Drouhin
   1970/71 *$14.50*
Volnay, Prosper Maufoux 1969/70 *$14.50*
Santenots, Domaine des Comtes Lafon
   1970 *$15.00*
Chassagne-Montrachet, Abbaye de Morgeot
   1969 *$12.50*
Mercurey, Sichel 1970/71 *$12.50*
Grand Cru Beaujolais
Brouilly, Château des Tours
   1971/72 *$7.50*
Juliénas, Perrachon 1969/70 *$8.50*
Moulin-à-Vent, P. Maufoux
   1969/70 *$8.50*
Fleurie, A. Barolet 1970/71 *$9.50*
Chénas, Chassagnol, Depagneux
   1971 *$8.00*
Morgon, Pillet, Depagneux 1971 *$7.50*
Beaujolais-Villages, Louis Jadot
   1971/72 *$8.50*

Country Wines of Burgundy
Pinot Noir, Lugny 1971 *$5.50*
Pinot Noir, Sichel 1970/71 *$7.50*
Moulin-à-Vent, Paul Bocuse 1971 *$7.00*

White Wines of Bordeaux ⑨
Château d'Yquem 1959
   Premier Grand Cru de Sauternes $52.00
Château d'Yquem 1967/68
   Premier Grand Cru de Sauternes $42.00
Château Bouscaut 1970 *Graves* $11.50
Château Laville-Haut-Brion 1968/69
   Graves $9.50
Château Haut-Brion Blanc 1970
   Graves $27.50
Château Suduiraut 1966/67
   Sauternes $9.50
Prince Blanc *Barton & Guestier* $5.50
Mouton-Cadet
   Baron Philippe de Rothschild $7.50
Blanc de Blancs, Sauvignon *Sichel* $5.50

White Wines of Burgundy ⑩
Chablis, Grand Cru, Vaudésir Pic
   1971/72 *$13.50*

Chablis, Grand Cru Les Clos, J. B. Simon
   1970/71 *$13.50*
Chablis, Grand Cru Bougros,
   Domaine de la Maladière 1971 *$12.50*
Clos Blanc de Vougeot, L'Héritier Guyot
   1970/71 *$15.50*
Corton-Charlemagne,
   Remoissenet Père & Fils 1970 *$24.50*
Beaune, Clos des Mouches, Jos. Drouhin
   1970/71 *$17.50*
Savigny-les-Beaune 1970/71 *$11.50*
Meursault-Perrières, Comtes Lafon
   1971 *$19.00*
Meursault, Potinet-Ampeau 1971 *$13.50*
Meursault-Charmes, Hospices de Beaune,
   Cuvée de Bahézre de Lanlay
   1966/69 *$24.50*
Puligny-Montrachet, Louis Jadot
   1970/71 *$16.50*
Montrachet, Domaine du Baron Thénard
   1969/70 *$35.00*
Chevalier-Montrachet, Jean Charton
   1966/70 *$34.00*
Chevalier-Montrachet, Louis Jadot
   1969/70 *$26.50*
Chassagne-Montrachet, Abbaye de Morgeot
   1971 *$22.50*
Pouilly-Fuissé, J. Drouhin 1971 *$12.00*

Country Wines of Burgundy ⑪
Beaujolais Blanc 1971/72 *$8.00*
Saint-Vérand, Paul Bocuse 1972 *$7.50*
Pinot Chardonnay Ninot 1971/72 *$5.50*
Macon Blanc, Barton & Guestier
   1969/71 *$5.50*

Wines of Alsace ⑪
Riesling, Clos Ste. Hune 1970/71 *$13.50*
Gewürztraminer, Reserve Exceptionnelle,
   F. E. Hugel & Fils 1970/71 *$9.50*
Sylvaner, F. E. Hugel & Fils 1970/71 *$6.50*

Wines of the Loire Valley ⑪
Sancerre, Frères Troisgros 1971/72 *$9.50*
Blanc Fumé de Pouilly, Domaine de Riaux
   1972 *$10.50*
Muscadet, Domaine de l'Hyvernière
   1971/72 *$8.50*

Wines of Provence ⑪
Blanc de Blancs, Domaines Ott
   1971/72 *$9.50*
Château de Selle, Rosé 1970/71 *$8.50*
Château de St.-Martin,
   Comte de Rohan-Chabot 1969/70 *$9.50*

Wines of the Rhône Valley ⑪
Red
Côte Rôtie, Domaine Gerin 1968/69 *$12.50*
Châteauneuf-du-Pape,
   P. Avril, Clos des Papes 1971 *$14.50*
White
Hermitage Blanc, Chante-Alouette,
   Chapoutier 1970/71 *$10.50*
Châteauneuf-du-Pape,
   Domaine de Mont-Redon
   1970/71 *$11.50*

Rosé Wines of France ⑪
Rosé de Marsannay, Clair Dau
   1970/71 *$8.50*
Tavel, Les Vignerons 1970/71 *$8.50*

Champagnes of France
Prince de Venoge, Cuvée Four Seasons,
   Decanter . . .
Ayala, Brut, Special Cuvée n/v *$18.50*
Bollinger, Extra Quality 1966 *$25.00*
Bollinger, Brut n/v *$22.00*
Dom Ruinart, Blanc de Blancs
   1964/66 *$30.00*
Krug, Private Cuvée, Brut n/v *$25.00*
La Belle Epoque, Brut n/v *$15.50*
Lanson, Red Label, Brut 1969 *$23.00*
Louis Roederer Cristal, Brut
   n/v 1969 *$36.00*
Moët et Chandon, Cuvée Dom Pérignon
   1964/66 *$37.00*
Mumm's Renée Lalou 1964/66 *$37.00*
Mumm's Cordon Rouge 1964/66 *$24.50*
Mumm's Cordon Rouge, Brut
   n/v *$22.00*
Perrier-Jouet, Blason de France
   1966 *$30.00*
Piper-Heidsieck Pink, Brut 1964/66 *$26.00*
Pol Roger, Brut 1966 *$22.50*
Salon, Brut 1966 *$26.00*
Taittinger, Blanc de Blancs
   1964/66 *$37.00*
Taittinger, La Française n/v *$19.50*
Veuve Clicquot, Gold Label, Brut
   1964/66 *$25.00*

Sparkling Wines of France
Kriter, Brut de Brut *$10.50*
Seyssel, Le Duc, Blanc de Blancs
   1970 *$10.50*
Chauvenet, Red Cap
   $15.50

Left: Vino with trumpet, guitar,
and accordion at a characteristic trattoria
in Rome. *Below:* Argentine steak and full-bodied
country wine at a Buenos Aires carrito.
Right: Wine at dinner in a London club.
Bottom: At a pub in Chelsea.

taurant price is more than 50 percent over retail, plus a $2 corkage allowance, the wine is overpriced.

Having made your selection—or selections— it's a good idea to order the wine as soon as possible. This will permit the sommelier to begin cooling a white and to open a red in time for it to "breathe" and be ready for drinking when your food is served. If there is no sommelier—or only an incompetent one—you'll have to give instructions about some of these basics. We approach it this way:

Having selected a wine, we tell the server when and how we want it served. For a red, we ask that it be brought to the table and opened immediately. For a white, we ask that it be put in ice immediately and opened when our appetizer is served. Some waiters, unless you instruct them to the contrary, will leave the red wine unopened until the main course.

The usual tip for a competent sommelier is $1 per bottle served, unless he steers you onto something sensational, in which case $5 is not out of line.

Wine Service in Restaurants

The serving ritual through which most sommeliers go can be befuddling to the newcomer. At its most complex, here are its steps and the rationale behind them:

1. The sommelier displays the bottle—so that you can examine the label. You'll want to insure that, first of

Diners at Barcelona's famed
Los Caracoles (The Snails) restaurant
may buy wine by the bottle or
order a carafe of Spanish country
wine "from the wood" (note barrels in
upper right corner).

all, you've been served the wine you ordered, that the vintage is correct, and that the bottle has not been opened previously. This latter point is very important; though the practice is illegal, some restaurateurs are not above refilling a used bottle with a cheaper wine, recorking it, then selling it as the expensive wine. The sommelier should display the bottle in such a manner that you can both read the label and see the unbroken seal over the neck and mouth of the bottle. If necessary, don't hesistate to take the bottle from him and examine it more closely.

If you've ordered a wine with which you're unfamiliar, take your time reading the label—noting such details as whether château-bottled, whether produced under specific governmental regulations (the appellation designation on French wines can be very revealing), and who the shipper and importer are. This information is especially important when you've ordered from a wine list that gives only a regional or varietal name for a wine. A sommelier may try to give you only a quick peek at the label before the bottle is opened so that you'll be intimidated into accepting it. But remember, you don't have to accept the bottle until you've tasted the wine.

How does one reject a wine? Simply state that it's unsatisfactory and ask for another bottle.

2. The sommelier opens the wrapping over the mouth. Watch him do it. It's not difficult, especially with foil wrapping, to make an opened bottle appear as if it has not been touched. Most restaurateurs, we believe, would not try this. But some would, especially with very expensive bottles.

3. The sommelier next may clean the top of the bottle with a cloth if it contains cellar deposits or other matter. The presence of this matter doesn't mean there is anything wrong. Even a moldy cork top is common with wines that are more than a few years old.

4. The sommelier uncorks the bottle, then feels the cork for dryness, and sniffs for mustiness or the odor of acetic acid—all indications that the wine has been spoiled by air seepage. If he believes this is the case, he should take the bottle away and bring you another.

5. If the sommelier is satisfied that the cork is good, he normally will hand it to you or—the preferable approach, at least for us—place it bottom end up near you on the table. A few will hold the cork to your nose, but this is widely regarded as improper. If you want to sniff and feel the cork, you may—and if you believe you have found evidence of spoilage, you may decide to reject the wine. But most experienced drinkers will prefer to reserve decision until they've nosed or tasted the wine. Having accepted the cork, tell the sommelier he may pour.

6. The sommelier pours about an ounce in your glass. Look at the wine for clarity and color, then swirl and nose it. You may choose also to taste it, but we rarely do unless we want to confirm that our nose identified a defect. When you taste, of course, you are not approving character but quality. A wine is not rejected because it fails to inspire your enthusiasm, or because you simply do not like it; it is rejected because there is something wrong with it. If you have doubts about a particular wine, order one you're better acquainted with and sample the doubtful one later by buying a bottle at a retail store. If we don't think the wine defective, we tell the sommelier he may pour.

If we do think it defective—because of oxidation, acescence (making the wine smell and taste like vinegar), lack of clarity, or some other reason—we reject it, asking either for a different vintage or a different wine.

Most sommeliers eliminate or make a perfunctory attempt at steps 3, 4, and 5—which is no great crime, since the ultimate test comes when the wine is poured into your glass.

9.

9.
ESTABLISHING A WINE CELLAR

*Opening pages: Old bottle
of Château Cheval-Blanc on tasting
table in San Francisco cellar of Peter Salz.
Note vertical bin dividers, sherry barrel
on bench at rear. Left: Beautifully carved
wine cask as Schloss Speyer, Germany.*

A wine "cellar" need not be subterranean. Originally wines were stored in the basements of buildings because there was no other place in the house where temperature was constant, light minimal, and vibration nonexistent. These three conditions are essential to the safe storage of wine. But any other room or area within a room is a good storage place if it meets these conditions.

Why bother to store wine? There are several good reasons. The first and most obvious is convenience. It's nice to know that an assortment of wines is handy when you want a bottle. Another is economy. Wine is cheaper by the case, and often cheaper still in multicase lots. If you store it yourself, you reduce the per-unit cost. But third and most important to the typical wine lover, keeping your own "cellar" permits you to lay away quantities of certain wines that improve with age. The prime vintages of these wines usually go out of circulation within a few years after they've been released by the winery. Some may be bought subsequently at auction—at prices tens or hundreds of times the original selling price—but others are unavailable at any price. By buying the wines young and laying them away, you insure continued access to them. You also create a valuable property. While some states forbid resale of alcoholic beverages by someone who is not licensed, such transactions are legal in others. Cellars have been sold at substantial multiples of the owner's initial investment.

There is another good reason for cellaring, but newcomers to wine will not always appreciate it. It is, simply, very satisfying to have a collection of things that are dear and important to you in your home, and to wander among them from time to time, either alone or in the company of friends who can share your appreciation of them. Anyone who prizes a library of books or phonograph records knows exactly the feeling we refer to. What are the ideal conditions for wine storage?

1. *Temperature.* The ideal temperature for a cellar is somewhere between 50 and 60 degrees Fahrenheit (between 10 and 15.6°C). French wine professionals suggest 50 to 54 degrees (10 to 12.2°C). Italians and Spaniards prefer it slightly warmer: 53 to 58 degrees (11.7 to 14.4°C). Actually, tests have shown that wine can be stored safely for long periods at anywhere from about 45 to about 70 degrees (7.2 to 21.1°C). The main thing is that there shouldn't be sharp fluctuations in temperature.

G-1 and G-2's own cellar, in the mountains of northeastern Pennsylvania, averages 56 degrees year-round. During the summer, it gets as warm as 58 degrees and in the winter as cold as 54 degrees. But the temperature's movement between these points is very slow, and our wines seem to live very comfortably in their environment. G-1 has held bottles for over forty years without damage.

Our cellar temperature is strictly natural. A thick stone and concrete wall insulates the cellar from outdoors. Other keepers of wine cellars—especially those not actually in basements—favor air conditioning, which makes it possible to keep the temperature virtually constant.

If a cellar is neither subterranean nor air conditioned, there are other approaches to minimizing temperature fluctuation. A refrigerator, with its temperature set in the 50's, can store up to a hundred bottles of wine. A second refrigerator doubles the capacity and also makes it possible to store at two different temperatures, slightly warmer for reds than for whites. A subterranean cellar achieves this effect by storing whites below reds.

A closet might also be used for wine storage, or one of those blind areas that exist beneath stairways in some houses. Or a cabinet can be built in a corner of a room—

*Left: Still life and
bouquet of flowers provide focal
point in cellar of Californian Albert Meyer.
Note hollow core of corkscrew in foreground.
Below: Stacked cases of prime Bordeaux.
Right: Bins of older vintages at Ernie's.*

preferably an interior corner, to minimize the effect of temperature changes out-of-doors. A cabinet of this sort might be made extra stable with double walls and an insulating layer of fiberglass between them.

In these room-temperature storage arrangements, the temperature will usually be above 65 degrees Fahrenheit (18.3°C). That precludes laying away wines for several decades, but they can be held without too much deterioration for about ten years.

Whether cellaring above or below the ground, be sure to stay away from heating units or motors of any kind. In addition to affecting room temperature, they create vibrations.

2. *Vibrations.* Wine cannot live long with them. They accelerate its aging, create sediment, and may induce cork problems that lead to oxidation. In most homes, avoiding vibrations is simply a matter of keeping away from areas containing motorized equipment.

When using a cabinet in an upstairs room as a minicellar, select one that permits stationary storage of wine rather than storage in drawers that are opened and closed to get to the wine. Label bins and compartments so that you know which wine is where, rather than having to take a number of bottles out of their caches to find the one you want.

The ideal position for bottle storage is near-horizontal, with the mouth a few degrees higher than the bottom of the bottle. When a bottle is held for many years, sediment will form in the lower portion; if this is at the bottom of the bottle, it will not cloud the wine as it is

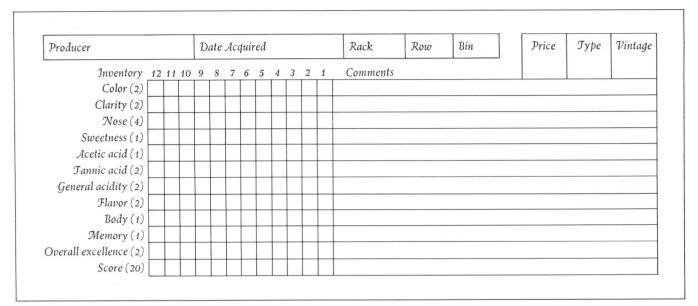

Producer						Date Acquired						Rack	Row	Bin		Price	Type	Vintage
Inventory	12	11	10	9	8	7	6	5	4	3	2	1	Comments					
Color (2)																		
Clarity (2)																		
Nose (4)																		
Sweetness (1)																		
Acetic acid (1)																		
Tannic acid (2)																		
General acidity (2)																		
Flavor (2)																		
Body (1)																		
Memory (1)																		
Overall excellence (2)																		
Score (20)																		

poured. If the neck is lower than the base, the wine cannot be poured without disturbing the sediment. But the mouth must be at least low enough for the cork to remain covered with wine. If the cork is not kept moist, air will enter and the wine will oxidize. That's why the bottles should not stand upright—unless they're screw-cap types, which you won't keep for very long anyway, or fortified wines, which are strong enough to withstand oxygen.

Some cellar owners use wooden wine cases, placed on their side, to hold bottles. Others build caches for individual bottles. Still others prefer bins. G-1 and G-2 prefer bins with a 24-bottle capacity. We store only one batch of wine in a bin, with the bottles directly on top of each other.

3. *Light.* It should be kept at a minimum. We have one small window in our cellar, and it's covered with a shutter. There is one electric light with only a 100-watt bulb, and we use it sparingly. We've been told that we're slightly fanatic about darkness, but we like it that way.

In any case, it's well known that a lot of light changes both the color and the acid balance of the wine.

Light acts even more quickly on whites than on reds, which is one reason why whites that have been improperly handled during shipping become obviously defective while still fairly young.

The effect of both light and heat on wines rules out displaying them openly—for example, on a rack in one's living room. It may please your eye and those of your guests, but it's not good for the wine.

4. *Odors.* The cellar should be protected from strong smells like paraffin, vinegar, and fuel oil. These can get into the wine through the cork and ruin it.

Stocking the Cellar

Not long ago a friend who is a professional wine man was asked for advice by a prominent physician. The physician had built a new house, complete with 100-case wine cellar designed by a leading architect. The temperature was kept constant, there was neither light nor vibration, and no odor-emanating materials were anywhere nearby. Nevertheless, he was having a problem: his bottles were leaking.

The wine man was baffled. He had heard of an occasional oxidized bottle leaking when its cork dried up—usually after many years in storage. But he had never heard of an epidemic of leaking bottles. He went to the physician's cellar to see if he could figure out what was wrong.

He found leaking bottles, all right—several dozen cases of them. They were leaking because they were filled with screw-cap bottles. These bottles, used for inexpensive wines intended for immediate consumption, normally are stored upright for the brief period between their departure from a winery and the time they are emptied by a consumer. The doctor had spent $30,000 on his wine cellar, to stock it with $1.29 bottles of wine! We're not knocking his taste. But it is pointless to take great pains stocking wines that do not benefit from bottle-aging.

Which wines do? As a rule, those made predominantly from Cabernet Sauvignon or Pinot Noir grapes benefit most. These include the château-bottled reds of Bordeaux and Burgundy, usually bottled under the vineyard name rather than the varietal name. Some of these wines continue to improve for twenty or thirty years after bottling. Wines from Nebbiolo, Sangiovese, and Zinfandel don't last as long, but the more carefully made of these can improve for ten or fifteen years after bottling, a few last twenty years or more. As a rule, Gamay-based wines, and most blends sold under regional rather than varietal names, are best consumed within five years.

Whites usually are best drunk young. The exceptions are those made from late-picked grapes—notably the German or German-style Spätlese, Beerenauslese, and Trockenbeerenauslese—and those wines made predominantly from such low-yield varieties as Chardonnay, Sémillon, and Sauvignon Blanc. These may continue to improve for up to ten years.

Our procedure in buying wines to lay away is first to sample one bottle of a producer's given vintage, then, based on our appraisal of it, to buy a number of cases (anywhere from two or three to forty or fifty, if we really are impressed with the wine). Our appraisal, by the way, is not based solely on our own evaluation of the wine. We visit regularly the wineries whose product we admire, and we maintain regular contact with winemakers, shippers, and importers. We solicit their opinions about which of their wines are best to lay away and for how long. (Most wine men are quite hospitable to inquiries of this sort. They want you to like—and buy—their wines.)

Having laid a wine away, we taste it a year later and fill out a rating card. G-2 uses the 20-point rating presented earlier, applied to twelve bottles (a full case of wine). He fills out a separate card for each case and one line for each bottle we sample. When we open our first bottle from the case, he circles the figure 12 (there are 12 bottles in the standard case) and fills in his numerical ratings along that line. He then comments to the effect that a given supply of wine need not be tasted again for two or three years, or should be drunk immediately, or whatever he feels about it. G-1 then adds his comments. Usually we taste each batch once a year. The other material on the card—vintage, date acquired, etc.—was filled in when we got the case. The rack, row, and bin numbers tell us how to locate the supply quickly.

Each line filled out on the rating file represents one bottle less in that particular case. We execute a separate card for each case, no matter how many we may have bought at a given time. And every time we take a bottle from the case, we rate it.

We also have a system of colored tags for different years. For example, we designate orange as this year's color, and we put orange tags around the necks of the bottles that must be drunk this year. Then, every time we

*A corner in the wine cellar
of G-1 and G-2. Color-coded tags indicate
when aging bottles should be sampled.
Card file on table contains tasting notes.
Upright bottles on shelf at rear will
be consumed before any others.*

walk into the cellar to select a wine, these orange tags remind us that these wines should be drunk fairly soon. The same thing happens with the wines we've decided to let mature for at least two years. Let's say we have assigned purple as the color for that year. We'll purple-tag it, then forget about it. Then, when the year comes where all current wines have purple tags, we're ready to taste this one again. Meanwhile, the oranges—and reds and yellows and whites—have been cycled on to future years.

By the way, when we speak of "tasting" a wine, we don't mean that we simply take a sip, then recork the bottle and put it back in its bin. We mean we drink the entire bottle. Wines can be recorked, and very old wines usually are. But there always must be a full bottle of wine, or oxygen will turn the less-than-full bottle to vinegar. To recork, combine the wine from one or more bottles (same vintage) until you have filled a bottle to the neck, then apply a new cork (which has first been soaked in another—presumably inexpensive—wine to moisten it) with a corking machine of the sort available in most wine hobby stores. If you open a 23- to 26-ounce bottle and taste it, you can store the remaining wine in a 12-ounce bottle. But recorking at home is always risky, and rather than take a chance on spoiling the wine, we'll drink the whole bottle, even if it is a bit young.

Of course, there are wines in our cellar other than those being aged for decades. In fact, about one-third our supply is given over to wines intended for consumption immediately or in the near future. These include, in addition to our homemade wines: all our jug-wines, which we usually buy in six-case lots (for reasons of economy as well as convenience); several cases of once-a-week wines of different types; special-occasion and super-special-occasion sparkling wines; an assortment of fortified wines; and such wine specialties as vermouth, Dubonnet, other apéritif wines, and nongrape wines.

These occupy what we think of as our "daily cellar," a phrase from the lexicon of the restaurateur. We buy in lots of at least one case, and when we get down to our last three or four bottles, we order another case.

We have an additional half-dozen once-a-week whites and once-a-week reds which usually change from year to year. One constant among them is Sebastiani Gamay Beaujolais. Another is Beaulieu Vineyard's Pinot Chardonnay. A third is A. Willm's Cordon d'Alsace.

Beyond this, we keep two cases each of perhaps thirty white wines from various regions, selling under $35 a case (mostly California varietals), and another two cases each of about thirty readily consumable reds, selling under $45 a case (an assortment of U.S., French, Italian, Chilean, Hungarian, and Spanish, mostly Cabernet Sauvignon or Gamay varietals).

The remaining two-thirds of the cellar is given over to wines we are keeping for the long run—mostly Cabernets, but also some Pinot Noirs, Nebbioli, and Sangiovesi. Among those we recommend to readers planning to start a cellar are the following.

Shown here are typical U.S. retail case prices at the time the wine is released
by the producer—usually after five or six years of aging. The vintages identified here were, in our opinion,
prime buys in 1974. For advice on prime vintages in later years, consult the producer
or importer of the wine, or any wine merchant whom you trust.

United States

Concannon Vineyards Cabernet Sauvignon 1967 $100

Concannon Vineyards Petite Sirah 1968 $36

Mayacamas Cabernet Sauvignon 1969 $110

Freemark Abbey Cabernet Sauvignon 1968 $90

Hanzell Pinot Noir 1968 $140

Souverain Cabernet Sauvignon 1970 $96

Souverain Mountain Zinfandel 1971 $60

Heitz Cellars Cabernet Sauvignon 1968 $96

Ridge Vineyards Cabernet Sauvignon 1969 $96

Wente Bros. Pinot Noir 1970 $39

Robert Mondavi Petite Sirah 1970 $48

Robert Mondavi Pinot Noir 1970 $54

Robert Mondavi Cabernet Sauvignon 1970 $58

Paul Masson Pinot Noir 1970 $32

Paul Masson Cabernet Sauvignon 1970 $32

Sebastiani Vineyards Cabernet Sauvignon 1968 $48

Sebastiani Vineyards Pinot Noir 1968 $42

Mirassou Pinot Noir 1967 $48

Louis Martini Barbera 1970 $30

Louis Martini Pinot Noir 1968 Special Selection $52

Christian Brothers Zinfandel N.V. $30

Beaulieu Vineyard Beaumont Pinot Noir 1969 $50

Inglenook Cask Cabernet Sauvignon 1968 $75

Inglenook Charbono 1969 $50

Inglenook Estate-Bottled Zinfandel 1971 $35

France

Château Margaux 1970 $430

Château Palmer 1966 $270

Château La Mouline 1970 $51

Château Lascombes 1970 $180

Château du Tertre 1970 $120

Château Lafite-Rothschild 1970 $620

Château Latour 1970 $610

Château Mouton-Rothschild 1970 $450

Château Pichon-Lalande 1970 $280

Château Haut-Brion 1970 $540

Château Pape-Clément 1967 $140

Château Larrivet-Haut-Brion 1966 $85

Château Cheval-Blanc 1970 $480

Château Pavie-Decesse 1971 $95

Château Cos d'Estournel 1969 $160

Château Pétrus 1967 $400

Château Petit-Village 1969 $124

Domaine de Chevalier 1971 $210

Château Léoville-Las-Cases 1964 $300

Château Beychevelle 1970 $240

Château Maucaillou 1970 $75

Château Teyssier 1970 $130

Château Calon-Ségur 1970 $140

Domaine des Comtes Lafon-Volnay Santenots,
    Reserve Numerotée 1970 $100

Louis Jadot Corton-Pougets 1971 $100

Louis Jadot Beaune Clos des Ursules 1971 $75

Domaine Maurice Dugat Gevrey-Chambertin 1969 $100

Domaine G. Roumier Chambolle-Musigny 1970 $110

Domaine Voarick Corton-Bressandes 1969 $160

Guigone de Salins Hospice de Beaune 1966 $180

Domaine Gros Richebourg 1970 $270

Domaine Bart Chambertin 1970 $300

Domaine Henri de Villamont Grands Echezaux 1966 $170

Domaine Dufouleur Clos de Vougeot 1970 $260

Germany

Steinberger Riesling Trockenbeerenauslese,
    Verwaltunger Staatsweingüter 1971 $700

Graacher Himmelreich Beerenauslese,
    Freiherr von Schorlemer 1971 $540

Schwarzhofberger Spätlese, Egon Müller 1971 $85

Piesporter Goldtröpfchen Auslese,
    Lehnert Matheus 1971 $108

Hattenheimer Nussbrunnen Riesling Spätlese,
    Langwerth von Simmern 1971 $85

Eltviller Sonnenberg Spätlese,
    Langwerth von Simmern 1971 $65

Italy

Borgogno Barolo 1966 $65

Borgogno Barbaresco 1966 $60

Calissano Barbaresco 1966 $60

Fontanafredda Barbaresco 1965 $65

Bersano Barbaresco 1970 $60

Bersano Barolo 1965 $65

Antoniolo Gattinara 1967 $54

Travaglini Gattinara 1970 $44

Travaglini Spanna 1965 $30

Negri Castel Chiuro Riserva 1964 $65

Negri Castel Chiuro 1970 $30

Polatti Grumello 1971 $32

Polatti Inferno 1971 $32

Negri Sassella 1969 $40

Polatti Sassella 1971 $32

Enologica Sassella Riserva 1964 $65

Pio Cesare Grignolino 1970 $44

Pio Cesare Barbera 1970 $44

Mirafiore Bardolino 1971 $30

Nozzole Chianti Classico Riserva 1964 $65

Chile

Concha y Toro Cabernet Sauvignon 1970 $30

Spain

Jean Leon Cabernet Sauvignon 1970 $55

Marques de Riscal 1970 $32

One of the most impressive wine cellars we've ever seen belongs to Victor and Roland Gotti at Ernie's in San Francisco. To provide a sort of anchor against which our own choices might be weighed, we asked the Gottis to draw up a list of wines they would stock if they were just beginning a cellar. We further asked them to divide their list into cellars valued at (if purchases were made in 1974 at approximate per-case U.S. retail prices) $1,000, $5,000, $10,000, and $100,000. The total list is that of the $100,000 cellar. The wines marked with ❖ are those of the $1,000 cellar. The wines of the $5,000 cellar are marked ❖, and those of the $10,000 cellar are marked ▣.

Red California

Foppiano Vineyards, Zinfandel	$24	❖▣
Russian River–Sonoma		
Foppiano Vineyards Petite Sirah, 1969	24	❖▣
Estate-Bottled, Russian River–Sonoma		
Robert Mondavi, Petite Sirah, 1970	48	❖▣
Napa Valley		
Paul Masson, Pinot Noir	32	❖▣
Santa Clara–Saratoga		
Foppiano Vineyards Pinot Noir, 1970	37	❖▣
Estate-Bottled, Russian River–Sonoma		
Robert Mondavi, Pinot Noir, 1970	54	❖❖▣
Napa Valley		
Paul Masson, Cabernet Sauvignon	32	❖▣
Santa Clara–Saratoga		
Foppiano Vineyards Cabernet Sauvignon	37	❖❖▣
Estate-Bottled, Russian River–Sonoma		
Robert Mondavi Cabernet Sauvignon, 1970	58	❖❖▣
Napa Valley		
Robert Mondavi Cabernet Sauvignon, 1968 Unfined	92	▣
Napa Valley		

White California

Foppiano Vineyards, Chablis, 1972	24	❖❖▣
Estate-Bottled, Russian River–Sonoma		
Robert Mondavi Chenin Blanc, 1972	32	❖▣
Napa Valley		
Robert Mondavi, Fumé Blanc, 1972	40	❖❖▣
Napa Valley		
Robert Mondavi Johannisberg Riesling, 1972	48	❖❖▣
Napa Valley		
Robert Mondavi, 1972 Chardonnay	70	❖▣
Napa Valley		

Bordeaux Wines of France
Graves

Château Ferrande, 1970	50	❖❖▣
Grand Cru		
Château Pape-Clément, 1967	134	❖▣
Grand Cru		
Château Haut-Brion, 1962	510	
Cru Hors Classé		
Château Haut-Brion, 1964	520	
Cru Hors Classé		
Château Haut-Brion, 1966	540	▣
Cru Hors Classé		
Château Haut-Brion, 1970	540	
Cru Hors Classé		

Saint-Emilion

Vieux Château d'Arthus, 1967	50	❖▣
Grand Cru		
Château Pavie-Decesse, 1967	94	❖▣
Grand Cru		
Château Pavie-Decesse, 1970	75	
Grand Cru		
Château Pavie-Decesse, 1971	94	
Grand Cru		
Château La Cluzière, 1970	75	
Grand Cru		
Château La Cluzière, 1971	134	
Grand Cru		
Château Cheval-Blanc, 1967	435	
Cru Hors Classé		
Château Cheval-Blanc, 1970	475	▣
Cru Hors Classé		

Pomerol

Château l'Evangile, 1969	101	
Cru Exceptionnel		
Château l'Evangile, 1970	183	
Cru Exceptionnel		
Château Pétrus, 1964	485	
Cru Hors Classé		
Château Pétrus, 1967	400	▣
Cru Hors Classé		

Margaux

Château La Mouline, 1967	50	❖▣
Cru Bourgeois		
Château La Mouline, 1970	51	
Cru Bourgeois		
Château Prieuré-Lichine, 1967	94	❖▣
Grand Cru		
Château Prieuré-Lichine, 1970	134	
Grand Cru		
Château Lascombes, 1966	270	❖▣
Grand Cru		
Château Lascombes, 1970	175	
Grand Cru		
Château Malescot-Saint-Exupéry, 1967	225	
Château du Tertre, 1970	120	
Château Margaux, 1964	405	
Cru Hors Classé		
Château Margaux, 1966	510	
Cru Hors Classé		
Château Margaux, 1967	430	▣
Cru Hors Classé		
Château Margaux, 1970	337	
Cru Hors Classé		

Saint-Julien

Château Beauregard, 1967	84	❖▣
Cru Bourgeois		
Château Léoville-Las-Cases, 1964	300	❖▣
Château Beychevelle, 1966	270	❖▣

Pauillac

Château Belle-Rose, 1970	50	❖▣
Grand Cru Bourgeois		
Château Pichon-Lalande, 1962	250	
Château Pichon-Lalande, 1964	400	
Grand Cru		
Château Pichon-Lalande, 1966	300	❖▣
Château Mouton-Rothschild, 1962	540	
Cru Hors Classé		
Château Mouton-Rothschild, 1964	534	
Cru Hors Classé		
Château Mouton-Rothschild, 1966	594	
Cru Hors Classé		
Château Mouton-Rothschild, 1967	460	▣
Cru Hors Classé		
Château Mouton-Rothschild, 1970	540	
Cru Hors Classé		
Château Latour, 1961	1,200	
Cru Hors Classé		
Château Latour, 1962	592	
Cru Hors Classé		
Château Latour, 1967	510	▣
Cru Hors Classé		

Château Latour, 1970	605	
Cru Hors Classé		
Château Lafite-Rothschild, 1961	1,500	
Cru Hors Classé		
Château Lafite-Rothschild, 1962	592	
Cru Hors Classé		
Château Lafite-Rothschild, 1964	640	
Cru Hors Classé		
Château Lafite-Rothschild, 1966	761	
Cru Hors Classé		
Château Lafite-Rothschild, 1967	640	
Cru Hors Classé		
Château Lafite-Rothschild, 1970	605	
Cru Hors Classé		

Saint-Estèphe

Château Calon-Ségur, 1970	134	
Grand Cru Classé		
Château Tronquoy-Lalande, 1970	50	
Cru Bourgeois		
Château Cos d'Estournel, 1966	300	
Grand Cru Classé		

Moulis

Château Maucaillou, 1967	100	
Cru Bourgeois		
Château Maucaillou, 1970	75	
Cru Bourgeois		

French White Bordeaux Wines

Château Carbonnieux, 1969	74	❖❖▣
Dry Graves, Premier Cru		
Château Coutet, 1969	77	❖❖▣
Barsac, Premier Cru		
Château d'Yquem, 1966	375	
Sauternes		

Red Burgundy Wines of France

Beaujolais-Villages, 1971	50	❖❖▣
Domaine Comte de Chabanne		
Moulin-à-Vent, 1971	78	▣
Tour de Bief		
Gevrey-Chambertin, 1969	97	❖❖▣
Domaine Maurice Dugat		
Chambolle-Musigny, 1970	111	▣
Domaine G. Roumier		
Volnay Clos des Ducs, 1970	120	
Domaine D'Angerville		
Nuits-Saint-Georges, 1970	123	❖▣
Clos de l'Arlot, Domaine Jules Belin		
Beaune Cent Vignes, 1964	126	❖▣
Domaine Coron		
Pommard-Epenots, 1969	145	❖▣
Domaine Gaunoux		
Musigny, 1969	135	▣
Domaine Moin Hudelot		

Musigny, 1971	275	
Domaine Dufouleur		
Vosne-Romanée, Les Beaumonts, 1969	146	
Domaine Grivot		
Corton-Bressandes, 1969	155	▣
Domaine Voarick		
Hospice de Beaune, 1966	172	
Guigone de Salins		
Hospice de Beaune, 1964	210	
Guigone de Salins		
Clos Vougeot, 1966	187	❖▣
Domaine M. Jean Grivot		
Clos Vougeot, 1970	259	
Domaine Dufouleur		
Gevrey-Chambertin Clos Saint-Jacques	195	
Domaine Clair Dau		
Grands Echezeaux, 1969	196	▣
Domaine Mugneret		
Chambertin-Clos de Bèze	250	▣
Domaine Clair Dau		
Richebourg, 1970	270	▣
Domaine Gros		
Chambertin, 1970	300	
Domaine Bart		

Red Rhône

Châteauneuf-du-Pape, 1970	75	
Estate-Bottled, Les Brusquières		

White Burgundy Wines of France

Chassagne-Montrachet-Ruchottes, 1970	91	❖▣
Domaine Pillot		
Meursault, 1970	97	❖▣
Domaine Michelot		
Pouilly-Fuissé, 1970	85	❖❖▣
Domaine René Guerin		
Chablis Grand Cru Vaudésir, 1970	70	❖❖▣
Domaine W. Fevre		
Puligny-Montrachet, 1970	104	❖▣
Domaine Carillon		
Puligny-Montrachet Le Refert, 1970	105	
Domaine Carillon		
Puligny-Montrachet, 1971	118	
Domaine J. Chavy		
Puligny-Montrachet, Perrières, 1971	119	
Domaine J. Chavy		
Meursault-Charmes, 1971	135	
Domaine Bouzereau		
Meursault Clos Saint-Felix, 1971	121	
Domaine Michelot		

Corton-Charlemagne, 1971	193	❖▣
Domaine Pavelot		
Le Montrachet, 1971	375	
Domaine Millan		

White Loire Valley

Sancerre, 1970	57	
Domaine Roblin		
Pouilly-Fumé, 1972	71	
Domaine Pabiot		

Italian Wines
Tuscany

Chianti Classico Tizzano, 1968	40	
Riserva, Conte Pandolfini		
Chianti Classico Tizzano, 1965	48	
Riserva, Conte Pandolfini		
Chianti Classico Castello Di Uzzano, 1967	48	❖❖▣
Contessa Albani Masetti		
Chianti Classico Castello Di Uzzano, 1965	58	
Contessa Albani Masetti		
Chianti Classico Fonterutoli, 1968	48	
Riserva, Prop. Massei		

Marches

Verdicchio Dei Castelli Di Jesi Classico	35	❖❖▣
Roberto Bianchi		

Lombardy

Grumello, 1967	48	❖▣
Valtellina, Produced by Enologica		
Inferno, 1964	75	
Riserva della Casa, Produced by Enologica		
Sassella, 1964	75	❖▣
Riserva della Casa, Produced by Enologica		

Verona

Bardolino, 1970	32	❖❖▣
Fratelli Poggi		
Valpolicella, 1970	32	❖▣
Produttori Associati Soave		
Amarone, 1969	56	
Fratelli Poggi		
Soave Classico, 1970	32	❖▣
Produttori Associati Soave		

Piedmont

Grignolino, 1970	42	❖▣
Pio Cesare		
Barbera, 1970	42	❖▣
Pio Cesare		
Castello Di Gabbiano, 1967	62	
Riserva (Barbera)		

Castello Di Gabbiano, 1964		67
Riserva (Barbera)		
Nebbiolo D'Alba, 1964	❖▣	75
Pio Cesare		
Barbaresco, 1964	▣	80
Riserva, Pio Cesare		
Barbaresco, 1964		121
Cru Montestafano, Alfredo Prunotto		
Barbaresco, 1967		80
Alfredo Prunotto		
Barolo, 1962	▣	97
Pio Cesare		
Barolo, 1964		121
Pio Cesare		
Barolo, 1965		78
Alfredo Prunotto		
Barolo, 1967		80
Alfredo Prunotto		
Gattinara, 1967		65
Pasquali Albertinetti		

Latium

Frascati, 1970		35
Vigneti di colle Portella, A. Desanctis		

Umbria

Orvieto Classico	❖❖▣	35
Barberani		

German Wines

Rhine

Liebfraumilch, 1971		40
Qualitätswein Abfüllung, R. Müller		
Hattenheimer Mannberg, 1970		72
Riesling Kabinett Blau Orange		
Originalabfüllung, Freiherr Langwerth		
von Simmern		
Hattenheimer Nussbrunnen, 1971		1,210
Riesling Trockenbeerenauslese,		
Qualitätswein mit Prädikat		
Erzeugerabfüllung, Freiherr Langwerth		
von Simmern		
Schloss Johannisberger, 1971		750
Beerenauslese, Qualitätswein mit Prädikat		
Erzeugerabfüllung, Fürst von Metternich		
Schloss Vollrads, 1971		115
Kabinett, Erzeugerabfüllung,		
Graf Matuschka-Greiffenclau		
Schloss Vollrads, 1971		205
Spätlese, Erzeugerabfüllung,		
Graf Matuschka-Greiffenclau		
Schloss Vollrads, 1971		253
Auslese, Erzeugerabfüllung,		
Graf Matuschka- Greiffenclau		
Winkeler Dachsberg, 1971		450
Beerenauslese, Qualitätswein mit Prädikat		
Erzeugerabfüllung, Landgraf von Hessen		

Mosel

Bernkasteler Kueser-Kardinalsberg, 1971		63
Kabinett, Erzeugerabfüllung,		
Winzergenossenschaft		
Bernkasteler Badstube, 1971		114
Spätlese, Erzeugerabfüllung,		
Wwe. Dr. Thanisch		
Piesporter Michelsberg, 1971		46
Kabinett, Abfüllung, Dünweg		
Piesporter Michelsberg, 1971		62
Spätlese, Abfüllung, Dünweg		
Piesporter Goldtröpfchen, 1971	❖❖▣	72
Kabinett, Erzeugerabfüllung, O. Tobias		
Piesporter Goldtröpfchen, 1971		108
Spätlese, Erzeugerabfüllung, O. Tobias		
Piesporter Goldtröpfchen, 1971		118
Auslese, Erzeugerabfüllung,		
Reichsgraf von Kesselstadt		
Graacher Himmelreich, 1971		1,065
Beerenauslese, Qualitätswein mit		
Prädikat, Erzeugerabfüllung,		
Joh. Jos. Prüm		
Bernkasteler Doktor und Graben, 1971		260
Spätlese, Erzeugerabfüllung,		
Wwe. Dr. H. Thanisch		
Bernkasteler Doktor und Graben, 1971		336
Auslese, Erzeugerabfüllung,		
Wwe. Dr. H. Thanisch		

Champagnes

California

Hanns Kornell Brut	62
Hanns Kornell Extra Dry	62
Hanns Kornell Sehr Trocken	75

France

Mumm's Cordon Rouge, V	160
Mumm's Cordon Rouge, V	180
(Magnums)	
Louis Roederer Cristal Brut, 1967	226
(Magnums)	
Louis Roederer Cristal Brut, 1966	242
Dom Pérignon Moët et Chandon, V	243
Dom Pérignon Moët et Chandon, V	248
(Magnums)	

Sparkling Wines

Italy

Asti Spumante	58

Dessert Wines

Findlater's Don Lorenzo	76
Sherry	
Findlater's Old Nathaniel	94
Port	

Vermouths of Italy

Bonardi Sweet	27
Bonardi Dry	27

Rare Bordeaux Wines of France

Château Cheval-Blanc, 1961		850
Saint-Emilion, Cru Hors Classé		
Château Cheval-Blanc, 1955		900
Saint-Emilion, Cru Hors Classé		
Château Cheval-Blanc, 1952		1,000
Saint-Emilion, Cru Hors Classé		
Château Cheval-Blanc, 1949	❖❖▣	1,100
Saint-Emilion, Cru Hors Classé		
Château Pétrus, 1955		885
Pomerol, Cru Hors Classé		
Château Pétrus, 1953		1,000
Pomerol, Cru Hors Classé		
Château Mouton-Rothschild, 1961		1,000
Pauillac, Cru Hors Classé		
Château Mouton-Rothschild, 1959		1,150
Pauillac, Cru Hors Classé		
Château Mouton-Rothschild, 1953		1,200
Pauillac, Cru Hors Classé		
Château Mouton-Rothschild, 1952		1,250
Pauillac, Cru Hors Classé		
Château Haut-Brion, 1961		1,100
Graves, Cru Hors Classé		
Château Haut-Brion, 1959		1,150
Graves, Cru Hors Classé		
Château Haut-Brion, 1952		1,200
Graves, Cru Hors Classé		
Château Haut-Brion, 1949		1,300
Graves, Cru Hors Classé	*(Magnums)*	
Château Haut-Brion, 1961		1,100
Graves, Cru Hors Classé		
Château Margaux, 1955		1,000
Margaux, Cru Hors Classé		
Château Margaux, 1952		1,050
Margaux, Cru Hors Classé		
Château Margaux, 1949		1,100
Margaux, Cru Hors Classé		
Château Latour, 1959		1,250
Pauillac, Cru Hors Classé		
Château Latour, 1955		1,200
Pauillac, Cru Hors Classé		
Château Latour, 1953		1,350
Pauillac, Cru Hors Classé		
Château Latour, 1952		1,400
Pauillac, Cru Hors Classé		
Château Lafite-Rothschild, 1959		1,650
Pauillac, Cru Hors Classé		
Château Lafite-Rothschild, 1955		1,750
Pauillac, Cru Hors Classé		
Château Lafite-Rothschild, 1953		1,775
Pauillac, Cru Hors Classé		

PICTURE CREDITS

(Credits read from left to right and from top to bottom)

INDEX
Italic numbers refer to caption locations